LONDON
TROLLEYBUS
ROUTES

Previous Page **796**, having spent most of its life at Bexleyheath depot, yielded a further eight months service to London's travelling public at Walthamstow depot, being withdrawn in November 1959. After storage for almost a year, it was presented to the Paris Transport Museum in October 1960. In this view in Seven Sisters Road, 796 takes on passengers for the last leg of its journey to Manor House. LT Museum

X2 class trolleybus 62 was one of the two prototypes (the other being 63) that London Transport considered for its standard trolleybus; 62 was chosen as the more suitable of the two. It was latterly allocated to Holloway depot and is seen here at Manor House. Hugh Taylor collection

Left **Trolleybus 468** turns from Upper Wickham Lane into the High Street at Welling Corner. The wire grille gives a touch of antiquity to the vehicle, whilst the paper route and destination blinds add a touch of modernity. The street scene is typical of the late 1950s. C. Carter

Facing Page **1057** nears the end of its southbound journey as it passes over Euston Road. The Tottenham Court Road trolleybus terminus was referred to as 'Euston' on schedules until the early post-war years; behind is Edmonton depot's 1170. Tony Belton

Below **The C Class vehicles** that were fitted with spats were always popular with students of London's road transport. **198** has been curtailed at College Park and is making the left turn from Harrow Road into Scrubs Lane. Stonebridge depot brought some AEC vehicles to this group of routes in the form of C, E and N classes on the 626 and 628. Fred Ivey

First published 1994

ISBN 185414 155 4

Published by Capital Transport Publishing
38 Long Elmes, Harrow Weald, Middlesex

Printed by the KPC Group, Ashford, Kent

© Hugh Taylor 1994

LONDON TROLLEYBUS ROUTES

Hugh Taylor

Capital Transport

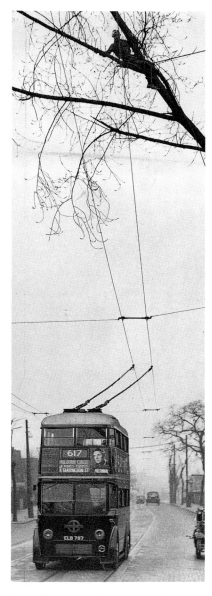

Above **Trolleybus wiring was usually closer to the kerb than tram overhead had been and so some additional tree lopping was necessary when trolleybuses were introduced. A member of a tree lopping team is seen above a brand new 787 on route 617.** John Aldridge collection

Upper Left **A splendid collection of vintage vehicles accompanies trolleybus 1006 heading north at Camden Town.** C. Carter

Left **A number of F class vehicles operated out of Hammersmith depot in later years. Here at Butterwick 753 continues its journey to West Croydon while 746 works into Hammersmith depot. The conductress of 746 has saved a bit of blind winding to show DEPOT HAMMERSMITH rather than HAMMERSMITH DEPOT.** Fred Ivey

Contents

THE KINGSTON ROUTES	9
ROUTES 657 AND 667	18
THE BEXLEY ROUTES	24
ROUTE 654	30
THE WANDSWORTH ROUTES	34
THE HANWELL ROUTES	42
NORTH WEST TRUNK ROUTES	48
THE HAMPSTEAD ROUTES	58
HIGHGATE HILL	62
THE FINCHLEY ROUTES	65
ROUTES 629 AND 641	72
ROUTE 653	76
THE KINGSLAND ROAD ROUTES	80
THE HERTFORD ROAD ROUTES	84
THE HACKNEY ROUTES	90
ROUTE 557	94
THE FOREST ROAD ROUTES	96
THE BOW ROAD ROUTES	102
THE ILFORD ROUTES	106
THE EAST HAM CIRCULARS	112
ROUTES 669 AND 685	114
THE DOCKS	120
THE COMMERCIAL ROAD	126
FOOTBALL SPECIALS	132
SYSTEM MAP	136
NIGHT ROUTES	138
STAFF TROLLEYBUSES	139
REVERSERS	140
BATTERY MOVEMENTS	142
NON-SERVICE MOVEMENTS	144
DELAYS AND DEWIREMENTS	145
DRIVER TRAINING	150
AT THE WHEEL	154
DEPOTS	160
MISCELLANEOUS MATTERS	162
THE SOUTH LONDON PROPOSALS	164
DESTINATION BLINDS	169

1218 on route 649A leads an RTW across Bishopsgate Junction. The operation of route 649A meant that three trolleybus routes served Liverpool Street on Sundays as opposed to two on weekdays. Lyndon Rowe

AUTHOR'S NOTE

Both in their life and in their death London trolleybuses have been a consuming passion for me. During preparation of this book I have learnt much more about their operation and I am very pleased to share it with you.

The opportunity is taken to cover in depth many of the facts about trolleybus operation in London that hitherto have been unpublished. As well as recording the changes to each route, there are a number of chapters detailing lesser-known aspects of the system. The photographic selection includes: all route numbers that operated, all main termini, all the preserved vehicles (apart from some of the Q1s in Spain), all rebodied types, all classes, all experimental vehicles and a Bournemouth vehicle on loan to London during the war.

The book could not have been written without the help of many people and they should be mentioned right at the start. Ken Blacker, Peter Carr, Frank Davis, Keith Farrow, Ken Glazier, David Kirk and John Price read through the original draft and offered many useful comments. Archival material owned by the London Omnibus Traction Society and the London Trolleybus Preservation Society was of great assistance. Other information also came from Ken Blacker, Peter Carr, Keith Farrow, Ken Glazier, Peter Nichols and Alan Nightingale. John Carwardine has carried out the artwork on the destination blind facsimilies and the many hours that he has spent on this are acknowledged. I am grateful to Keith Farrow and Mike Harris for the two maps. Frank Davis has provided much detail about the early movements of vehicles. There are many others who have contributed, including former trolleybus staff and a number of their anecdotes are included. An acknowledgement is also given to Terry Shaw of Isleworth depot; not only was it good to interview him, but also a pleasure to track him down and re-establish a friendship after 25 years.

During the preparation of the book I have been given access to many photographers' collections in order that the best possible photographic selection could be made. I am very grateful to all who have contributed in this manner and many of them have kindly accommodated me in their own homes; a bonus is that many new friendships have been made. John Fozard has literally printed thousands of photographs for me, often at short notice and most of the photos used herein are from his excellent standard of printing. I am also grateful to Sheila Taylor of the London Transport Museum for making their photographic collection available. Finally I must thank my wife Catherine for the many long hours typing the manuscript.

It became noticeable at an early stage that there was an element of conflicting information even within London Transport's official records. In such situations further research has usually brought an answer but there are a few matters that are still unresolved; where this is so, this is indicated. Some information is just not available: most early destination blind listings have not survived nor have all of the schedules, so some irregular journeys are probably unrecorded. Charlton works did not keep records of vehicle transfers; although cards existed for such data to be logged, they simply erased one entry and replaced it with another. Readers may observe that some dates quoted herein are at variance with those stated in other books on the subject, but it should be borne in mind that this new information has only recently come to light. The thorough checking of this book has hopefully resulted in an accurate record, but if you know otherwise, can clear up any unresolved matters or have any new information that may be able to be incorporated at some other time, please feel free to communicate with me via the publisher.

When there were but two trolleybus depots remaining, Fulwell and Isleworth, I had the pleasure to encounter two of the staff who were fiercely proud of working on trolleybuses, which they described as the 'Senior Service'. Ron Hadland was a driver at Fulwell depot and had conducted London's first trolleybus in 1931. It was his desire to drive London's last trolleybus and although this duty was available to him by the scheduled driver, an uncaring London Transport denied him his wish and he had to settle with conducting trolleybus No. 1 on its ceremonial run on 8th May 1962; despite this disappointment, he remained a faithful employee until retirement. Ron Hayward was a fitter at Isleworth depot and I recall with great affection many Saturday evenings in 1962 spent helping to shunt trolleybuses there. He would be in the cab and I would be on the bamboo pole, banging down trolleybooms under retaining hooks or hoisting them on to the wires. Here was I, a mere schoolboy, working with the living London trolleybus which to me was 'Queen of the road'. I am very grateful to him for allowing me those precious times.

Both these men are unfortunately no longer with us but it gives me the greatest of pleasure to dedicate this book to them.

Ron Hadland with 1837 in Fulwell depot; he described the Q1s as the 'Rolls-Royces' of the trolleybus world.
London Transport Magazine

Ron Hayward stands beside 1060 in his beloved Isleworth depot.
Hugh Taylor

Edgware, Middlesex, December 1993

HUGH TAYLOR

'Father of the fleet' trolleybus No.1 is seen outside Fulwell depot on a trial run of some nature. Trolleybuses 1 and 2 were initially fitted with a number of swivelling slats which had a destination painted on one side. These boards were fitted at the front and rear of the vehicle; an oval metal route number stencil was mounted on the roof, front and rear, with another one being positioned over the nearside entrance. These stencils were mounted between two brackets on the roof, while that over the doorway was placed into a slot. This early destination equipment was removed in favour of conventional blinds before they entered service. Trolleybus 1 was officially withdrawn in 1949 but ran again in London on a ceremonial run on the last day of trolleybuses in the capital, 8th May 1962. Despite 28 years inactivity, she successfully operated at the East Anglia Transport Museum, at Carlton Colville in 1990 by means of a loan agreement between the London Transport Museum and the London Trolleybus Preservation Society.

Charles Klapper

Trolleybuses 4 and 3 prepare to formally inaugurate the London trolleybus system at Twickenham on 16th May 1931. The motorman of LUT car 300 looks on, knowing that he too will be a trolleybus driver before long. The turning circle here was unattainable on two occasions; during the war due to bomb damage and for a short time in the mid-fifties due to road works. At both times, a special circle was constructed a hundred yards short, in King Street. John Aldridge collection

THE KINGSTON ROUTES

The 1930 London United Tramways Act became law on 1st August that year and gave the London United Tramways Ltd the authority to convert some of their tramway routes to trolleybus. It was not, however, the LUT's policy to abandon all of their tramways, for they were about to introduce a new type of tram on the busy and highly profitable trunk route 7 which ran from Uxbridge to Shepherds Bush; this was the 'Feltham', which was of expensive and ultra-modern design for its time. It had been decided that it was uneconomic to invest in track relaying and new trams for use in the Kingston area, where passenger use was not high, and the alternative of trolleybus operation was therefore adopted. Just as the LUT had been the first concern to introduce electric trams to London, so they were the first to introduce trolleybuses to the capital. The LUT wasted no time once their Act had been passed and on 1st October 1930 enough wiring had been erected in Twickenham for the first vehicle to make a trial run with a hired vehicle that day; the LUT had previously been involved with a trolleybus experiment in Haydons Road, Wimbledon in 1922/23.

At midday on Saturday 16th May 1931, after an opening ceremony at Twickenham involving two vehicles, trolleybus operation came to London. At the ceremony, trolleybus 4, the leading vehicle, was started by the Mayor of Twickenham; trolleybus 3 followed and a journey was made to Fulwell depot where lunch was given to civic dignitaries and officials of the company. Six vehicles were then placed into service that day. Route 1

Trolleybus 2 on route 3 heads a line up of vehicles in the Stanley Road side of Fulwell depot in September 1934.
London Transport Museum U15903

operated between Twickenham and Teddington, a 2½-mile stretch, with a through fare of 2d. Progress was rapid and on 15th June 1931 the Kingston Hill loop wiring was commissioned; this consisted of joining the two short tram routes of Kingston Hill and Richmond Park Gates by way of Park Road, which was the first road to be served by trolleybuses that had not been served by trams previously. Wiring was opened to trolleybuses between Teddington and Kingston on this date and route 1 was also extended to operate round the loop in both directions. On 15th July 1931, route 2 was introduced and operated from Tolworth 'Red Lion' to Richmond Park working round both loops; route 1 was diverted at Kingston to run to Tolworth at the same time. During the conversion period, shuttle tram services operated and the last to be withdrawn was that between The Dittons and Kingston. It was replaced on 29th July 1931 by route 2 which now operated from The Dittons to Tolworth working anti-clockwise around the loop. On the same date, route 3 was introduced and operated from Tolworth to The Dittons clockwise round the loop.

On 2nd September 1931, trolleybus route 4 was started between Hampton Court and Wimbledon Hill (St Georges Road); trams continued to operate until October when sufficient trolleybuses had been delivered. An exact date is not known, but the LUT November 1931 Traffic Circular stated that from Monday 26th October 1931 the pull frog at Norbiton Church was set for trolleybuses to Wimbledon, implying that the final trams had been withdrawn a few days earlier. Special instructions were in force for trolleybuses at Malden Bridge with vehicles travelling towards Kingston being required to keep to the centre of the road when passing under the bridge. A regulator was stationed on the Kingston side of the bridge to hold up traffic proceeding towards Wimbledon, so as to give trolleybuses travelling towards Kingston the unrestricted use of the roadway. He was equipped with red and green flags in daylight and red and green signalling lamps during darkness; the roadway beneath the bridge was lowered at some stage as these restrictions were later rescinded. The only extension opened by the LUT occurred when the 4 was

extended to Wimbledon Town Hall on 15th December 1932, with trolleybus route mileage now totalling 17.26. Routes 1-4 ran daily. A variation of route 4 was introduced (believed to be in 1932) operating on Saturday afternoons and evenings between Teddington and Malden; it was later renumbered route 5. Routes 1 to 5 were operated by Fulwell depot and meant long depot journeys for routes 2 and 3. There were a number of restrictions to the 'Diddlers' (the nickname given to vehicles 1-60). A 25 mph top speed was allowed with only 15 mph permitted in Kingston and Teddington; 10 mph was the top speed under bridges, although reducing to 5 mph under Malden Bridge. Routes 1-5 were renumbered 601-605 in the summer of 1935, a fare chart for route 604 appearing in August 1935.

Above **Trolleybus 35 stands on a wood-blocked road surface in Clarence Street, Kingston, bound for Twickenham on route 1 in September 1934. The overhead wiring has been changed from 18ins to 24ins width by now. The small child is fascinated by this form of transport and points it out to his mother.**
London Transport Museum U15914

At Norbiton, 55 heads for Wimbledon on route 4, while trolleybus 4 heads into Kingston. Just seen in the picture is a re-set skate for the Richmond Park trolleybuses to operate. John Aldridge collection

Right **Trolleybuses 6 and 37 on route 2 at Kingston in early days of the system; the original 18ins overhead wire spacing is still in use.** AEC

The trolleybus routes were an immediate success in many ways and a 26% increase in gross revenue over the trams was the reward. In terms of finance, they cost less to run than the trams and the operated mileage was 24% higher. About a third of the London United Tramways tram network had been converted to trolleybus operation in a very short time. The LUT obtained Parliamentary powers to extend trolleybus operations at Tolworth from the 'Red Lion' to the Kingston By-pass with a loop via Ewell Road, then using a service road alongside the Kingston By-pass to return via Warren Drive, this totalling 1500 yards. On much of this extension, use was made of concrete traction standards, but they remained unique in London. Work had commenced under LUT auspices but it did not open until 20th September 1933, by which time the London Passenger Transport Board was in being. Route 1 was extended to Tolworth By-pass and so became the second route to run over roads previously unserved by trams. It cost £11,000 to construct. On 20th September 1933, route 2 was revised to operate to and from The Dittons, working anti-clockwise round the loop with route 3 now operating to and from Tolworth, 'Red Lion', working clockwise round the loop. In November 1934 a notice was issued to trolleybus drivers that they were to cease treating the service road along the side of the Kingston By-pass as a private right of way belonging to the Board!

No.61, classified X1 yet carrying A3 on its platform wall, waits at the 'Tramways' trolleybus stop at Hampton Court in February 1935. Already different blinds are being printed (compare with photo of trolleybus 55 on the previous page) and the conductor is using a paper ticket issuing machine; the LUT were the first transport authority in London to use them. No.61 gained the nickname 'Bessie'.
London Transport Museum U16836

In pre-war years, routes 602 and 603 were known officially as 'Crosstowns' and 'The Loop' was quoted on schedules. From inception on 15th July 1931, there were short workings between Tolworth 'Red Lion' and Surbiton Station in weekday morning peak hours; operating as route 1A, two vehicles were allocated from Fulwell depot. This was renumbered 601A in the summer of 1935 but the route number was not displayed on the blinds; SURBITON STATION was all that was shown. The Saturday service was withdrawn in November 1939; but was restored in May 1940. The 601A last operated on 19th October 1943 when the Surbiton journeys were placed on the 601 schedule where they lingered until October 1948. A few weekday journeys on route 603 reached Tolworth By-pass with a Saturday journey being retained until May 1962. A general restriction at Tolworth allowed only one bus on the stand at a time but it was an instruction that was regularly

broken. On 9th November 1945, Surbiton-bound trolleybuses were diverted from St James's Road and Eden Street to run via Brook Street instead; £720 was spent on the erection of the overhead equipment. The diversion was made under one of two Parliamentary powers granted to London Transport in their last Trolleybus Bill in 1939 (the other being at Peckham Rye).

The January 1936 schedule gives insight into some particular needs which were met by London Transport in those days; a journey was projected from Fulwell depot to Tolworth By-pass to pick up dance-hall traffic on the return trip. There were also, at different times, 601s entering the depot from the Twickenham direction via the 667 route (quoted as London Road Gate). Another odd working between April 1944 and March 1946 was a 603 Sunday journey which returned to the depot via Hampton Court; it was the last 603 journey of the day so presumably served

a passenger need. Routes 602, 603 and 605 normally worked to and from Fulwell depot via Teddington while route 604 worked to and from Fulwell depot via Hampton Court. On Christmas Days some 604 running-in journeys operated from Hampton Court to Fulwell depot via Teddington, with boom shunting at Kingston Bridge. For a number of years on Sunday and Bank Holiday mornings, a 602 turned at Kingston Bridge roundabout from The Dittons. For the Christmas Days of 1960/61 the last 601 from Twickenham turned at Kingston Bridge roundabout, employing the little used link wires towards Hampton Court. Only one bus was allowed on the stand at Twickenham and if a second vehicle arrived then the first was to depart irrespective of scheduled time. This instruction was given as early as March 1934 and may have been in force since inception: it was quite usual, though, to see two vehicles on the stand.

No. 33 turns from Kings Road into Richmond Road in this September 1937 view. The pedestrian in his 'plus fours' gives little thought to the fact that the 'Diddlers' were now antiquated in comparison to the standard trolleybuses now coming into service in their hundreds. When the Diddlers first entered service, some drivers were discovered to be adjusting their brakes themselves. In March 1932, the LUT instructed drivers to cease this practice and that if adjustment was needed to call a fitter. G.H.F. Atkins

Routes 601-604 were very consistent performers over the years with regard to their routeing and they always operated daily, but route 605 underwent continual changes. From 8th May 1940 it became a daily route running from Teddington to Wimbledon in Monday to Friday peak hours, with the rest of the time working to Malden only; it ran to Wimbledon all day Mondays to Fridays from November 1947. From 16th November 1940, the Saturday service operated all day between Teddington and Wimbledon. From 16th May 1937, route 605 ran as and when required on Sunday afternoons and evenings between Hampton Court and Malden, but commencing on 2nd November 1941 was revised to operate between Teddington and Malden on this day, although the Hampton Court to Malden service was reintroduced in the summers of 1942 and 1943. There was no summer Sunday service in 1944 or 1945 and

it did not operate on Sundays between April 1945 and November 1947, when it began on winter Sundays between Teddington and Wimbledon. The reason for route 605 not operating during various summers was that it allowed resources to be concentrated on the Hampton Court service; in fact for the summers between 1943 and 1954, there was a higher 604 Sunday allocation on the route than on any other day of the week. There was no Sunday service on route 605 between May 1952 and January 1959. On Sunday 11th January 1959 (and also on Boxing Day 1958), route 605 was restored on Sundays, operating between Twickenham and Wimbledon. By doing this it served to temper cuts which occurred on routes 601 and 604 on Sundays at this time and was the last extension of a trolleybus route. The terminus at Teddington was alongside the Savoy cinema; upon its closure, the terminus became known as

Teddington Post Office and most destination blinds showed this henceforth; some 'Savoy' blinds continued to be used and 'Savoy' was retained on the schedules until the end. London Transport's allocation books for a number of years describe this location as 'Savoy Street' which had originated from 'Savoy Street Strand' tram terminus.

Routes 602 and 603 were the least patronised trolleybus routes; despite this, an eight-minute service operated on them as late as Christmas Day 1959; this was as generous as that on route 601 and almost as frequent as route 604 on that day. By now, however, London Transport was looking very closely at economies that could be made and from October 1961, early morning and late evening Sunday services on routes 601-605 were running at 28-minute intervals which was the widest that ever occurred on the system. From 7th January 1962 this led to public timetables being displayed at bus stops for the complete services on routes 602/603 and were the only trolleybus timetables. Only three vehicles were required on these routes on Sundays henceforth. The 601 suffered heavily on Sundays between 1950 and 1959 with the allocation falling from 18 vehicles to 6 – a two-thirds reduction; generally speaking though, routes 601, 604 and 605 were moderately well patronised. The terminus at The Dittons had the smallest number of departures from any terminus: from 95 departures in 1952 this became a mere 64 in 1962 – a one-third reduction.

Between 1935 and the delivery of the second batch of Q1s, there was an allocation of C1 class vehicles at Fulwell depot for route 667 which occasionally worked on routes 604/605 and very rarely on 601/602/603. Trolleybus 171 is seen outside Wimbledon Town Hall on route 605. The paper blind for this display had 'via Kingston' and 'Savoy' transposed. Behind 171 is a brand new 1768 on driver familiarisation duties. Lens of Sutton

Route 604 was at its busiest on summer Sundays and Bank Holidays when supplementary services were run; in the immediate post-war period much of the summer Sunday service was running at a two-minute interval and even in 1960 a three-minute service was operating on these days (in the summer of 1953, route 604 used double the number of vehicles on Sundays compared with Mondays to Fridays). The boosted schedules catered for visitors to Hampton Court which was just a nine-minute journey from Kingston. The last schedule compiled for trolleybuses was for Easter Sunday and Easter Monday, 22nd and 23rd April 1962, when five supplementary vehicles worked on route 604 between Hampton Court and Malden. The vehicles left the depot displaying EXTRA on the blinds but on inspectors' instructions were changed to 604. These five vehicles proved hopelessly inadequate to convey the crowds as a winter service was in operation at the time.

Kingston was served by all these routes and was their focal point; a well-known landmark passed on the Wimbledon run was Carters seed factory at Raynes Park opposite which Southern Region railway tracks paralleled the trolleybuses. The area around Surbiton was sylvan and in autumn the speed of the trolleybuses scattered leaves over the pavements; for many years, special LUT-style trolleybus stops abounded in the area. The antiquity of the 'Diddlers' was synonymous with these routes and they survived until the first batch of 8ft wide Q1s were delivered in 1948. Routes 601-605 were the recipients of these fine vehicles which first went into service on 1st March 1948, but their talents were somewhat wasted considering the low passenger carrying potential of some of the routes on which they worked. The Q1s made a complete contrast with the 'Diddlers', with dual operation of the two types persisting for some time. The Q1s incorporated the most up

to date equipment and were extremely fine vehicles; they were by far the best trolleybuses London Transport ever owned. There had long been voltage problems in the Kingston area and these became accentuated with the use of the Q1s; the vehicles were fitted with the customary rheostatic braking but regenerative control was omitted, for the power supply would not have stood up to this type of braking. As the Q1s often overloaded the power supply in this area, London Transport had to modify the substation equipment. Loadings taken shortly after the introduction of this class to routes 604/605 showed that the Q1s were not so productively used as the 'Diddlers' for the loadings had not increased significantly. The Q1s were popular with the staff and passengers, but from 1st February 1961 their places started to be taken by L3 vehicles ousted from north London routes. The Q1s were sold to Spain where they worked in new territories for many years.

Due to their width, Q1s were not allowed to pass at the junction of St Mark's Hill, Ewell Road with Surbiton Hill Road; vehicles proceeding towards Kingston had priority.

There was an air of complexity about routes 601, 602 and 603 as there was much changing from route to route and the very last 603 of all to operate on 8th May 1962 worked as a 601 from Twickenham to Kingston where it became a 603 to work around the Richmond Park loop before returning to Fulwell depot, also as a 603. Interchanging among the routes was as follows:

601 to 603 at Tolworth, 'Red Lion'
603 to 601 at Tolworth, 'Red Lion'
601 to 603 at Tolworth By-pass
603 to 601 at Tolworth By-pass
604 to 605 at Wimbledon
605 to 604 at Wimbledon
602 to 601 at Kingston
601 to 602 at Kingston
603 to 601 at Kingston
601 to 603 at Kingston
605 to 603 at Kingston

There were also a number of unusual journeys which operated as:

601 Twickenham to 603 Kingston Loop
605 Twickenham to 603 Kingston Loop
601 Twickenham to 602 Kingston Loop
602 Twickenham to Dittons
602 Dittons via Richmond Road (603) to Tolworth, 'Red Lion'

603 Tolworth 'Red Lion' via London Road (602) to Dittons
601 Depot to Loop to Tolworth By-pass
603 Depot to Loop to Tolworth By-pass
601 Depot to Loop to Twickenham
602 Depot to Loop to Twickenham
603 Depot to Loop to Twickenham
602 Dittons to Loop to Twickenham
603 Twickenham to Loop to By-pass
602 Dittons to Twickenham

There was not a consistent point for blind changing; it depended on the inclination of the conductor. However, it was normal practice for 602/603 Richmond Park to be displayed from Twickenham.

One Fulwell driver, answering to the nickname of 'The Galloping Major' had perfected a means of travelling through troughing (traction wires in wooden channels) at Raynes Park railway bridge at 28mph. This was done by centring his cab interior mirror with the troughing. Some of his colleagues tried to emulate him, but without success and many a trolleybus dewired here, with only 'The Galloping Major' continuing to sail through without mishap!

Just as these routes had been the first to open in 1931, so they were to be among the last to close in 1962. It had been the specific intention of London Transport to continue operating Q1 trolleybuses from Fulwell and Isleworth depots until the vehicles were life-expired in the late 1960s. Near the end of

Generally speaking, loadings around the Kingston loop were small, but on this occasion a reasonable number of people are using 1516. It is waiting at the stop in Park Road and the driver has correctly positioned the trolleybus beyond the section breaker, thus giving him an unbridled getaway. As can be seen on traction standard 74, the location of section breakers was designated to drivers by supporting standards being marked in white about a third of the way up. Peter Moore

1959 the London Transport Executive decided to convert the routes from these two depots to motorbuses and on 10th March 1960 provisional approval was given by the British Transport Commission. It was announced on 16th May 1960 that the routes operating from Fulwell and Isleworth depots would form the 14th stage of the trolleybus abandonment programme on 23rd May 1962 and the staff union was informed on 22nd December 1960 that the Q1s, about to be sold, would be replaced by standard vehicles. Due to advancing other routes, stage 14 was revised to a new date of Wednesday 9th May 1962 which was one week short of 31 years of trolleybus operation in London; the final roll-call would be on the traffic day of 8th May.

1511 speeds along the service road alongside the Kingston By-pass where bowstring support arms were fitted to the concrete traction poles. Ron Lunn

1389 turns onto The Dittons turning circle where 'fairy lights' assisted drivers when the light was dim. The driver's hat is placed in a favourite position, in the nearside of the cab. Don Thompson

The longest fast section of track on the trolleybus system was on the 604 between Hampton Court and Kingston; this was due to stops rarely being made and drivers having their vehicles flat out on the top controller notch on this straight road. In this view of 1392, Bushy Park is on the left and Home Park is on the right. Michael Dryhurst

1386 and 1437 squeeze past each other in Stanley Road, Fulwell. Not so long before, the space between passing trolleybuses was much tighter as 8ft wide Q1s worked these routes for many years. Stanley Road has now been cut off at Hampton Road. Peter Moore

ROUTES 657 and 667

Routes 657 and 667 first operated on Sunday 27th October 1935, this being the first stage of London Transport's tram to trolleybus conversion programme. The LPTB had decided that the £13 million invested in electrical plant could not be wasted and at an early stage had decided to replace the trams by trolleybuses; London Transport were eventually to have a maximum of 255 miles of trolleybus route. It was logical to choose tram route 67 first as this would rid Fulwell of its remaining trams. By converting tram route 57 simultaneously, trams would be removed from Chiswick High Road. (Trolleybus powers were granted to Chiswick Council in 1911 which would have seen trolley vehicles operating in Chiswick High Road but the powers were not utilised). This conversion brought trolleybuses to the County of London (at Hammersmith) for the first time.

It was planned for both routes to commence on 6th October 1935 but this was delayed due to the lack of vehicles. Comments made on the Ministry of Transport Inspector's report stated that "London Transport undertook to continue with the trolley vehicles the existing tramcar restriction over the Southern Rail-

way bridge at London Road, Twickenham, in that no two heavy vehicles will be on the bridge at the same time. Also at Gunnersbury Station Bridge, that no two heavy vehicles, including trolleybuses, would cross the bridge in the same direction at the same time". At mid-morning on 27th October, a special trolleybus carrying the press and senior London Transport officials travelled from Hounslow depot to Hammersmith where lunch was served at the Clarendon Hotel. In the first three days of operation receipts had increased by 30% over the earnings of the trams in 1934; there was a 13% increase in mileage at this time. Prior to the introduction of the 657, it was necessary to remove the horse trough at Shepherds Bush in order that there would not be any disturbance to the trolleybus services. London Transport paid for its removal but did not provide a replacement! The LPTB also considered constructing a trolleybus station at the east end of Shepherds Bush Green, but nothing was done.

Having figured in London Transport's first tram to trolleybus conversion, these two routes were to remain until the last stage of the trolleybus to bus conversion programme.

Both routes were initially allocated C1 class vehicles although a few B2s were allocated to the 667 prior to the delivery of sufficient C1s. At times 'Diddlers' worked on the 667, but this was rare. In 1952 the second batch of Q1s replaced the C1s which were transferred elsewhere.

Route 657 operated daily from Shepherds Bush to Hounslow, Wellington Road and worked from Hounslow depot; route 667 worked daily from Hammersmith Broadway to Hampton Court, being operated by Fulwell depot. Local feeling was divided as to whether the trolleybuses should follow the same one-way turn as the trams had done at Hammersmith which was via Glenthorne Road, or whether the direct route through King Street should be used. The inspecting officer, Colonel A.C. Trench, on behalf of the

Above **If necessary, Fulwell depot would press into service any licensed vehicle that was on the premises, including the works; this particularly applied on summer Sundays and Bank Holidays. 205, due to be allocated to Hendon depot, is used in this way in August 1936 and has almost a full load for Hampton Court as it takes on passengers at Kew Bridge. It is a very hot day and both windscreens are open.** G.H.F. Atkins

Ministry of Transport, made specific reference to the improvement that would be realised in King Street once the trams had been removed. This routeing was adopted. Initially route 667 operated both ways in King Street and terminated via Hammersmith Grove and Hammersmith Broadway to stand in King Street. During the summer of 1936 two diversions took place on this route for short periods. The first diversion was from Youngs Corner via Goldhawk Road to Seven Stars Junction, from where trolleybuses ran via Paddenswick Road to Hammersmith. The second was from King Street via Studland Street and Glenthorne Road to Hammersmith Grove. Both diversions were only in the easterly direction and were for the duration of the removal of tram tracks. The route via King Street was altered by October 1941 so that vehicles travelled in a one-way system via Glenthorne Road to turn via Hammersmith Grove, although it was thus utilised from time to time before this. From 6th January to late May 1936 while the tram tracks were being removed along its main line of route, eastbound 657s were diverted from Seven Stars Junction via Askew Road and Uxbridge Road to reach Shepherds Bush, with special link wires being put in for the purpose at 'Askew Arms' and Seven Stars Junction.

At Hounslow the 657 was extended half a mile beyond the tram terminus and although there was a proposal to extend the route around Hounslow via a $1\frac{1}{2}$ mile loop, it never materialised. A unique feature at Hounslow was a special conductor-operated signal which gave departing trolleybuses priority over other vehicles at the traffic lights. By operating a button on trolley pole 368, a white signal light on this pole signified that the traffic lights were now set against westbound traffic and that a clear departure from the terminus could be made; trolleybuses were given a maximum of 15 seconds to make the manoeuvre. Route 657 was the last trunk route to operate, always worked to a high frequency headway and was the more important of the two routes. On Christmas Days from 1936 until 1959 a five-minute service was run. The 657 was so busy on Saturdays that eastbound passengers would board westbound vehicles in Hounslow and travel to the terminus to ensure they would get a seat.

Top **Initially, trolleybuses operated northbound via Hammersmith Grove for their Hammersmith terminus. 177 and 180 are seen operating in this manner.** London Transport Museum U18749

Centre **61 was allocated to Hounslow depot for a time and was often to be seen working 'shorts' on route 657 between Hounslow and Brentford. Photographed at the Hounslow terminus, the special light mentioned in the text is in view. 61 was the first trolleybus in the country to receive three letters for its registration.** F.G. Reynolds

Left **The lone member of class X3, trolleybus 63, was used likewise by Hounslow depot; viewed in Hounslow High Street in July 1949 it is on the final leg of its journey.** Alan Cross

At 'The Nelson', Fulwell, this special trolleybus sign was still to be seen on 8th May 1962.
R.F. Mack courtesy Trolleybus Museum Company

There was only one location on the system where the trolleybuses ran alongside the River Thames; this was at Hampton where 1848 passes a number of boats moored thereon. Sid Hagarty

The two routes had a common section between Youngs Corner and Busch Corner which was always busy; westwards from here they were on their own apart from a short section in Twickenham on the 667. The famous rugby ground is situated here and extras would be lined up at Twickenham Station after the match to take supporters away; extras were also laid on for Brentford Football Club matches and in both cases vehicles from Hanwell and Hammersmith were used as well as the home depots.

Both routes, with the 655, underwent wiring alterations in 1957 when the Chiswick flyover was being constructed and trolleybuses picked their way through changing layouts. From time to time it was necessary to turn trolleybuses here by battery and even today troughing marks can still be discerned under the flyover, particularly in the westbound direction. The roundabout was first commissioned for trolleybus wiring from Sunday morning 6th September 1936, over 20 years earlier.

All year round from October 1942 until withdrawal, the 667 required fewer vehicles on Saturdays than on Sundays. Both routes were easy to operate for conductors as regards frog operation, with only one frog needing to be pulled for each of the routes (657 at Youngs Corner and 667 at Busch Corner). Fulwell and Hounslow tram depots featured in the first regular use of TIM paper ticket issuing machines. The trolleybuses inherited them and these two routes, along with the others operating from Fulwell, saw very little use of the punch and ticket rack system. Special sets were used by Hanwell until 1953 for their 667 workings and emergency sets were available at Fulwell and Hounslow depots. Cheap returns were available on some former London United Tramways' routes and it was the only area in which such tickets were issued.

London Transport has always been ready to accommodate specific needs and for a time from February 1939, turned a 657 at Kew Bridge so that it provided for the Busch Corner school end of day. A very unusual journey on Mondays to Saturdays, shown on the 1939 timetable, gives the last 667 journey of the day working from Hammersmith to Hounslow depot, having operated from Hounslow on its eastward journey. On the afternoon of 22nd April 1944, a schedules dispute arose on route 657 and army lorries were used. In the early fifties, a scheduling exercise gave Fulwell a share in operating route 657; it gave 24 minutes running time from Fulwell depot to Isleworth depot including a battery manoeuvre at Busch Corner. This was not put into practice.

An instruction issued to trolleybus drivers on 19th November 1948, stated that when using the stand at Hampton Court terminus they were to ensure that their vehicles were parked clear of the roadside water trough at this point. There must have been complaints from its users! There were two separate stands here (no doubt broken by the horse trough); one for two vehicles and one for one vehicle at trolley poles 307 and 306 respectively. On Sundays, Bank Holidays and on occasions when race meetings were held at Hurst Park, the accommodation at pole 306 was increased to four vehicles. Should a fourth or seventh vehicle arrive at the stand at these respective times, then the first vehicle was to proceed on its journey and the remaining vehicles move up accordingly.

1884 is seen at Seven Stars Junction on its journey to Shepherds Bush; it crossed the 660/666 wires at this location. The United Dairies shop, a taxi, various motor cars and another Q1, complete the scene. Don Thompson

A similar arrangement was in force here for route 604, in that if a fourth vehicle arrived on the stand which allowed three vehicles, then the first was to proceed on its journey and the remainder move up accordingly. It was reported at the General Manager's traffic meeting of 16th June 1938 that a number of public complaints had been received in that passengers were finding difficulty in securing accommodation on journeys proceeding to Hampton Court. Checks indicated that on fine evenings in the summer an inadequacy existed over a considerable period. Such was the importance attached to meeting the public demand, that events moved speedily and on 6th July the service was augmented on Monday to Friday afternoons and evening peak hours.

Hampton Court has always been an attraction for Londoners; not only was there Hampton Court Palace to view, but a fair was held on Bank Holidays with race meetings on these days at nearby Hurst Park. Large crowds were therefore attracted on Bank Holidays and the trolleybuses played a very important part in moving them. From 1936 a special 667 service operated on Bank Holiday Mondays from Shepherds Bush to Hampton Court and replaced a similar tram route. Fulwell depot ran it in 1936 with Hanwell and Hounslow depots joining them in 1937. Operations were only on three days a year (from 1959 only on Whit and August Mondays) and it worked in addition to the main 667, with Fulwell, Hanwell and Hounslow operating on both 667 services. In the early 1950s, Isle-

worth dropped out of these arrangements, followed by Hanwell's workings to Hammersmith and in the late fifties by Fulwell's workings to Shepherds Bush. This left just Hanwell depot to operate the Shepherds Bush to Hampton Court service as the last vestige of these interesting Bank Holiday journeys. On these trips, 657 was displayed to Shepherds Bush and 667 to Hampton Court; other permutations occurred and on August Bank Holiday 1960, the last occasion these journeys worked, EXTRA was displayed. On this day only three of the eleven scheduled Hanwell vehicles were operating, priority being given to cover 607 duties and those 667s that did run, did so to inspectors' instructions. On this occasion crew reliefs were at Fulwell depot when normally the relief point was at Busch

Corner with crews travelling to Isleworth depot for meals. These occasional outings found Hanwell drivers negotiating unfamiliar overhead and conductors were at a loss with the fares; this special route was not advertised and carried few passengers *from* Shepherds Bush. This service along with the main 667 one, which was always boosted on summer Sundays as well as Bank Holidays, meant that on any given Bank Holiday until 1958 and on Whit Mondays 1959/60 and August Bank Holiday 1959 twenty trolleybuses per hour were being operated to and from Hampton Court. Hanwell often used Q1s on their 667 runnings; when they used their native F1s though, they looked out of place with Fulwell's 8ft wide Q1 vehicles. After Hanwell depot had been converted to motorbuses, the special service ceased. From Bank Holidays 1961 the summer Sunday service sufficed on those days. To cater for the number of people requiring transport some 667s worked 'shorts' to Brentford instead of scheduled Hammersmith trips on these occasions.

In the immediate post-war period when the use of public transport was at its peak, large crowds needed to be transported on summer weekends to and from Hampton Court; this was particularly so on Sundays and Bank Holidays. The combined special and ordinary 667 services, with supplementary vehicles, were providing arrivals and departures at about one a minute. After their standard vehicles had been allocated, Fulwell depot pressed into service 61-63, any vehicles that were in the works but licensed and finally the 'Diddlers'. So great were the crowds on Bank Holidays that the inspectors had to send away a few trolleybuses prior to scheduled departure time, thus getting a queue to form. Once this was observed, the public knew that they should get in the queue, for otherwise they might have a problem getting home. This plan always worked, but so great were the crowds on some occasions that the inspectors knew that the remaining trolleybuses would not be sufficient to transport them. Consequently after the last Hammersmith had departed, crews were asked to take Fulwell depot-bound vehicles to either Twickenham, Brentford or even Hammersmith. This was a request that was always answered in the affirmative, such was the rapport between inspectors and crews.

During the summer and on Bank Holidays, large crowds needed to be carried to Syon Park at Brentford and to Kew Bridge for Kew Gardens. On Bank Holidays the special and ordinary 667 service helped in accommodating them as did the 657 whose service was boosted on summer Sundays until 1957. On Bank Holidays, a four-minute service operated on route 657 to cover requirements until August Bank Holiday 1960, although generally speaking Bank Holiday services did not operate on Easter Mondays from 1959. The 657 was one that did and augmented services operated. On Easter Monday 23rd April 1962, four extra vehicles ran, all correctly display-

Top **Bank Holiday workings were a special feature of route 667. Hanwell's 731, amid crowds at Hampton Court, sets off to Shepherds Bush; blind displays were provided for their 667 workings despite infrequent use.** Martin Brown

Above **Isleworth contributed EXTRAs on Bank Holidays on their sole route, the 657. This one is seen with 'grey socks', for some depots (Isleworth being one) added a touch of class to their vehicles by embellishing the ends of the trolley arms with grey paint. 1888 is photographed at Youngs Corner; from their delivery in 1952, Isleworth were stocked mainly with the higher numbers of this batch of Q1s until January 1961. Also working as an extra is a Thames Valley bus on relief duties.** Fred Ivey

ing EXTRA (some EXTRAs were operating on the 667 but 667 was turned up on inspectors' instructions). This was the last occasion that the EXTRA display was used and rather strangely the last extra (vehicle 1270) had to be curtailed at Stamford Brook Station. Extras being curtailed were extremely rare; another 'last' quirk of this particular journey was that it was driven by the last man to be trained as a trolleybus driver. A provision made from October 1950 until October 1961 for visitors to West Middlesex Hospital on Sunday and Bank Holiday afternoons brought two 'light' journeys into operation. On a journey from Hampton Court to Hammersmith one vehicle was to show TWICKENHAM and from there show PRIVATE and run empty to the hospital gates, while a journey which left Brentford, Half Acre, was to show PRIVATE and run empty to the hospital gates before picking up passengers; both ran for visitors' departure times.

As with so many other trolleybus services, route 657, which London Transport considered as one of its most important, suffered from traffic congestion. To alleviate the gaps that were caused in the service, the battery turn at Stamford Brook Station was wired up in 1957 and was frequently used to the benefit of this route in particular. The 657 and 667 were to prove very long lived, though it had been London Transport's stated intention to retain the routes operating from Fulwell and Isleworth depots until the late 1960s. However, big economies had been forthcoming in the early stages of the trolleybus conversion programme and the Q1s were sold to Spain in 1961. Older class vehicles were then used on the routes out of Fulwell and Isleworth depots henceforth, which was not popular with either the public or the staff. Routes 657 and 667 ran for the last time on Tuesday 8th May 1962; this was part of the 14th stage of the conversion programme and the last day of trolleybus operation in the capital. The amount of route mileage left at this time on the system was the same as that being operated on 27th October 1935.

The original wiring layout at Bexleyheath Market Place saw all vehicles working south of the Clock Tower. To enable the Bexleyheath conversions to take place on time, a few C1s were used for a while; 106 and 175 pass in the Broadway on 16th April 1936. The 'Boots' sign outlasted the trolleybuses as this sign was still extant in March 1959; their logo has stayed the course too.
London Transport Museum U20097

THE BEXLEYHEATH ROUTES

When London Transport was planning its tram to trolleybus conversion programme, the routes operating in the area centring on Bexleyheath came under early consideration. The determining factor for an early conversion was the condition and layout of the tram track, much of which was single track with loops. The elderly tramcars themselves had been replaced by newer ones.

A new depot was built and as such remained the only entirely new trolleybus depot to be constructed; local residents' protests did not prevent its commissioning. An amusing anecdote concerned some London Transport officials who were attempting to find the traffic potential in the area. They came across what they thought was a large factory being built near the centre of Bexleyheath; this was reported to their superiors who later found out that the 'factory' was in fact their own new trolleybus depot! 60-seater B2s were used initially on these routes but some C1s were drafted in at an early stage to provide require-

ments before a number of new D2s were allocated towards the end of 1936. A few 'Diddlers', on loan from Fulwell for training duties, were pressed into service using boards instead of blinds in the earliest days of operation. The B2s were appropriate, for there were various awkward turns in the area around Belvedere and Erith and projected passenger demand deemed that they would suffice. Between Woolwich Ferry and Plumstead Corner, trams used the same positive wire as trolleybuses. Six poles length from Wickham Lane the wiring split and the trams ran on their own wire to and from Abbey Wood, trolleybus conductors being required to pull the frog for this operation. This was the only instance of this type of dual working operating on a permanent basis in London and lasted from 1935 to 1952. It was anticipated that the 698 would commence on 13th October 1935 and the 696 on 17th November 1935 but the necessary vehicles were not delivered in time.

On Sunday 10th November 1935, route 698 began operating between Bexleyheath Market Place and Woolwich Ferry via Abbey Wood. This provided a very useful link, as tram 98 had only worked as far as Abbey Wood and passengers had to change there for Woolwich. This link had been much sought after by the Erith Council Tramways. On Sunday 24th November 1935, route 696 commenced and ran from Dartford Market Street to Woolwich Ferry via Welling; by operating to Dartford it was the only trolleybus route to work in a town that Central buses did not reach. (Route 698 had the sole timed connection with Country buses, a 480 at Erith, Wheatley Arms). Both routes worked out of Bexleyheath depot and, along with the yet to be introduced route 694, were the only London trolleybus routes in Kent; at Dartford the terminal stop was a request stop until such time as the tram and trolleybus departments were amalgamated with Central Buses. Throughout the system, request stops

Above Left **Some 'Diddlers' were used for training duties at Bexleyheath depot, and one member of the class is seen in this role at Bexleyheath Market Place.**
Courtesy David Packer

Above Right **384, the only D1 class vehicle, worked from Bexleyheath depot in 1936/37 and is seen leaving Dartford on the original anti-clockwise routeing which was used until August 1952.** John Aldridge Collection

Right **106, a Workman 696, heads towards West Hill, Dartford in the earliest days of the Bexley network.**
London Borough of Bexley, Local studies centre

Below Right **Viewed on inauguration day of route 698, 10th November 1935, is 94 — the first of the B2 class; it is welcomed with great interest at Woolwich Ferry.** LT Museum U18909

predominated in areas where trolley-buses operated and motorbuses did not, apart from the former London United Tramways area. Where buses and trolleybuses operated alongside each other, they used the same stops. Within two months of introduction it was necessary to augment the 696 between Woolwich and Bexleyheath; the service had been inadequate and it had been necessary to operate spare trolleybuses as extra vehicles.

At Dartford, the most easterly point of the trolleybus system, vehicles turned from High Street into Market Place and then proceeded from Market Street back into High Street; the terminal working was reversed to operate in a clockwise fashion in 1952. In autumn 1937, London Transport declined a proposal from Dartford Borough Council to extend the trolleybus service to the eastern boundary of its area to provide a through facility between the western and eastern areas of the Borough. In May 1946, Dartford Rural District Council co-operated with Dartford Borough Council in the former's efforts to persuade London Transport to extend the 696 to Gravesend; again the proposal was declined. Over the years there were many short workings on route 696 only as far as Bexleyheath Market Place from the Welling direction, but there was always a high-frequency service to Dart-ford. It was possible to see five vehicles together on the stand here, for drivers would put their foot down once Bexleyheath and supervision had been passed.

Although initially loadings were not high on both routes, passenger traffic grew considerably in due course, particularly on the 696. This was due to the housing and property boom taking place in the area and the army camps and munitions works at Woolwich. Consequently the 60-seat vehicles were soon superseded by 70-seater D2 and H1 types, although a few of the 60-seaters did remain until their withdrawal in the early fifties. Thirty vehicles were originally allocated to the 696 but this was soon increased to 39. Due to war requirements this was continually added to, culminating in 59 vehicles being used and it was not until 1955 that this figure started to decrease. Route 696 was always the more frequent and busier of the two routes. This was because it gave a quicker journey from Woolwich and Plumstead to Bexleyheath, and there was higher passenger use in the area around Welling than in the quieter backwaters of Belvedere and Erith.

On Sunday 16th May 1937, route 694 first ran, operating between Woolwich Ferry and Erith Station Road via Welling; it worked on Sunday and Bank Holiday afternoons and evenings and was operated by Bexleyheath depot. There are reports that these journeys had worked as an unnumbered service prior to this but London Transport's Traffic Circular for 21st May states that blinds were not available and lists which displays were to be used: on leaving Woolwich, 'BEXLEYHEATH MARKET PLACE via Welling' was to be shown with 'ERITH Station Road' to be shown on arrival at Welling Corner. On return the 696 Woolwich display was to be shown throughout and 696 was to be used at all times on the number blinds; when new blinds arrived, 694 and relevant destination details were used. The 694 operated until 28th January 1940 when it was withdrawn but it was reintroduced on Sundays and Bank Holidays for the summers of 1940 to 1944; it last worked on 28th May 1944.

Top **Trams 192 and 575 receive attention at the plough change pit at Woolwich Ferry. Trolleybus 415C and another trolleybus are in view as is a motorbus on route 75.** D.W.K. Jones

Centre Left **In the Abbey Wood and Plumstead areas, a number of combined tram and trolleybus stops existed. They were illuminated at night, as shown by this one at Basildon Road, Plumstead.** John Gillham

Centre Right **407B stands at Woolwich, Parsons Hill. No loop wire was ever constructed here despite the likely arrival of 696s and 698s out of turn. Consequently much boom lowering took place and for convenience a bamboo pole hung from a traction standard; 429 waits behind.** Alan B. Cross

Right **Route 694 continued to be displayed for the odd workings that took place on this network. It would be used on such a journey as 393 is about to make from Dartford to Erith.** Lens of Sutton

Route 694 continued to be shown, though, as conductors wound up this route number for the many unusual workings, mainly in peak hours, which occurred on routes 696 and 698, but the practice ceased as the blinds wore out. Some of these unusual workings had operated from very early days but with the onset of war, many more such journeys were introduced which remained in operation until the routes were withdrawn. Many of these workings catered for staff at Vickers' factory at Crayford, with special journeys commencing to Princes Road early in the war, for the factory was heavily involved with war work. Some 696 journeys to and from Crayford and Dartford were worked via route 698 and went variously to and from short working points on the route; one went from Crayford to Plumstead Station thereby performing two reverse manoeuvres in one journey and simultaneously using the only two scheduled reverser points on the system. The out-muster from the Vickers works needed a high-density trolleybus departure from Princes Road and an inspector supervised reversals and ensured punctuality for the six trolleybuses that left here to various locations in the evening peak. There were three at 5.07pm, although one of these was from Dartford. There were also some 696 journeys working both ways from Woolwich via Abbey Wood to Dartford Market Street; these operated in Monday to Saturday morning peak hours. There was also an unusual 698 midday journey out of the depot which turned at Erith, Wheatley Arms on battery (not an approved point) before returning to Welling (shades of a 694), from where it operated to Dartford; also a wartime Sunday midday 696 journey operated in the same fashion but in the reverse direction. The most unusual journey on these routes, however, was a wartime Sunday midday 696 journey from Woolwich to Welling Corner via Abbey Wood (it then went to Dartford before returning to the depot). The reason for such a journey seems obscure but the schedules regularly refer to connections at specific factories at various locations; no doubt this was the function of this journey. Due to the wiring layout, all 698s operating into the depot had to go via Bexleyheath Market Place which was the centre of activities for these routes; as early as February 1938, London Transport wanted to operate the 698 as a self contained route but this turned out to be impracticable. Despite the small nature of operations of the routes there was changing from one route to another with 696s changing to 698s and vice versa at Woolwich, Plumstead Station and Bexleyheath Market Place.

Centre **793** heads five of the 'Crayford Six' which await the outmuster from Vickers works. The loop wire cannot accommodate these six, so some have to wait with poles under retaining hooks. Denis Battams

Left **786B** and **799B** pass at 'The Harrow Inn' at Abbey Wood. 799B is on one of the special 696 workings from Abbey Wood to Dartford. Fred Ivey

In 1938 the possibility of acquiring some spare land adjacent to Plumstead bus garage for a turning point was looked into but enquiries did not bear fruit. Instead a turning loop was erected at Villacourt Road in Wickham Lane in 1941, accommodating passengers on the section from Plumstead to Woolwich; uniquely the turning circle was at a traffic island in a housing estate. In the early postwar period, management became aware that crews were reversing into the loop here from the wrong direction and then coming out on battery, thus missing out the remainder of the journey to Woolwich; they took steps to prevent it continuing. At Welling Corner, the short working facility was available from both directions and was useful for providing an intensive service to Woolwich.

With the onset of war with Germany, Woolwich Arsenal played a very important part in the war effort. The 696 and 698 transported many of its workers, but there was a perennial problem of matching crew schedules to the fluctuating finishing times of the workers' shifts. Although there was no successful bombing on Woolwich Arsenal, two bombs fell on Bexleyheath depot; the first was on 7th November 1940 and four vehicles needed to be rebodied. The depot received a direct hit by a doodlebug flying bomb at 3.20am on 29th June 1944 and was set on fire. The damage was so catastrophic that none of the 84 vehicles were fit for service. Twelve were completely destroyed, 26 needed rebodying

and the remainder required major attention. London Transport rose to the occasion, though, and drafted in enough buses and trolleybuses to run an almost normal service that evening.

The section from Crayford to Dartford became a restricted area in wartime and became part of the south east coastal zone. Trolleybuses were stopped at a control point at Crayford, Princes Road for checking of papers and those without the necessary documents were turned off. After the end of hostilities, Woolwich Arsenal continued to be active and the transporting of its workers continued to be an important task.

The terminus at Woolwich Ferry became too cramped to accommodate all the turning vehicles comfortably (the Police too, were concerned about the congestion) and routes 696 and 698 were extended to Parsons Hill on 14th July 1943 with the 694 following on 18th July 1943; it was the last new wiring for an extension of trolleybus routes. It is conceivable that the extension may have been constructed under powers for the South London conversion scheme; however, it may have been constructed under Defence regulations. The extension was for an experimental period of three months, but was deemed successful and remained as the terminus thereafter.

Above **440 at West Street, Erith; route 698 trolleybuses negotiated two sets of level crossings in the space of less than half a mile; these were over freight lines. It is believed that these were the only level crossings that were crossed by London trolleybuses.** Fred Ivey

Left **Descending West Hill, Dartford is 451B; the blinds are already changed as it passes beneath bowstring traction standards. By using this means of support, money was saved on rentals to local councils; an annual fee, varying with the councils concerned, had to be paid on each one.** Don Thompson

Drivers were not allowed to leave their cabs at Parsons Hill until conductors had scotched a wheel. In 1955, 52 vehicles an hour left Parsons Hill between 7 and 8am on Mondays to Fridays which included 41 on the 696; two vehicles departed at the same time for Bexleyheath Market Place. At Woolwich Ferry (Nile Street on early schedules), the vehicles were in sight of trolleybuses at North Woolwich directly across the River Thames. At Beresford Square there were disused tram tracks which outlived vestiges of trolleybus operation by many years and also a market and trolleybus passenger queueing pens.

Extra vehicles were run for Crayford dog track on race meeting nights and extras were also run to Welling for Danson Park fair and fireworks. On Saturday afternoons, right until 1959, extras were provided on the 698 from Bexleyheath to Station Road, Erith to cater for the volume of shoppers; these journeys had been part of the schedule from early 1940 until May 1954. In September 1958 when a number of vehicles were out of action due to having been driven through floodwater, B3 class 489 and a number of withdrawn D3 class vehicles were allocated to Bexleyheath depot for a few days. A significant factor in the post-war period was the large number of re-

bodied vehicles working on the routes; about every third trolleybus was of the rebodied variety.

London Transport intended to link these routes to others that were to be converted from tram to trolleybus operation in south London but this did not happen and the routes' isolation was a factor for including them at stage one of the trolleybus to bus conversion programme. Serious consideration had been given to converting routes 654, 696 and 698 to RT operation in July 1955 as a preliminary stage of the conversion programme; this was not proceeded with due to the high prices that could be obtained for the surplus buses that existed at the time and which could be used by other operators.

In February 1957, thought was given to converting route 698 to Routemaster operation in the spring of 1958 in order for the engineers to gain experience of this type of vehicle, but too many complications were foreseen. An inefficient 698 schedule would have resulted and the 696 and 698 would have worked under different staff agreements, as those of central buses and trolleybuses were not the same. The idea was dropped. It had always been planned for Bexleyheath and Carshalton depots to form the first stage of the conversion scheme and the varied proposed conversion dates quoted for route 654 apply equally to the 696 and 698 which survived until they were withdrawn after operations on Tuesday 3rd March 1959.

Above **Four trolleybuses were just able to squeeze onto the shunt wire at Bexleyheath Market Place. On the last Saturday of operation, 28th February 1959, No.480 heads a line-up of four. 480's driver is experienced enough to know how far he can run up the loop without fouling the 696 through wires from Dartford; close inspection of the photo shows that there is very little gap between the positive trolley boom and the negative wire from Dartford. Some drivers did not gauge this properly and 696s hit shunt buses' poles.** John Gillham

Right **553, the last D3, was transferred into Bexleyheath at a very late stge, the second half of January 1959. Pictured under the oddly constructed Plumstead reverser on 28th February that year, it only had another three more working days after this; the horse was destined for a longer life!** Denis Battams

84 has climbed to the top of Ringstead Road, Carshalton on its way to Crystal Palace; the original wire grille valance has been replaced by a newer model. The traction standards here look as if they could do with a new lick of paint.
Don Thompson

ROUTE 654

When London Transport took over the operation of the capital's public transport on 1st July 1933, it inherited a motley collection of vehicles. This included a number of elderly tramcars and some of the most decrepit were those operating on the former South Metropolitan Electric Tramways network. When London Transport made the decision to replace the trams by trolleybuses, among the earliest withdrawals were these trams, which at the time of conversion were the last open-top cars in regular service. Another factor in this early conversion was that for much of the way the route was single track with passing loops. Consequently on Sunday 8th December 1935, trolleybus route 654 from Sutton depot was inaugurated, running between Sutton, Bushey Road and West Croydon.

As not enough B1 class vehicles were available for the conversion, that had already been put back from October, a few 'Diddlers' had to be used. The B1s were 60-seaters (standard vehicles seated 70) and had short wheelbases which were ideal, as there were a number of awkward bridges and narrow roads en route. It was intended to link up two separate tram routes which had been operating and this occurred on Sunday 9th February 1936 when

the 654 was extended to Crystal Palace. Upon the 654's introduction an experimental roundabout was constructed at Crystal Palace which was retained, as it improved the traffic flow; the vehicles were to see the Crystal Palace for only a short time as it was destroyed by fire on 30th November 1936. At Crystal Palace, the traction standards were set in four boroughs (Camberwell, Penge, Croydon and Lambeth) such was the complexity of trolleybus infrastructure. The tram route had terminated at 'The Grapes' in Sutton so there was a small extension to Sutton Green. The 1924 Croydon Corporation Act gave powers to operate trolleybuses from George Street, Croydon to Woodside via the Addiscombe tram route and for a turning loop in Croydon via George Street, High Street, Katherine Street and Park Lane. None were taken up.

Due to its steepness, 1 in 9, Anerley Hill required special braking equipment for the trolleybuses that were to be used on the route. Run-back and coasting brake equipment was fitted to them and extensive trials were made on the hill with this equipment in preparation for the introduction of trolleybuses. Drivers were not allowed to leave their cabins at

Crystal Palace and conductors had to place a scotch (which was carried under the staircase on the vehicle) in front of the nearside central wheel which was returned to its position at departure time. As soon as the vehicle had arrived at Crystal Palace, the driver had to switch in the coasting brake equipment. This was by means of a special lever marked 'run' and 'brake' or 'power' and 'brake' (this also applied to vehicles operating on Highgate Hill). On departure from the terminus, braking was by handbrake (rescinded at some stage) until the coasting brake came into operation which limited the speed to 10mph. Power was cut off from the control pedal during the time the coasting brake was functioning (the use of the handbrake being to ensure a full reservoir of air for possible emergency stops). This equipment was switched off at the compulsory Brunswick Place stop at the bottom of the hill (pole 24). There was also a compulsory stop halfway down the hill on the descent at pole 15. On the ascent of the hill a run-back brake automatically operated in the event of a trolleybus running back due to a power failure or the circuit breaker tripping which limited the speed to 2mph. Trolleybus 65 was deliber-

ately dewired in trials two days before opening to satisfy the Ministry of Transport about the efficiency of the equipment. The MoT inspecting officer stated "the Board will arrange that the rules for the descent of this hill are most scrupulously followed and operation will be limited to drivers qualified by special instruction". However, drivers did descend the hill without the coasting brake in operation, hoping that there would not be an LPTB inspector observing whether the MoT stipulation was being obeyed. No passengers were allowed to stand on the ascent of the hill or on the descent as far as Brunswick Place. In February 1936 the MoT withdrew the restriction of standing passengers on the ascent (it had been difficult to enforce). From July 1936, eight passengers were allowed to stand on the descent but this was rescinded by the Regional Transport Commissioner; on 22nd January 1943 staff were notified twelve standing passengers were now allowed on the descent. The MoT report also stated that it would be necessary that the road authorities did not raise the level of the road surface at all in the course of any reconstruction at Selhurst Bridge, where there was a minimum clearance of 16 feet between the road surface and the trolley wire.

The first B1, trolleybus 64, makes a trial run around an incomplete trolleybus roundabout at Crystal Palace; trams are still running for one can be seen in the right hand corner. Trolleybuses were to pass the Crystal Palace building for less than a year (it was burnt down on 30th November 1936), so such a view is rare. Courtesy David Packer

Below **Extract from a Tram & Trolleybus Dept Traffic Circular regarding Anerley Hill.**

884.—ANERLEY HILL.

INSTRUCTIONS FOR TROLLEYBUS DRIVERS AND CONDUCTORS.

All trolleybuses operating on the Crystal Palace Section are equipped with special braking apparatus consisting of :—

    (a) A run-back brake which will come into operation automatically in the event of a bus commencing to run back when ascending the hill.

    (b) A special electric coasting brake which will automatically control the speed of the bus when descending the hill. The brake is controlled by a switch placed on the right-hand side of the cab and marked " Run " and " Brake."

The following instructions must be rigidly observed :—

Ascending the Hill.

Should the power fail or a circuit breaker blow the driver must immediately apply the foot brake and hand brake. In addition the run-back brake will come into operation automatically. The reversing key must be kept in the forward trolley position for the run-back brake to operate.

At the Terminus.

After turning at the top of the hill the bus must be brought to a standstill at the stopping place ; the driver must fully apply the hand brake, and then operate the coasting brake switch, turning the handle from the run position to the brake position. The reverser must be in the forward trolley position. The conductor must then place the scotch in front of the nearside centre wheel.

Descending the Hill.

When ready to descend the hill, the conductor must remove the scotch, place it under the staircase and give the signal to proceed. The driver must then gradually release the hand brake, allowing the bus to coast without power, but still controlled by the hand brake until the coasting brake comes into action automatically. This will control the speed of the bus to less than 10 miles an hour. Any additional braking must be done with the hand brake, except in emergency when the air brake must be applied.

Power is cut off from the control pedal during the time the coasting brake is in operation.

At the compulsory stop half-way down the hill the trolleybus must be brought to rest on the hand brake. On re-starting, gradually release the brake as before.

Upon reaching the compulsory stop at the bottom of the hill, the bus must be brought to a standstill and the coasting brake switch moved to the running position. The bus can then be operated as under normal conditions.

Special Notes.

    (1) The coasting brake switch must not be moved except when the trolleybus is stationary.

    (2) The coasting brake is inoperative when the reverser is in the battery position.

    (3) A bus must not be driven in service if the air pressure is below 50 lbs.

Above **Trolleybuses were not allowed to stop on the ascent of Anerley Hill, so this special sign was placed at the foot of the hill.** Frank Mussett

Above Right **The driver of 1051 is disengaging the coasting brake at Brunswick Place, Anerley Hill; the J3s had a slightly higher descending speed than the B1s that they were supplementing at this time.** Denis Battams

Arrangements for the turning circle at West Croydon Station from 7am on Wednesday 10th March 1937 stated that the frog was electrically operated. Two push buttons were provided on pole 224 marked 'branch' and 'straight' (elsewhere, they could be marked 'curve' and 'straight') and an indicator on pole 221 showed the direction for which the frog was set. London Transport's Traffic Circular stated that in the event of failure, 'call for tower wagon and change poles over by hand'. During the war it was necessary to operate motorbuses on the 654 when a bomb fell outside the depot, preventing the use of trolleybuses for a time.

Route 654's only link with the remainder of the system was between West Croydon and Pitlake Junction where it ran alongside the 630. The junction was controlled by two colour-light signals which were installed from the use of this junction for trolleybuses in 1937 (a similar practice had been in force for tram operation and no doubt a system was in operation for the time of dual tram/trolleybus operation). One was installed at pole 246 in Tamworth Road and the other on pole 2 in Lower Church Street and each was activated by the conductor operating a push button. They were reset by the trolley head activating a skate as it passed out of the section. The signal showed a white vertical repeater arrow for 'proceed' and a red horizontal arrow light for 'trolleybus approaching; wait for white light to proceed'. The signals were arranged to allow more than one vehicle through the section at a time. The light system was specially for Croydon-bound 630s but they also

controlled the movement of westbound 654s although a priority was given over them to eastbound 630s. Eastbound 654s were at the driver's discretion. While an adverse signal was showing, operation of the frog was prohibited. This special system remained in operation until 1956 when ordinary traffic signals were installed. By April 1946, the facing frog here had become interlaced (a unique feature on the system) and remained so until January 1956. Experiments were also carried out here with driver-controlled frog operation by radio control, with three B1s on the 654 being specially equipped.

Route 654 operated a frequent service through Norwood, Selhurst, Croydon and Wallington; at Wallington the most southerly point of the trolleybus system was reached. At Waddon Station a complete circle of wires was constructed with no centre pole for support as the circle was within the running wires with all support coming from the span wires. It was used by a few journeys each week from the Sutton end. Traffic for Crystal Palace FC at Selhurst Park was carried by the ordinary service.

A very interesting situation occurred in September 1958 when a number of B1s were out of action due to having been driven through heavy floodwater, thereby damaging the motors. Three J3s (1049-1051) were drafted in from Highgate depot to make up the 654's quota and were used for a few days. Carshalton drivers had never driven full-length trolleybuses before and did so on a voluntary basis, no familiarisation being given to them beforehand. The drivers also had the unusual task of changing the front destination blind, receiving instructions from their conductors about the order of displays. The J3s, with their special brakes, had a slightly higher speed to descend Anerley Hill.

From 1949 the route operated the oldest trolleybuses in the fleet and this was a determining factor in including the 654 at stage one of the trolleybus conversion programme. Thought was given to converting the 654 to RT operation as early as July 1955 along with routes 696 and 698 as a preliminary stage of the trolleybus conversion programme, and it would have eliminated isolated pockets of trolleybus operation. By April 1957 consideration was given to using the 654 as a test bed for the Routemaster bus as the engineers wanted to have some operational experience with the production model. However, route 654 was considered not to be arduous enough and route 611 was considered a better possibility, though this was not proceeded with either. It was thought that January 1958 was the latest that the B1s could last in service and 1st January 1958 was the date set for the conversion of the route. When it became obvious that this date would not be adhered to, a revised date of 1st January 1959 was given. This was later changed to 1st March 1959 but was retarded by three days to coincide with the start of the crews' payroll week. In complete contrast to the farewells given in each stage of the tram to bus conversion programme, very few people turned out to see the conclusion of the first stage of the trolleybus to bus conversion. Vehicle 65 was hired on the final night of operation by the proprietor of a local paper for a trip from the depot to West Croydon and back. The participants attempted to make 65 the last vehicle into the depot but the driver of trolleybus 83, the last service trolleybus, was having none of it and ensured that 83 was 'last man home'. Timewise, route 654 was the first casualty of the £10.5 million conversion programme and vehicle 83 closed the route in the early hours of Wednesday 4th March 1959.

Left **493** passes beneath a bowstring bracket arm in Penge Road, Norwood. Due to the narrow roads, there were a number of locations on the route where this type of overhead support was installed; it was less obtrusive and cheaper than the traditional method.
Denis Battams

Below **86** with a wire valance stands at the Sutton terminus. There were **42** silver painted fluted traction poles between here and Benhill Avenue; they were painted silver for amenity reasons, although by the time that the route was to be withdrawn, they looked very grim indeed. Alan Cross

THE WANDSWORTH ROUTES

Sunday 12th September 1937 saw the introduction to the area of daily trolleybus routes 612, 628 and 630, with a fourth route, 626, commencing on the following day. When the inspection of the Harrow Road route had taken place on 17th August 1936, the MoT was informed that the conversion of the Wood Lane trams to trolleybuses would take place at the end of January 1937.

Route 612 operated from Wandsworth depot and worked between Battersea 'Princes Head' and Mitcham, Fair Green, being the southern portion of tram route 12 which continued to run from Wandsworth to the Borough at London Bridge; it was intended to link the truncated tram route 12 with route 612 as one through trolleybus route between Mitcham and London Bridge at a later stage. A large turning loop, via Battersea Park Road, Candahar Road and Cabul Road was constructed at Battersea to enable route 612 to terminate; the stand at Cabul Road was on the offside of this thoroughfare.

Route 628, working from Hammersmith depot, operated from Clapham Junction to Harlesden, Craven Park on Mondays to Saturdays but on Sundays ran only as far as

Harrow Road, Scrubs Lane. It, too, broke a tram service in two, with tram route 28 continuing to run from Clapham Junction to Victoria. Again it was the intention to join the two routes as one trolleybus route in due course with route 628 operating between Wembley and Victoria.

Route 626 first ran on Monday 13th September 1937 and was also allocated to Hammersmith depot, working between Acton Market Place and Clapham Junction via North Acton and Shepherds Bush in Monday to Saturday peak hours (Saturday peak hours during the trolleybus era meant morning and midday). The partly replaced tram route 26 now ran between Clapham Junction and London Bridge, Borough. The level of service between Clapham Junction and Hammersmith in off-peaks was maintained by an all-day service on an extended 655 route. It was intended in due course to join tram route 26 and trolleybus route 626 as a daily trolleybus route between Hammersmith and London Bridge, Borough. The through running services on routes 612, 626 and 628 would have taken place in the proposed South London Tramway conversion scheme.

Suitable turning arrangements had to be found for the trolleybuses at Clapham Junction. The wires were directed along Falcon Road to turn into Meyrick Road and stand in Grant Road with return via Lavender Road; this meant running beneath the two main bridges of the Clapham Junction rail network and, at over 100 yards, carried the longest piece of troughing on the system (wiring was fixed in wooden channels attached to the underside of bridges and could also be seen in depots). A 5mph speed limit was in force beneath bridges, for if a boom dewired at speed it could bend against the bridge girders.

Above **No.429 is seen at Clapham Junction, although its blinds are turned for the trip back to Craven Park; tram 1501 on the truncated 28 tram route is also in view. No.429 did not stay at Hammersmith depot long, for it was transferred to Bexleyheath depot in early 1938. In March 1959, this vehicle gained an unwanted tag of being the first trolleybus to be dismantled by Cohen's at Colindale.** John Aldridge Collection

No.511 has parked up in Candahar Road on the Battersea turning loop. In the background, a tramcar passes under the railway bridge in Battersea Park Road. Wandsworth was the only depot to retain tram operations during its life as a trolleybus operator. David Packer

Wandsworth High Street Junction was the location for some experimental wiring to be constructed in the immediate post-war period. One of the two D2s allocated to Wandsworth depot waits at the traffic lights. C. Carter

From 4th August 1938, the Monday to Friday evening (7-11pm) service on route 628 was extended to Wembley for greyhound and speedway racing at Wembley Stadium though this lasted only until 21st November 1939 with Craven Park becoming the northern terminus again the next day. This was due to the Government placing restrictions on services specially laid on for sporting events. At the same time the Monday to Saturday evening service was curtailed at Scrubs Lane. This was restored in October 1949 and the 628 also commenced to operate to Craven Park on Sundays. The 628 now operated daily between Clapham Junction and Craven Park. Much of the Monday to Friday peak hour service to Craven Park was withdrawn after 6th January 1959, the 628 ceasing to run at these times. A wider headway was also required at the Clapham end and these cutbacks were met by increasing the number

of 626s. The schedule file for route 628 provided for it to operate to Sudbury but this never occurred. Until at least the 1946 issue, 'Sudbury' and 'Wembley' were included on Hammersmith destination blinds.

Initially, special arrangements were necessary for southbound trolleybuses at The Lawn, Shepherds Bush for they used this road which was otherwise one-way northbound for all traffic. It was agreed with the police that a line of 'keep left' markers should be positioned appropriately in order to define the route for the southbound trolleybuses and to debar northbound traffic from using this portion of the roadway. These were to be in place before the opening on Sunday 12th September. It was understood that these

arrangements were intended to be of a temporary nature only, pending a decision by the London Traffic Advisory Committee and other authorities concerned with permanent arrangements for traffic at Shepherds Bush. The whole question of traffic circulation at Shepherds Bush had been under consideration for some time, but London Transport had objected to the suggestion of the Wood Lane trolleybuses working right round Shepherds Bush Green itself on the grounds of cost. Such was the pressure on London Transport that by the summer of 1939, all Wood Lane trolleybuses circled The Green on their journey south. Between May and October 1938, the trolleybuses had been diverted around The Green utilising temporary wiring.

Above An unusual allocation to Hammersmith depot in 1954 was short wheelbase 484 of the B3 class. Photographed at West Croydon, it is heading for the nondescript NR WILLESDEN JUNCTION. Geoff Baddeley

Right A fast run across Mitcham Common was always guaranteed and the driver of 1705 is making no exception to this. The 'Buses for Trolleybuses' notices are on every traction standard, detailing route 630's imminent withdrawal — but was it really necessary for them to be placed on every single pole when the pavements were little used here! Tony Belton

Route 630 from Hammersmith depot operated between West Croydon and Harrow Road, Scrubs Lane. The tram terminus here had been at the junction of these roads, but the trolleybus terminus was in Letchford Gardens, a side road nearby. London Transport were not happy with this terminus as it was not in a main area. Following tramway practice, it was known as NR WILLESDEN JUNCTION on the destination blinds, a description which was far from accurate as this was half a mile away. It was not until well into the 1950s that the terminus became known as HARLESDEN, (COLLEGE PARK) on blinds; NR WILLESDEN JUNCTION continued to be shown for many years however, with vehicle 656 retaining this display in its rear

box until almost the end of these routes. It was intended that Thornton Heath depot, which had worked on tram route 30, would have an allocation on the 630 when its other tram routes were converted to trolleybuses. This did not happen, but staff at Thornton Heath were asked to volunteer to transfer to Hammersmith depot to work the 630, with the intention of their returning to Thornton Heath upon that depot's change to trolleybuses. Consequently, provision was made to transport such staff to Hammersmith depot and very early staff trolleybuses were run. Some staff were still working at Hammersmith in 1960 and then returned to Thornton Heath! While rebuilding continued at Hammersmith depot, it was necessary for

some vehicles on routes 626, 628 and 630 to park daily at the former Chiswick tram depot for a few weeks; journeys were made out of service.

Route 630 increased in stature over the years. In 1941, it required 32 vehicles on Mondays to Fridays; in 1951 it needed 52. During the same period, the Saturday allocation jumped from 32 to 51 (for a short time it had been 53) with the Sunday allocation moving from 20 to 33; these all meant a 50% increase. On post-war Bank Holidays, 54 vehicles were allocated to the route which operated a three-minute headway throughout, from midday until close of traffic. Route 630 was by far the busiest of the Wandsworth routes.

Above **Three 630s have arrived at Mitcham from West Croydon together. A small number of F1s were latterly allocated to Hammersmith depot; 749 was one such example and is about to pass under the trailing frog here.** Fred Ivey

Left **There were only two places on the system where trolleybuses crossed the River Thames; these were at Kingston and Putney bridges. No.422 on route 628 crosses Putney Bridge and is followed by another D2 on route 630.** Denis Battams

On Wednesday 2nd April 1941, a bomb fell in Garratt Lane severing the trolleybus route. It was expected that repairs would take several months so it was decided to divert routes 612 and 630 around the neighbouring streets. Traction standards and overhead wiring were in position by 5th April and the diversion was brought into use the following day. Southbound trolleybuses operated via Wilna Road and Atheldene Road back into Garratt Lane while northbound vehicles travelled via Atheldene Road, Farlton Road and Wilna Road, the split running being necessary owing to the narrowness of the roads concerned. This diversion remained in use for much of that year. On 22nd November 1944, the 612 terminus at 'Princes Head' was destroyed by enemy action; 612s had to travel via Falcon Road and Clapham Junction to pick up line of route at Wandsworth.

The main function of route 626 was to give essential peak hour augmentation for factories in the North Acton area and to give a direct link to them from the Scrubs Lane vicinity. It operated on Sunday mornings from 9th February 1941 until 7th April 1946 for munitions journeys from Clapham Junction to Acton and return. The route did not have many through journeys and there were always more of these in the evening than in the morning; it last ran on Saturdays on 4th June 1949.

Routes 612 and 630 operated in heavy tram-occupied territory until 1951 with the conversion in 1937 being the first to replace conduit-equipped tram routes. It was also the only occasion when a tram to trolleybus conversion programme was carried out in two different areas, another scheme being carried out in east London simultaneously.

1085 turns into Fulham Palace Road while road and wiring layouts are realigned in 1960. In this view both Riverside bus garage and Hammersmith trolleybus depot can be seen. Due to the march of progress both are now demolished.
Denis Battams

After withdrawal from the 628 in January 1959, Stonebridge depot continued to contribute to the route on some Bank Holiday Mondays. No.1636 and 1602 sit their time out at the Clapham Junction terminus on the last such occasion, 6th June 1960.
Norman Rayfield

Below **There were always a number of P class vehicles at Hammersmith depot. 1707 passes through North Acton on the peak hour 626 route. Fred Ivey**

Facing Page **1273 has just started its long haul from West Croydon to Harlesden. Until April 1951, trams crossed routes 630 and 654 here at London Road, Croydon. Tony Belton**

There were some changes to the routes' allocations over the years with the 628 gaining a daily allocation from Stonebridge depot from 3rd January 1951 along with some 626 workings (it had been the intention to commence this at tram conversion stage one in October 1950). This continued until 6th January 1959, though Stonebridge continued to work the 628 on Bank Holiday Mondays until Whitsun 1960 and trainee drivers were taken over this routeing almost until the 628 withdrawal. The 628 worked out of Wandsworth depot on Bank Holiday Mondays from Easter Monday 1938 until August Bank Holiday 1950; on Bank Holiday Mondays from 1939 Hanwell operated 628s with the vehicles working via route 655 to Hammersmith. Hanwell's workings were handled by Hammersmith staff and conductors were issued specially with route 655 tickets; Hanwell also provided trolleybuses for the 630 on Bank Holidays in 1939/40 with the same provisions applying. As a 'Hanwell Broadway' display was not available, PRIVATE was to be shown on depot runs made in service. The 630 gained a Monday to Saturday Wandsworth depot allocation from 19th April 1944, supplying three peak-hour vehicles which continued until 30th September 1950 when they lost all their tram and trolleybus workings. These runnings were transferred to Hammersmith depot from 2nd October 1950. Over the years, some of the Wandsworth-operated journeys worked via Falcon Road and Clapham Junction to pick up service at Wandsworth thus bringing into passenger operation the link wires between Battersea 'Princes Head' and Clapham Junction. Other depot journeys made a battery manoeuvre at Wandsworth High Street. 628 Bank Holiday depot runs to Wandsworth ran via Wandsworth High Street, meaning that the northbound wiring in Falcon Road was never used by passenger trolleybuses.

Although route 630 was widely reported as London's longest trolleybus route this was not so (655 Acton Vale to Clapham Junction was the longest), but at 14.65 miles it was the longest trolleybus route to operate its full length daily. Seventy-seven minutes were allowed on the trip to West Croydon and 76 minutes on the way back and this figure was standard throughout, whether it was Christmas Day, the staff trolleybus or peak-hour working. The allowance was 82 minutes southbound from Harrow Road to West Croydon when blackout running time was in operation (9.30pm-6am). Blackout running time on the system commenced in November/December 1940 and was withdrawn between February and April 1946. Route 630 hosted the longest journeys on the trolleybus network. As part of the war effort there were three direct journeys on Sunday mornings from Acton Market Place to West Croydon which took 90 minutes to complete – these had taken up from 626 munition journeys which had ran from Tooting to Acton. The first journeys on the 630 started from the depot in the region of 3.15/3.30am so as to provide for a return from West Croydon at 4.40am or thereabouts. At West Croydon, two vehicles only were allowed on the stand together. However, it was common to see three vehicles together here. For a number of years the bell punch tickets referred to West Croydon terminus as fare stage 0; this was unique but the reason is unknown. Route 630 was the only route that required a frog pull (semi-automatic) at both termini.

Another unique fact about route 630 was that it was the only one where a road was specifically wired for trolleybuses to serve a sports stadium. This was from the junction of Garratt Lane and Wimbledon Road up to Summerstown, where greyhound racing took place at Wimbledon Stadium on Monday, Wednesday and Friday evenings. It was brought into use on 15th January 1940; trams had operated over the otherwise disused tracks on these journeys from September 1937. SUMMERSTOWN was displayed on the blinds but it was an obscure definition as Summerstown is a road linking Garratt Lane with Wimbledon Road. It was possibly used to avoid misleading the public, for if 'Wimbledon Stadium' had been used, people might have been misled into thinking it was Wimbledon's All England Lawn Tennis and Croquet Club. Different schedules were worked on Tuesdays and Thursdays. Known as 'dog specials', unnecessary mileage was run, as the vehicles had to operate to and from the depot while events were on. Having been worked as overtime for many years, these schedules started on 31st May 1950 and from the early fifties, 630 was displayed instead of EXTRA which had been shown hitherto. The journeys were made from Tooting Broadway to Summerstown before and after the events, although for a short time until January 1951 the first two trips operated from Mitcham, Fair Green. Two vehicles were scheduled for this work and a mere five minutes was allowed each way, so conductors had to be quick in collecting fares from punters. There were eight journeys before the meeting and six afterwards. Stonebridge depot ran vehicles to Summerstown in the immediate post-war period (EXTRA was displayed with a blank

Two vehicles were allocated to the Summerstown-Tooting 'dog specials'. In this instance two others have been curtailed from the opposite direction, 659 being one of them, thereby giving punters an unscheduled facility to Summerstown from the Wandsworth direction. The Summerstown wiring was constructed under the 1937 Act for South London routes. Denis Battams

destination being shown). Although the reason for this has not been ascertained, one possibility is that they were laid on when Wembley and Wimbledon speedway teams met. Summerstown was also used for vehicles which having been turned short at Mitcham, Fair Green (where no lay-by wire was available) found themselves in advance of their time. They would run in service to Summerstown and pick up their time from there. This was approved by the supervisory staff; what was not approved was a 'lost' 630 one Saturday afternoon. An inspector despatched a breakdown wagon as he thought that assistance was required; the wagon could not find the vehicle but by chance went up to Summerstown. There was the 'lost' vehicle with the crew sitting out a journey!

The White City Stadium in Wood Lane was served by routes 626, 628 and 630 and on occasions as many as 25 extras were supplied for boxing events, some of which would not see the last people away until 1.30am. Dog racing took place here and at Wandsworth with the ordinary service sufficing. The wires in Wood Lane were used occasionally when the 660/666 service was unable to work via Acton and on such occasions they also used the wires from Hammersmith to Shepherds Bush; these two sets of wires were not retained for emergency use after the withdrawal of the Wood Lane routes as had already happened in some instances.

The most intriguing feature concerning route 630 was the operation of three trolleybuses by Carshalton depot on Christmas Days from 1937 until 1958. It was instituted to provide a late service to West Croydon: all vehicles had to be in their depots by 4pm and this was the only way that a late service could be provided. Sets of Hammersmith linen destination blinds were kept at Carshalton and these were usually fitted for these journeys with EXTRA being shown in the route box. At times Carshalton blinds were used but 'WEST CROYDON via Wallington' was hardly appropriate. Nine journeys were operated although only the last three were required as

Hammersmith vehicles were working to West Croydon as late as possible; by providing nine journeys it meant that a reasonable amount of mileage was worked on the Carshalton crews' duties. The journeys were from West Croydon to Mitcham, Fair Green, although the trolleybuses worked a half mile further north and reversed on battery into Lavender Avenue which was at Figges Marsh; depot journeys were worked in service. Carshalton depot was converted to motorbuses in March 1959 so arrangements were made for Carshalton garage to perform nine 630 journeys with RTs; special blind displays incorporating 630 were printed but this number was painted out.

When Mitcham Fair took place, Carshalton, Hammersmith and Wandsworth depots ran extras to Fair Green from August 1948 with as many as 30 extra vehicles being operated. In later years only Carshalton worked these journeys. On one occasion, 2nd June 1953, Queen Elizabeth II's coronation, four Carshalton vehicles operated from West Croydon to Wimbledon Stadium (Summerstown) giving a rare outing to the B1s and Carshalton crews. They are shown specifically as operating to 'Wimbledon Stadium' in the timetable issued for that day. A union agreement saw first trolleybuses out of their depots at 2.11am that morning with the last returning at 2.49am the next day; routes 630 (Carshalton), 663 and 687 operating to the traffic days' total extent.

Extra trolleybuses were run for the Boat Race and Fulham FC at Craven Cottage; Stonebridge vehicles, on loan to Hammersmith and displaying EXTRA, provided some of the Craven Cottage requirements. The Boat Race was well patronised.

Route 630 had a very fast section over Mitcham Common and a number of would-be trolleybus drivers first 'learnt the ropes' when, as conductors, their drivers gave them a go at the wheel on the staff trolleybus journeys. On one occasion a conductress was doing her stint when out of nowhere in the middle of the night sprang an inspector with

hand outstretched at a request stop. Braking occurred further up the road with the conductress climbing back into the saloon via the flap in the front bulkhead, the driver gaining his correct position and the boarding inspector being none the wiser! The routes served the major areas of Hammersmith, Shepherds Bush, Putney, Wandsworth, Clapham, Tooting, Mitcham and Croydon and provided important links between these districts. Major overhead junctions were negotiated at Shepherds Bush, Hammersmith and Wandsworth. At the railway bridge in Putney Bridge Road, the troughing for the overhead leading into and out of the bridge was held by wooden battens on both sides. This bridge was liable to flooding and vehicles had to be turned on both sides when this happened with some vehicles being stranded on the Wandsworth side. Some in-town termini (Bloomsbury and Holborn) were referred to as 'London' on early schedules; others to fall into this category, rather obscurely, were Hammersmith, Paddington and route 612's terminus at Battersea. As part of the war effort, Hammersmith 628s were kept at Stonebridge depot in off-peak hours.

There were a number of unusual journeys on these routes and on Monday to Saturdays from at least 1942 there were some 628 journeys from Tooting to Craven Park and some 626 journeys from Tooting to Acton Market Place; these worked until November 1951. For ten months in 1951, Stonebridge depot operated one of these journeys to Tooting Broadway, returning to Craven Park thus explaining BROADWAY TOOTING's inclusion on their blinds even until 1960. On Thursdays, route 630 operated a single journey from College Park to Clapham Junction before returning to Hammersmith depot; 626 changed to 628 at Clapham Junction and 628 changed to 626 at the same place. 626 changed to 628 and 630 at Scrubs Lane. Shortly after route 628 was introduced, it had to be given two minutes extra running time and an extra trolleybus on each day of the week (from 4th December 1937). In its

infancy this route had a very long operating day; on Monday to Saturdays the first vehicle left the depot at 3.59am with the last one returning at 2.16am on Mondays to Fridays, 2.35am on Saturdays and 1.56am on Sundays. All such journeys were to and from Clapham Junction.

Route 612 succumbed to the motorbus at an early stage, as it had been decided to rid Wandsworth depot of all electric traction in one fell swoop. It had never been a particularly important route as the 630 covered it for most of the way. Its only odd working was a Sunday morning journey departing from Wandsworth depot at 4.09am via Falcon Road with a battery manoeuvre being required at Wandsworth Junction (where three minutes was allowed for this), on its journey to Fair Green. Route 612 was replaced by bus route 44, the last day of operation being Saturday 30th September 1950, the first stage of the South London tramway conversion scheme.

Route 630 operated on a high-frequency basis and these routes adequately served the areas through which they ran. However, in later years they suffered from traffic congestion which resulted in bunching of vehicles and curtailments were commonplace. In 1954, Wandsworth Borough Council made overtures to London Transport to divert trolleybuses via Armoury Way; it could not have been considered important at the time as the proposal was soon dropped. Towards the end of 1955, one option that was bandied about was to close Hammersmith depot and replace the trolleybuses by RT vehicles; the Cromwell Road extension scheme was the dominating factor for this idea but it was not thought economical. Between 1958 and 1960 the routes underwent continual wiring alterations at Hammersmith due to the construction of Hammersmith flyover and southbound vehicles were diverted away from Queen Caroline Street into Butterwick commencing on Sunday 13th July 1958. No extra running time was allowed for this or for vehicles running into the depot from the south which perforce had now to circle The Broad-

way. A Statutory Instrument regulation was made for the use of Butterwick so an Act of Parliament for this trolleybus re-routeing was not necessary. During this construction the approach to Hammersmith depot was altered drastically. This major construction work at Hammersmith was a factor in the routes operating from Hammersmith and Hanwell depots being advanced in the conversion programme. It was originally intended to retain the depots operating nearest to Fulwell, which was the main works and stores, until the very end (Hammersmith would have been last in the original conversion programme). Another factor dictating a premature withdrawal was that it would do away with long sections of wiring that were utilised in the main by single services, this being applicable to both of the depots. At Wandsworth in 1960, a no right turn procedure came into operation for all vehicles except trolleybuses and a special sign allowing 630s to make this manoeuvre was placed in the road stating 'NO RIGHT TURN EXCEPT TROLLEY BUSES'. D class vehicles predominated on the routes until April 1959 when they were replaced by K classes. Along with some resident P class at Hammersmith, the Ks remained until the routes' demise.

Routes 626, 628 and 630 figured in stage seven of the conversion programme and last ran on Tuesday 19th July 1960. There was an element of vying between the staff as to which would be the last trolleybus to enter the depot. Trolleybus 1158, a 628 from Clapham Junction, was scheduled to be last home, but 1121, the last 630 from West Croydon, followed it in.

However, the last trolleybus to operate on these routes was 1161 which had run a special trip on the 630. The reason for this was that there was not to be a replacement service for the night 630 trolleybus that had operated until this time, although the daytime replacement service would run later than the trolleybuses had done. It was necessary, therefore, to run one later journey that night to provide continuity of service to the public and consequently 1161 left Hammersmith at 11.46pm (the time of the first night journey) for a return trip to BROADWAY TOOTING. It was timed to arrive back at 12.45am, but when 1161 reached the feeder in Fulham Palace Road, Hammersmith it ground to a halt because the power had been switched off: the crew whipped down the poles and in so doing unceremoniously concluded conversion stage seven.

THE HANWELL ROUTES

The busy tram service on the Uxbridge Road was replaced by trolleybuses on Sunday 15th November 1936, when route 607 was introduced daily between Shepherds Bush and Uxbridge; it had been hoped to introduce the route the previous August. It was just under six years before, on 5th January 1931, that new Feltham trams had been introduced to LUT service 7, but this was of little consequence to London Transport who were making concerted efforts to replace many of the trams by trolleybuses as soon as possible. The Felthams were transferred to south London at this conversion. In July 1933, Uxbridge Development Committee (a consortium of local councillors and businessmen) had been informed that trolley vehicles were not entirely suitable for the route but in October that year, London Transport were considering the practicability of using them on it, which gives insight into the Board's early intentions to use trolleybuses. At Uxbridge, the trolleybuses were extended beyond the tram terminus, down the hill to a specially constructed turning circle at Frays House on property acquired by London Transport. It was the busiest single trolleybus service and operated only out of Hanwell depot, apart from a short period from December 1936 until March 1937 when Acton depot ran a few vehicles. In March 1937, Hanwell depot was fully rebuilt and able to take its full allocation on route 607. From Wednesday 2nd June 1937, the 607 was temporarily diverted westbound via Goldhawk Road and Askew Road while tram tracks were being removed.

Route 607 is remembered for its long straight run along the dual carriageway of the Uxbridge Road from Hanwell to Hillingdon; short workings at Stratford Bridge, Hayes End Road, Delamere Road and Southall bus garage (where the unattached circle of wires was within the main running track) utilised gaps in the reservation. It had been intended that a further short working should be constructed at Hayes Post Office by means of a service road, but objections were made and London Transport were prepared to drop this proposal. A police ruling allowed four vehicles to stand at Shepherds Bush Green but if a fifth vehicle arrived, then the first vehicle was to proceed on its journey and the remaining vehicles were to move up accordingly. There were many vehicles terminating here so early departure was enforced at times, no doubt to the delight of the staff!

The 607 coped with large volumes of passengers through Southall, Ealing and Acton and also connected with many bus routes. It was initially provided with D2 class vehicles but these were soon replaced by the F1 class as these had higher horse-power motors which were more suitable for the route. The class were synonymous with the 607 and 655 until their last day and were so sound that they outlasted many vehicles their junior. In the very earliest part of the war, London Transport withdrew sections of motorbus routes which paralleled tram and trolleybus services. By doing this they maintained levels of services on electrically operated routes. This was done so as to conserve fuel and

rubber during the war and it was deemed better to make deeper cuts on these parallel services than on roads that were served only by motorbuses. There was little or no augmentation at all, but in the case of route 607, ten extra trolleybuses were added to the Monday to Friday schedule commencing on 22nd November 1939, to cover the withdrawal of bus route 17 between Hanwell and Shepherds Bush on 18th October 1939 (and on route 83, withdrawn between Ealing and Southall on 8th November 1939). From January 1953, a number of Q1 vehicles were allocated to the 607; some were almost brand new, being of the 1952 batch. As progressive service cuts reduced vehicle requirements at Fulwell and Isleworth, the number of Q1s at Hanwell was increased to a final total of 20. It was necessary to obtain MoT approval for the use of the 8ft wide Q1 vehicles on this and all other routes on which they operated.

Above **At Southall, route 607 passed near to the AEC works where a trolleybus test track existed on the premises; the only AEC trolleybuses to operate on this route were vehicles on loan. 728 has just passed beneath the Iron Bridge at Southall.** Ken Swallow

Above **724 is impeded at the stop at Hayes End Road by indiscriminate parking which was a factor that was coming to the fore in the latter days of trolleybus operation; the girls who have just left 724 are no doubt wearing the latest fashions. 724 has been curtailed at Stratford Bridge, so the crew no doubt will have checked to ensure that they are carrying a bamboo pole, for a trolley swing was required at this location.**
Denis Battams

Seen on the north side of Shepherds Bush Green is 1671, a regular on the 607. Classified X7, it has a Lancastrian registration number and was the only trolleybus to receive a non-London designation.
Lens of Sutton

1768 has been delayed outside Hanwell depot; its negative boom has been placed on the 655 wire and a still sound looking 710 overtakes. The six-inch width difference is noticeable and the two destination printings for UXBRIDGE are of interest. 1768, being the last trolleybus to be overhauled was put aside for preservation. Last operating on 24th April 1961, its trolleys were placed on the Carlton Colville Museum overhead wires on 8th May 1992 — and off she went first time! Tony Belton

715 and 1849 at the Uxbridge terminus of route 607. In the earliest days of trolleybus operation, at least one traction standard was painted with three white bands at its base, to assist drivers at night to know where the turning circle was. In July 1948, a dangerous chestnut tree, situated in the middle of the turning circle here, was felled without removing the overhead. Fred Ivey

Viewed on the 30th May 1954 are three trolleybuses using the temporary terminus at Uxbridge Station, the leading vehicle being 674; at the rear is 95A which was allocated to Hanwell depot at the time. John Gillham

The section that had the most frequent service was between Southall, Delamere Road and Acton Vale, Bromyard Avenue. Even at the end of its life, route 607 was operating a one-minute service interval for much of the time during Monday to Friday peak hours and Saturdays. In 1952, 75 vehicles were needed on Monday to Friday, with 80 for a Saturday and 69 on a Sunday. From October 1954, apart from a few odd journeys, all vehicles ran through to Uxbridge on Sundays at a three-minute service interval! In the summers of 1949 and 1950 the route had more vehicles (76) running on a Sunday (41 buses per hour ex Shepherds Bush) than it did on a Monday to Friday (75). The service was so intense that 45 trolleybuses an hour each way passed through Hanwell Broadway between 3.30 and 4.30pm on Saturdays in 1953 while at the height of the Monday to Friday morning and evening peak hours in 1954, 42 vehicles an hour passed towards Shepherds Bush and Uxbridge respectively with 10 vehicles an hour on the 655 to and from Acton Vale and 11 vehicles on the 655 turning in the depot thrown in for good measure. As late as bank holidays 1960, a 2-3 minute service

operated between Shepherds Bush and Uxbridge. Until Christmas Day 1958 there was a 2-3 minute service operating as far west as Hayes End Road. When route 607 finished, there were still 66 vehicles allocated on Mondays to Fridays, 68 on Saturdays and 43 on Sundays. Even route 607 suffered from service cuts in the fifties and on Sundays between 1950 and 1959 the allocation dropped from 76 vehicles to 43 – a 45% reduction. The maximum fleet total of scheduled vehicles on Monday to Fridays was 1616 in 1950; for Saturdays the peak was reached in 1944 with 1553 vehicles required, with the highest Sunday requirement being in 1949 when 1112 vehicles were needed. These totals for an intact system reached their all-time low in January 1959 when 1340, 1190 and 718 vehicles respectively were required.

Conductors were instructed to be on the platform at Uxbridge terminus to warn overtaking traffic before turning from the main road into the stand; very few of the staff ever did this here. However, throughout the system many conductors would assist their drivers by giving hand signals when making nearside and offside turns. One flamboyant

conductor gave leg signals when his trolleybus was making a turn at Hayes End Road; traffic took heed of him when he did this here and at other bus stops en route. In July 1953, a circle of wires was erected outside Uxbridge Station so that 607s could turn during roadworks between there and the terminus. This new terminus was operational from 3rd March to 27th July 1954 (it had been planned to use it from August 1953); the proper terminus at Uxbridge, which was the most westerly on the system, then returned to becoming the main terminus although the station loop was used occasionally to correct late running.

There was always good camaraderie between the trolleybus staff and of course there were the jokers. One driver, on returning to his trolleybus at Uxbridge found a tree trunk in the cab; there was no sign of any of the culprits, his colleagues, who were hiding in the foliage that abounded there. By the time that he and his conductor had removed the wood from the cab, the vehicle was ten minutes late and had to be curtailed at Bromyard Avenue. It would be interesting to know what was entered on the log sheet as the cause of curtailment.

1851 turns into the Uxbridge Road at Shepherds Bush; very noticeable is the driver's cab mirror to view into the lower saloon.
Fred Ivey

On the last day of dual working in Queen Caroline Street, Hammersmith, 12th July 1958, trolleybus 678 heads for Clapham Junction. To the left, another 655 is having its booms attended to following a dewirement. Apart from Leylands of various classes at Hanwell depot from time to time, route 655 was always operated by the F1 class.
Norman Rayfield

Route 655 commenced on Sunday 13th December 1936 and was a vast improvement on tram service 55 which had mainly operated from Hanwell to Brentford. It ran on Monday to Saturday from Hammersmith to Acton Market Place via Brentford with an extension to Craven Park in Monday to Saturday peak hours which catered for factory workers in the North Acton area. The Sunday service worked from Hammersmith Broadway to Hanwell, Hospital Gates (Southall bus garage). These journeys to Hanwell Asylum, as it was known, were run out of service and conductors on route 655 were told to show HANWELL BROADWAY on these workings. This was due to the fact that London Transport did not want to advertise a service that it would not be continuing. This was necessary as the entrance to the depot in Jessamine Road, Hanwell which would form part of the turning loop for route 655, was not ready. However, building work continued apace, allowing the Sunday service to turn there from 14th March 1937.

London Transport's planning was so advanced that by September 1936, as part of the tramway conversion programme which was

to occur twelve months later, frequencies had been planned for a re-vamped 655 which would have worked from Clapham Junction to Craven Park in Monday to Saturday peak hours. These journeys never materialised. At the MoT inspection of route 655, the inspecting officer, referring to the short working facility being provided at Brentford, Half Acre, made arrangements to approach the police to enforce the prohibition of parking vehicles on days when Brentford Court was sitting. He made arrangements to ensure that motorbuses, which were using this turning facility in the reverse direction to the intended trolleybus direction of travel, should now reverse their direction of turn so that all large vehicles worked in the same direction. In all MoT Inspector's reports, there is little reference to the need for guard wires. These were set above the running wires and protected them from other wires such as those of the General Post Office. However, on the inspection of the Hanwell to Brentford route, there were a number of instances where guard wires had necessarily to be fitted. Hanwell and Acton depots initially operated the 655 on Mondays to Saturdays with Hanwell

having total responsibility on Sundays; from 10th March 1937, Hanwell took control daily. On the same date it was cut back from Craven Park to Acton Market Place, also being withdrawn between Acton and Hanwell during Monday to Saturday off-peaks. It was intended to use the 655 route number at this time for the Monday to Saturday short workings from Craven Park to Acton Market Place, but 666 was used instead. A display of 'via Horn Lane ACTON MARKET PLACE' was given and was still being printed in August 1960!

On Sunday 12th September 1937, route 655 gained a lengthy extension to Clapham Junction daily. It now operated in Monday to Saturday peak hours from Acton Market to Clapham Junction and from Hanwell Depot to Clapham Junction for the rest of the time. The weekday evening and Sunday services to Clapham Junction were withdrawn in November 1939; in April 1943 the Monday to Friday daytime service followed suit, but the Sunday service to Clapham Junction was reinstated from 9th June to 10th November 1940. On 5th April 1942 it was further reduced on Sundays to just working a shuttle service from Hanwell to Brentford; on 16th

June 1946 the Sunday service to Hammersmith was restored. Occasionally, when it was becoming obvious that a gap would appear on route 655, an inspector at Hammersmith would phone a colleague at Shepherds Bush and arrange for a 607 to be sent via route 630 to Hammersmith to cover the gap. The vehicle operated as a 607 to its scheduled destination, being curtailed at Acton on return. On the trip westward, such journeys entailed carrying passengers through Hanwell depot.

On Wednesday 10th July 1946, a small number (nine initially) of Monday to Friday 655 evening peak hour journeys were extended from Acton Market Place to Acton Vale, Bromyard Avenue and at 14.8 miles it became London's longest trolleybus route, with 77 minutes running time allowed each way. The extension to Clapham Junction was essential to meet traffic requirements and the extension to Bromyard Avenue catered for the heavy industrial traffic in the Acton Vale area. Also served at Bromyard Avenue by this and the other Acton trolleybuses were the Government offices in this road. On Wednesday 8th June 1949, the morning peak hour service was extended to Acton Vale too and on the following Saturday, 11th June, the Saturday service was extended there in the morning shopping hours and for the midday peak. As motor traffic increased considerably during the 1950s, the reliability of the 655 over the whole section was reduced and steps were taken to improve this in peak hours. It was done by splitting the route into two sections, with one section working from Bromyard Avenue to Brentford, Half Acre and the other from Hanwell to Clapham Junction. It meant that between October 1956 and October 1959 there were no through journeys on Mondays to Fridays between Clapham Junction and Bromyard Avenue. However, from October 1959 three journeys in the morning peak hour did work the full length of the route, but from the Clapham Junction direction only; during this time the Saturday through service was not affected. As part of the service cuts following the 1958 bus strike, the service to Clapham Junction was curtailed at Hammersmith on Saturdays from 10th January 1959. The Saturday journeys to Acton Vale were also withdrawn at this time with the Sunday service to Hammersmith being restricted to working from 1 to 6pm and the rest of the service operating between Hanwell and Brentford. The 655 now became Acton Vale to Clapham Junction in Monday to Friday peak hours and Hanwell to Hammersmith for the rest of the time save for the Sunday curtailment at Brentford. Sunday reductions between 1955 and 1959 saw the allocation reduced from twelve to five – a 60% decrease. No further changes occurred to the route but a unique situation occurred from Wednesday 20th July 1960. Routes 626 and 628 had been withdrawn the previous day and the wires from Hammersmith to Clapham Junction therefore became used in the

peak hours only, having to be specially retained for such use. Of interest was the fact that from January 1959 until July 1960, Clapham Junction saw two trolleybus routes simultaneously operating in peak hours only, routes 626 and 655.

Q1 type vehicles were not allowed to work on the 655 due to the narrowness of Boston Road. However, when they were being tested, moved to and from Fulwell for various reasons or when Hanwell depot was operating 667s, they used this thoroughfare. This re-

Operational snippets are: on Saturday afternoons 655s became 607s at Bromyard Avenue. To economise on the consumption of rubber during the war, some 655s were stabled at Hammersmith depot in off-peak hours. On Mondays to Saturdays from September 1937 until May 1938 one Monday to Friday morning peak hour 607 operated from Acton Market Place to Brentford, Half Acre from where it worked to Hanwell, Hospital Gates. For a number of the middle years there were some Monday to Friday peak hour 607 journeys from Shepherds Bush to Brentford, Half Acre via Hanwell from where they returned to the main line. At the same time some Hanwell 660s/666s ran from Southall, Delamere Road to Craven Park before working on these routes.

Due to its intense service it was common to see 607s travelling in convoy. Despite the number of scheduled vehicles turning short at Hayes End Road, it was quite usual to observe four vehicles together at Uxbridge terminus, although three were often scheduled to be there at the same time. Once past Hayes End Road and supervision route 607 drivers just put their foot down. The 607 was the epitome of trolleybus operation, for it provided a speedy, reliable and high-frequency service operating in urban areas throughout.

Route 655 almost had a stay of execution, for there was an investigation in 1958 by the Central Road Services operating department on instructions from the London Transport Executive to look into the possibility of making use of Q1s that would become surplus to requirements after the Hanwell conversion, thereby deferring the conversion of a route. They reported that only one route was worthy of consideration, the 655. This could have worked from Isleworth depot, although only operating from Hanwell to Hammersmith – no doubt the restriction in Boston Road could have been overcome. Twelve vehicles could have been slotted into Isleworth and would have been sufficient to work the truncated route. There were no main obstacles for this. The only physical problem was that the overhead would have had to be retained in Hanwell bus garage, but the idea was not proceeded with.

Both routes figured in stage eight of the trolleybus conversion programme and were operated for the last time on Tuesday 8th November 1960.

A smart and happy looking trolleybus conductress looks skywards to see 717's trolleys take the frog into Edgarley Terrace short working. Before pulling the frog handle down, she will give it two taps against the traction standard to indicate to her driver that she is ready. Once 717 has cleared the points she will run after 717 and re-board in Edgarley Terrace, no doubt calling out "Okay Jim", so that he will know that she is on board. Once the vehicle is in the turning loop she will have to turn two destination blinds. All this trolleybuswork was just an accepted part of the job and was done without whim or whimper. Denis Battams

striction was strictly adhered to and there are no recorded instances of Q1s operating on the 655. However, on the Hanwell 667 workings that perforce had to use Boston Road to get to line of route, most depot journeys operated to and from Shepherds Bush (as opposed to Hampton Court) via Brentford. To avoid confusing the public, these journeys sometimes showed 655. Depending on the whim of the conductor as to where the blind was changed it was possible to see route 655 at Shepherds Bush.

NORTH WEST TRUNK ROUTES

Sunday 5th April 1936 saw the introduction of route 660 daily between Hammersmith and Acton Market Place. It replaced tram route 89 on what was one of the busiest sections of road on the London United Tramways network; this short route became the first stage towards the elimination of trams from north west London. The route worked out of Acton depot until 4th July that year being replaced on Sunday 5th July 1936 by route 666 which operated daily between Edgware and Hammersmith and was worked by Acton, Hendon and Stonebridge depots; this was the first incursion of trolleybuses into the Metropolitan Electric Tramways network. From Sunday 23rd August 1936 the 666 operated only in weekday peak hours and Sunday afternoons/evenings, working on Sundays until 7th April 1940. It was reintroduced on Sundays on 23rd April 1944 continuing until 22nd October 1944; it was introduced again for Sundays on 6th May 1945. At Edgware terminus, trolleybuses stood in the service road adjacent to the main Edgware Road; by the time of the introduction of the route from Canons Park, the service road had become the

main thoroughfare. Conductors were required to pull the frog for the mainline to Canons Park here which was an unusual feature on the system. At Hendon depot and Edgware, conductors had to warn traffic that a turn was about to be made. On Sunday 2nd August 1936 route 645 commenced to operate daily between Edgware and North Finchley, being worked by Hendon and Finchley depots; on the same day, the 660 was reintroduced, working daily between North Finchley and Hammersmith, now with Finchley and Stonebridge depots operating it. Bus route 26 followed the 660 from North Finchley as far as Askew Road; regarded as superfluous it was withdrawn piecemeal in 1937/38. The Hammersmith terminus was in King Street; vehicles encroached on Hammersmith Broadway when terminating. The terminus was re-located to Hammersmith Grove after a short time. To complete the changeover to trolleybuses on this network, two new routes were introduced on Sunday 23rd August 1936. Route 662 from Stonebridge depot worked daily from Sudbury to Paddington; route 664 worked daily from Edgware to Pad-

dington and was operated by Hendon and Stonebridge depots. The piecemeal introduction of trolleybuses meant that tram services had to be run as well on a temporary basis, which was unsatisfactory; they were instances of the trend to replace trams as soon as practically possible.

Throughout MoT inspections of the system, the inspecting officers continually made reference to protection barriers being needed outside schools along the new trolleybus routes. As an example they commented that protection was required at the boys and girls exits of St Mary's school in Church Road, Willesden due to the quietness of the trolleybuses. It was stated that a man would be in attendance to control the movement of trolley vehicles re-entering the traffic stream from the turning loop at Golders Green tube station. At a number of the short working turns, North Acton Station, Craven Park, St Gabriels Road and Wembley Hill Road, it was the practice initially to dispense with as many frogs and crossings as possible and trolley heads would be shifted from one set of wires to the other.

Hendon depot's 302 turns into Hammersmith Broadway on 25th September 1936, the original trolleybus routeing here; both of 302's windscreens are open, giving ventilation to the cab and saloon, for at this time there was a seat adjacent to the driver at the front of the vehicle. The nearside route plate is visible over the rearmost lower deck windows as is the trolleybus bullseye by the platform.
LT Museum U21508

260 departs from Paddington on 15th August 1959; three days later it will be withdrawn for forwarding to the Museum of British Transport. Ousted in favour of trolleybus 1253 in 1962, it avoided a visit to the scrapyard due to a successful literal last-minute rescue attempt and 260 now operates at the London Trolleybus Preservation Society's museum premises at Carlton Colville. Lyndon Rowe

The original plan had been to extend the 662 at Sudbury along the Watford Road to its junction with East Lane. This would have been for about half a mile and although Parliamentary approval was granted, it was not proceeded with and vehicles turned at the Sudbury roundabout. The turn at Paddington was made anti-clockwise round Paddington Green which was made one-way for all traffic on the introduction of trolleybuses. The terminus at Paddington was located further from Edgware Road than the tram terminus which had been close to the Edgware Road,

and difficulties were encountered in finding a suitable turning point; at one time it was proposed that a turntable should be used here. The terminal was unsatisfactory from a traffic point of view as it fell short of the central area and contact with the Underground at Edgware Road station; it was considered to be an inconvenient trolleybus terminus. It was envisaged originally that movements were to be clockwise and at one time a turning loop via Harrow Road, Edgware Road, Church Street and Paddington Green was considered, but approval was not

given. Also investigated in 1936 was an extension of the route along Euston Road to link up with other routes that were to be introduced at Kings Cross. Route 662 ran for its whole length along the Harrow Road, although parts of it were under the guise of various local thoroughfares. The parallel 18 bus route group was considerably reduced along the Harrow Road in March 1937. In the early years, the section between Sudbury and Wembley was regularly used for trainee trolleybus drivers and a circle of wires at Wembley facilitated this.

In the initial planning stages for these routes, it was suggested that careful consideration should be given for all trolleybuses to work through the station forecourt at Golders Green, but nothing resulted. For many years until May 1956, there were peak hour short workings that operated variously as 645 or 660 between North Finchley and Golders Green. In fact for the first few years of operation, twenty vehicles an hour were working in Monday to Saturday peak hours, such were the requirements before the Northern Line was extended to Finchley. These workings catered for peaks in demand at these times at the Underground station; by May 1956, though, they were confined to a few 660 Monday to Friday evening peak journeys. A pre-war proposal would have brought about a short working point at Finchley Central which would have been most useful; nothing came of it and the battery turn at Holly Park sufficed.

From Sunday 13th December 1936, Acton depot ceased to work route 666, but it was allocated Monday to Saturday work on route 660 from 8th February 1937 until 9th March 1937, when the depot closed. From 10th March 1937, Hanwell depot received an allocation on the 660 on an all-day Monday to Saturday basis until 30th July 1937. They were shuttle journeys run as 660 Extras between Acton Market Place and Hammersmith Broadway, known as 'Acton swings' (vehicles going on short journeys in quick succession); these had comprised Acton depot's involvement. Hanwell depot started operating 666 Extras on 10th March 1937 in Monday to Saturday peak hours and were joined by Hammersmith Depot in Monday to Saturday peak hours from 22nd November 1939; all were on the section from Craven Park to Acton Market Place. Often quoted as running from Scrubs Lane, were some depot journeys operating directly from Hammer-

Above **Finchley depot's allocation on route 660 was always small so there was little likelihood of 954 appearing thereon; the photographer is renowned for his perseverance and it is seen here approaching Craven Park. It had been transferred from Highgate to Finchley in February 1957.** Fred Ivey

Above Right **Colindale's 323 approaches the top of Chichele Road, Cricklewood. The wheel spats fitted to a hundred C class vehicles gave them a streamlined effect. 323 was the last C class trolleybus to be overhauled (February 1958) and the last C class to receive an inter-depot transfer (CE-FY in August 1959). It was behind Colindale depot, on the site of Hendon tramcar works on 25th September 1909, that the first trolleybus trials in this country were held.** John Meredith

Right **No.1566 was a late addition to Stonebridge's fleet of N class vehicles. Here, at Jubilee Clock, it is about to pass under two of the three crossovers in the immediate foreground of the picture.** Fred Ivey

smith Depot via Wood Lane and Jubilee Clock. When the extras were extended to Hammersmith in April 1943 it meant in effect that such depot journeys became circular ones operating in both directions. Hanwell and Hammersmith depots operated no further north than Craven Park and from May 1943 their workings were transferred to the 660. Specific instructions were given to Hanwell conductors regarding blind displays to be used on 660/666 depot workings. On route 666 a blank number blind was to be shown on the Hanwell to Acton section with the final destination being displayed; 660s were to show HANWELL BROADWAY when leaving Hammersmith and HAMMERSMITH BROADWAY when leaving the depot. The Hanwell and Hammersmith Saturday workings were withdrawn in November 1947; the 660 Hanwell allocation continued until June 1949 with the Hammersmith allocation finishing in September 1950. Route 660 had five depots operating on it simultaneously between 1943 and 1949. The same happened to route 666 between 1939 and 1943; both routes had six depots working on them during their lives. Hendon depot operated just a few journeys on route 660 over the years, with the same applying to Finchley 666s and Stonebridge 645s.

On Sunday 6th March 1938, route 651 was introduced; it operated between Barnet and Golders Green in Monday to Friday peak hours, Saturdays and Sunday afternoons and evenings. It was extended to Cricklewood, St Gabriels Road in Monday to Friday off-peak hours (midday and evening). It was London's shortest lived trolleybus route, being withdrawn on Tuesday 31st May 1938; it was replaced the following day by an altered 645 route. Route 651 only appeared on one tram and trolleybus map: the No.2 1938 issue.

In the early days of trolleybus operation at Finchley depot some C1 class vehicles were used. Seen on route 651, operated solely by Finchley, is trolleybus 198 at Barnet. G.L. Newcombe

On Wednesday 1st June 1938, route 645 began operating its circuituous course between Barnet and Canons Park with Hendon and Finchley depots continuing to work it. This was the only simultaneous double extension of a trolleybus route. There had been some doubt as to whether the mile-long section to Canons Park would open to trolleybuses, as there was already a bus service on this section (it was withdrawn upon the 645 introduction) and it was anticipated that there would be a low demand. This turned out to be the case and it never reached its full potential. The tram wires and tram track had been left since its abandonment in 1936. Strangely enough, a junction had been made in the wires at Edgware at that time. The MoT inspecting officer referred to it as the 'Canons Park extension of the Edgware Road trolley vehicle route'. The determining factor that led to the restoration of electric road transport to Canons Park was the large number of vehicles turning at the Edgware terminus: 645 and 664 daily with 666 in peak hours. The police had made representations to the LPTB about the matter. To reduce the number of movements across the main road here, approval was given by the MoT in 1937 for the turning of trolleybuses via Manor Park Crescent and Station Road; this would have required equipping 1129 yards of single track (a 550 yard extension) on which little traffic would have been obtained. The alternative was to extend to Canons Park and a decision was taken on 23rd December 1937 to 'extend to the old tramway terminal at Canons Park' on the understanding that half the trolleybus service would continue to turn at Edgware. If the Manor Park Crescent routeing had been adopted it would have brought the trolleybuses very close to Edgware Station and it was strange that it was not taken up. If gaps occurred to Canons Park, 664s or 666s would be extended here or a crew would make two journeys between Canons Park and Cricklewood instead of a full journey on 645/664/666. In February 1950, thought was given to the withdrawal of the 645 between Canons Park and Edgware and diverting bus route 141 via Stonegrove to Edgware Station. This had been considered on a number of occasions, but the idea was not taken up as inconvenience would occur to the staff at De Havillands, Stonegrove and the government offices at Canons Park if a through service along the Edgware Road was broken.

Appearing in allocation books from 1st April 1942 were what were known as 'scheduled diversions'. These comprised three Monday to Friday morning peak hour journeys from Paddington to Acton Market Place although from 2nd May 1956 this was amended to four journeys with two of them being extended to Bromyard Avenue, Acton Vale (known colloquially to staff as 'Bromyard'). They were for factory workers in the Acton area, but no evening peak hour journeys operated in the reverse direction; they were variously known as 660, 662, 664 or 666

over the years and these, along with a blank aperture or EXTRA, were displayed.

Traffic-interval impulse and recording clocks were located at a number of points and included two at Golders Green which were sited on the northbound and southbound wires. The trolley head actuated a skate which recorded a mark on a circular paper clock, indicating the service frequency. Not only was this available for the public to see inside the Finchley Road entrance hall, but a headway clock also recorded these times in viewing cases in the main hall of London Transport's offices at 55 Broadway. Managers wanted to see regular intervals being recorded and a dodge concocted by an inspector at Golders Green led to the M.E.T. stores tram shunting back and forth over the skate to give a punch on the card! These clocks also existed at Ealing Common, Highgate, Green Lanes and Seven Sisters Road, Manor House and could also be seen at 55 Broadway; the recording cards were changed daily. There were 20 clocks; some were located inside depots (Sutton, Fulwell, Finchley, Isleworth, Wood Green, Stonebridge and Colindale) and there was one at Archway southbound. The one inside Sutton depot read: ROUTE 654 SUTTON DEPOT UP.

662s operating into Stonebridge depot from Sudbury had to travel via Craven Park Circle which was frustrating for the crews. Having passed the depot they had three frog pulls at Craven Park and another at the depot before they could park the vehicle as there was no link wiring from Sudbury. A battery manoeuvre was performed from Sudbury on Christmas Days, though. The turn at Paddenswick Road was so close to Hammersmith that some crews who were curtailed here would continue to Hammersmith, as they felt that by the time they had swung the trolleys and manoeuvred around the tight turning circle, it would not have saved any time. In icy conditions, trolleybus drivers were given instructions not to stop on the ascents at Willesden Green Station and Childs Hill. Fog could cause problems and sometimes instead of proceeding down Ballards Lane, a driver followed the kerbline to end up in Long Lane! On one occasion a number of trolleybuses followed each other in this manner and a convoy of them had to be towed out by a breakdown vehicle; apparently many of them thought they had only dewired when the orange neon light in the cab (which indicated that power was available) was extinguished. Another driver, following a cyclist, found himself in the Express Dairy entrance at College Farm opposite Holly Park; despite dewiring, he was able to move himself back to the wires by means of battery power.

An early example of support for noise abatement involved an old dog at Hammersmith terminus; it was necessary at times for 660s/666s to 'dip their sticks' to allow a 667 to pass. The dog took a dislike to the rumbling of the bamboo pole in and out of its holder and having made a mental note of the vehicle

concerned, would run to the back of the vehicle and start to tug at the bamboo pole's grappling hook, but the pole would only be withdrawn an inch or two. One day, a vehicle moved off as the dog was at the bamboo and to the dog's surprise the pole came completely out of the holder leaving the dog walking off with the bamboo! It was retrieved by the point inspector and the crew of the following trolleybus chasing the dog who dropped the bamboo in 'the thrill of the chase'. The tugging happened on a number of occasions but nobody knew when the dog would turn up. When it did, there was some 'eyeballing' between the dog and the inspector, with the dog only going for trolleybuses 'dipping their sticks'. Withdrawn bamboos were hung on a traction pole and were used for vehicles doing this; it obviated the need to withdraw bamboo poles, but surely it was a case of DOG 1, LONDON TRANSPORT 0!

For the Olympic Games at Wembley in 1948, seventeen extra trolleybuses were run between Paddington/Scrubs Lane and Wembley. Extras for sporting events at Wembley Stadium are mentioned in another chapter. On Bank Holidays, a 662 supplementary service was run in some post-war years between Wembley and Paddington and was one of a number of such augmentations on those days. They provided work for crews who would otherwise have been unoccupied, for generally speaking Sunday services operated on Bank Holidays.

Above **Virtually unaltered since trolleybus times is Henlys Corner near Temple Fortune; 1467 passes the Naked Lady statue. Just one stop to the north is the Holly Park battery turn adjacent to the Express Dairy farm.** Norman Rayfield

Below Left **Another location that is unchanged since the trolleybus era is Golders Green. From 1955-1959, a number of E1s were allocated to Stonebridge depot, 559 being one such example. There tended to be an unfortunate trait due to bad blind positioning or blind slip, that this display often read as illustrated.** Alan Cross

Below Right **1557 is operating on one of the four morning journeys from Paddington to Acton. The 626 wires were used at Jubilee Clock with this particular journey going to Bromyard Avenue.** Fred Ivey

1618, seen at Acton Market Place, is running very late and has been curtailed at Cricklewood where it will perform a battery reverse manoeuvre at Gillingham Road. The destination blind display is not actually correct for Gillingham Road is to the north of Cricklewood Broadway, whilst St Gabriels Church is to the south. However, it was considered to be 'near enough' and accepted by crews and passengers alike. Peter Moore

Extras were run for greyhound racing at Hendon Stadium, close to Staples Corner. Vehicles would park with poles down at the appropriate stop and after the event would be sent to various destinations by an inspector. Extra 645s operated on Saturday afternoons from 1949 to 1954 between Edgware and Cricklewood to cater for shopping traffic and on Bank Holidays supplementary 664s ran between Edgware and Cricklewood. Extras were also laid on for the annual air pageant at Hendon aerodrome. The Edgware terminus was considered to be a convenient turning point from which shopping and industrial traffic built up into the Burnt Oak, Colindale and Cricklewood areas, with many factories being served in between. In the area around

North Acton there were many factories and great provision was made for their workers. A circle of wires existed at North Acton Station and turns from both directions were made at various times over the years to accommodate these workers, some of whom had seen the changeover from trams to trolleybuses and then from trolleybuses to motorbuses. By the North Acton factories there was a railway bridge at Old Oak Common Lane where water tended to accumulate; at such times the services were turned back on each side of the bridge.

All these routes operated at frequent intervals due to high passenger loadings. Particularly busy was the section from Cricklewood, through Willesden and Harlesden to

Acton, passing railway marshalling yards at Acton, Harlesden and Cricklewood. Route 662 was always busy; the 664 shared its wires from Craven Park to Paddington, these routes being the main means of public transport along the Harrow Road. Greyhound and speedway events took place at Wembley Stadium and from the earliest days it was necessary to augment the service to cater for passenger requirements in the summer period; journeys to Wembley were built into the schedule on Mondays to Fridays to provide extras before and after events.

The Edgware Road loadings were heavy and the trolleybuses catered for the various factories alongside. The Edgware Road wires were also used by many vehicles making their

Dusk at North Finchley trolleybus station as 957 prepares to leave for Hammersmith. It will not be working for much longer though, as 1512 has been transferred in from Poplar; the East End conversions saw all but one (954) of Finchley's stock replaced and 957 will soon be making a one-way trip to the scrapyard. Fred Ivey

own way under power to the scrapyard at the rear of Colindale depot. The Edgware terminus was situated outside the primary school and many a time the children thought that playtime was over when they heard the inspector blow his whistle to send a 664 on its way! The authorised stand at High Street Edgware, which came under a regulation issued by the Commissioner of Police for the Metropolis, allowed three trolley vehicles to park here but should a fourth vehicle arrive at the stand, the first vehicle was to proceed on its journey. On the journey north at Edgware, conductors on route 645 would hand in their tea cans with a few pence inside at a cafe on the other side of the road. On return they would pick up the can full of piping hot tea to

be consumed later in the duty. This was just one example of a commonplace practice on the system. On the matter of refreshment, London Transport issued free supplies of barley water for the staff during the summer of 1938. They also nominated authorised refreshment places; in July 1950, Betty's Cafe of 118 Anerley Road, Anerley (route 654) was replaced by Stafford Ice Cream Parlour, Stafford Road, Waddon. The MET also made arrangements for providing coffee for their staff during the winter of 1926/27 and issued coffee tickets at nominated establishments.

Routes 660 and 666 served the industrial areas of Acton, Willesden and Cricklewood and the trolleybuses were well loaded most of the time. Major junctions were encountered

at Cricklewood Broadway, Craven Park and Jubilee Clock. At North Finchley trolleybus station, congestion tended to occur as not only was it a major terminus, but many crew reliefs took place. In 1956, London Transport considered purchasing land to the rear of the large cinema to ease the problem but nothing resulted. To make life easier for the crews, though, a new wiring layout with more loops was constructed in December 1956. The C2/C3 class trolleybuses predominated on this group of routes until the summer of 1958 when some N class vehicles were transferred to Stonebridge. Between then and November 1959 the rest of the C classes were withdrawn and the allocation thereafter was mainly of the L3, N1 and N2 classes.

An odd fact concerning the 645 was that on Christmas Days 1955-1959, more trolley-buses were allocated than on any single day of the week during that period and the three-minute combined 645/664 or 645/666 headway was superior to the five-minute headway on Mondays to Fridays at this time. Christmas Day duties did not exceed four hours; the shortest example was a 662 turn of 1 hour and 39 minutes, which included 20 minutes signing on/signing off time. The crew only had to work Stonebridge depot/Sudbury/Paddington and back to the depot – they had finished before the second duty started! In later years routes 645, 664 and 666 along with routes 557, 628, 661, 663 and 693 had a more frequent service on much of a Sunday than in Monday to Friday off-peaks.

There were a number of irregular journeys on these routes over the years: North Finchley/Edgware to Scrubs Lane, thence to Wembley and Stonebridge depot via Craven Park, operating as 660 or 666. Four evening peak hour 660 extras worked from Acton Market Place to Wembley before returning to Stonebridge. Time card instructions stated that 'CRAVEN PARK' was to be shown until Jubilee Clock, where the indicator was to be changed to 'STADIUM Wembley Hill Road'. There was one morning peak journey on route 660 working from Hammersmith to Wembley, returning to Hammersmith; similarly there was an evening peak journey on route 666 of the same configuration. Shown on the schedules was a 664 to Acton, a 666 to Wembley and a 662 to Edgware but in practice an appropriate route number for the journey was shown. The 666 Wembley journey operated directly to Edgware, although it had a six-minute layover at Craven Park. For a short time there was a Sunday evening Finchley depot 645 which operated from North Finchley to Willesden Green (this was the original terminology for St Gabriels Road) with the return journey being to Canons Park. The stand time was minimal at Willesden Green, but the reason for not operating directly through the Broadway was to enable a Hendon depot 645 to 'jump it' and run into the depot from Canons Park without breaking the required through frequency. For some unknown reason a Hendon depot 645 operated from Barnet to Willesden Green from where it worked almost immediately to the depot. A regular section operated on route 645 on Sunday afternoons and evenings from May 1945 until October 1949 between Willesden Green and North Finchley with a few journeys extended to Barnet. 645s had to change positions with others at Canons Park to maintain even headways. A bamboo pole was left resting in the trees here (some drivers would not handle a bamboo pole without using gloves, for bamboo splints could catch the hands and cause dermatitis). There were instances on the system of trolley booms needing to be lowered if vehicles got out of order. It also occurred when crews whose vehicles were returning to the depot would have a

preceding vehicle's booms lowered so that they could finish early! Another oddity was a Stonebridge depot working which ran as a 660 to North Finchley, then as a 645 to Edgware where it became a 664 to Paddington.

Changing from route to route occurred thus:

666 to 664 at Edgware
666 to 645 at Edgware
664 to 666 at Edgware
664 to 645 at Edgware
645 to 664 at Edgware
666 to 660 at Willesden Green
664 to 645 at Willesden Green
666 to 645 at Willesden Green
645 to 660 at North Finchley
660 to 645 at North Finchley
660 to 666 at Hammersmith
666 to 660 at Hammersmith
660 to 662 at Scrubs Lane
666 to 662 at Scrubs Lane
660EX to 662 at Wembley

316 starts to circle the roundabout at Canons Park terminus. It was necessary for many traction standards to be used here so that the wiring configuration could be accommodated. C. Carter

Trolleybuses 1633 and 1642 have arrived together at Sudbury. They will circle the roundabout and then park on the stand on the opposite side of the road. Peter Moore

Foreign stabling occurred as:
SE 660 stabled at Finchley
FY 660 stabled at Stonebridge
FY 645 stabled at Hendon
SE 664 stabled at Hendon, but returned to service as 666.
CE 660 stabled at Stonebridge, but returned to service as 664.

It was common practice for vehicles to change from one route to another within depot confines and this normally happened during off-peak hours. The shortest such operation involved a Colindale 664 which had a mere three minutes in the depot (7.44/7.47am), before emerging as a 645. This happened for a few years on Mondays to Fridays in the fifties.

Route 666 was withdrawn on Saturdays from 4th June 1949 and on Sundays after 16th October 1949; in both instances only slight augmentation was given on parallel routes. However, the odd 666 journey or two appeared on Saturdays and Sundays from time to time but only as far as Acton Market Place, the route now becoming Monday to

Friday peak hours only. On Wednesday 2nd May 1956 a revision of services led to route 666 operating all day on Mondays to Fridays, with route 664 running during Monday to Friday peak hours and all day on Saturdays and Sundays. The switch between the 664 and 666 enabled properly interworked headways to be scheduled throughout the north west trolleybus system. The 645/660/664/666 were all on common headways, whereas the 662 and 664 were not; by linking the 660 Hammersmith to Craven Park 'shorts' to the erstwhile 664 Edgware service, introducing 662 'shorts' between Craven Park and Paddington and reducing the service to Sudbury, it was possible to get full interworking. Despite its contraction the 664 operated on Bank Holidays between 1956 and 1958. As a repercussion of the 1958 bus strike, the 664 was withdrawn after operations on Tuesday 6th January 1959. There was a boosting on Mondays to Fridays on the 662 in 1956 but only a slight amount of additional work was given to the 662 in 1959. From Wednesday 7th January 1959, route 666 worked daily.

These were the most profitable trolleybus routes, which was the reason for leaving them till last in the conversion programme (before the addition of Fulwell and Isleworth). At one time it had been planned for routes 645, 660, 662 and 666 to survive until July 1962 but this was revised to withdrawal on 31st January 1962. However, with the advancing of route 629, further revisions were made to the abandonment programme and it was planned that these routes would be replaced on Wednesday 3rd January 1962. This was the only instance in the conversion programme of three depots closing to trolleybuses in one night. On Sunday 31st December 1961, the heaviest snowfall for many years swept across the Home Counties and consequently the remaining trolleybus services were greatly disrupted. For their last three days of life, routes 645, 660, 662 and 666 were subject to many curtailments and even on the last day, Tuesday 2nd January 1962, the routes did not operate normally, though the last vehicle into each depot did proceed in a normal manner. Despite the arctic conditions

the final evening was enlivened by two items of entertainment! During the late evening a number of Stonebridge vehicles were making their last journeys to the storage lines at Colindale depot. At Craven Park, the driver of one trolleybus signalled the author to pull the frog handle; as there appeared to be a number of vehicles making a similar journey to Valhalla he kept the frog handle pulled down. However he failed to observe that in the middle of the pack was a Paddington-bound 662 with the inevitable dewirement of trolleybus 1621! The last trolleybus of stage 13 was vehicle 1666 into Stonebridge depot. At Craven Park the driver paused for a respectful one minute with the vehicle broadside across the junction. As he carefully pulled away and to the amazement of trolleybus conductress Costello, the author literally had to haul aboard the redoubtable photographer Fred Ivey who was rapidly slithering on the still atrocious roads beneath the platform of 1666. All was well however, and at Stonebridge depot a bank of trolleybus staff across the road welcomed the vehicle home.

THE HAMPSTEAD ROUTES

The Hampstead routes were introduced on Sunday 10th July 1938; they replaced tram-car services operated from Hampstead depot in Cressy Road. London Transport were empowered to operate trolleybuses along Cressy Road, but Hampstead depot was never used as a trolleybus operating base. The new routes worked from Holloway depot, entailing a lengthy run from Kentish Town via Tufnell Park along which no regular service was advertised. This depot run was to remain unique on the system but passengers were allowed to be carried as far as Junction Road, Monnery Road. Some vehicles operated with a blank route aperture on these journeys. In January 1937 the question of whether the tram services should be replaced by buses or trolleybuses had been discussed. Loadings were a dictating factor and the margin in favour of trolleybuses was small. Route 513 operated from Hampstead Heath to Holborn Circus via Grays Inn Road returning to Parliament Hill Fields. Route 613 ran from Parliament Hill Fields to Holborn Circus via Farringdon Road and on to Hampstead Heath: both routes functioned daily. The services linking Parliament Hill Fields and Hampstead Heath with Holborn were initially allocated route numbers 613 and 637 respectively, with the corresponding 513 and 537 being added at a later

stage, and all these appeared on Holloway's blinds in anticipation of them being required. However, the pattern of service which was actually introduced, whereby trolleybuses which started out from Parliament Hill Fields returned to Hampstead Heath and vice versa, removed the need for route numbers 537 and 637 to be used. This must have been a fairly late change of plan as route plates were prepared. Initially the 613 took Kings Cross Road on journeys to Holborn, but this was altered to Swinton Street in the early part of the war. Conductors were instructed to show 513 when leaving Hampstead and this was to be retained until arriving back at Parliament Hill Fields; route 613 was to be shown on leaving Parliament Hill Fields and was to be retained until arriving back at Hampstead, where the process would start again. Front and rear destination and side blinds on routes 513/613 were to be turned on the inward journey after crossing Clerkenwell Road and before arriving at either Holborn, Grays Inn Road or Farringdon Street Station.

Route 615 operated from Parliament Hill Fields to Moorgate, while route 639 ran from Hampstead Heath to Moorgate; both routes ran daily. At Hampstead the trolleybuses followed the same one-way system as the trams had done, inward via Fleet Road and outward

via Agincourt Road. At Camden Road station, where the wires crossed the Euston services under the bridge, a unique crossing was installed bolted to the bridge itself. A Colindale depot driver who regularly visited this locality in his private car found himself taking his foot off the accelerator pedal and coasting under this junction such was his automatic reaction – he was never able to work out why it was only under this particular junction that he did this. Route 639 approached Kings Cross via Mornington Crescent while 513, 613 and 615 travelled via Kentish Town. There was little scope to adjust vehicles that ran late and there was no turning facility in the Hampstead direction, save for battery manoeuvres (which tended to be overlooked if possible) and the turn at Islington Green for 615/639. A detracting factor for routes 615/639 was that they paralleled the Northern Line from Kentish Town and Camden Town respectively, both serving Kings Cross, the 'Angel' and Moorgate. Christmas Day duties for the staff were traditionally brief. The first duty on the 513 ended at 6.17am at Fortess Walk and the crew were given a 'special walking time' allowance of 20 minutes back to the depot as there was not a bus service working at that time. Such practices would not be entertained today.

At the Ministry of Transport inspection it was stipulated that trolleybuses be subject to a 10mph speed limit under the arched Prince of Wales railway bridge (London Transport ruled this should be 5mph) and that initially they should stop at a compulsory stop on either side of the bridge. This was to remind drivers of the need for special care. Vehicles were to keep more or less in the centre half of the road here which was 35ft between the kerbs. The MoT inspector commented that "While the double track tramlines remain they will provide a very useful guide to the trolley vehicle drivers, as if they follow these they will have a comfortable margin". Arrangements were to be made for lines of studs in the carriageway directly below the lines of lamps installed here and an inspector was positioned to supervise movements. Instructions were given to the staff that trolleybuses were not to pass each other under the bridge in Prince of Wales Road and inward-bound vehicles had precedence up to 12 noon and outward-bound vehicles precedence after 12 noon. At night the underside of the bridge was illuminated by two incandescent strings of lamps denoting the clearway.

New 1015 on its way to Kings Cross passes beneath Kentish Town West railway bridge of the London Midland and Scottish Railway. Judging by the looks that 1015 is getting, this may well be a first day photograph. It was unusual to see standard length vehicles on these routes when the B2s were in residence. Charles Klapper

No.1389 turns from Monnery Road into Junction Road on a depot run to Hampstead Heath; this wiring was used almost exclusively for vehicles taking up service at Kentish Town. Tony Belton

The MoT report also stated that trolleybuses were not to stand in Fortess Walk or proceed through it in both directions at one time (there was a fire station located on one side while on the other side there was a public house requiring a daily delivery of beer and a garage requiring bulk petrol). Trolleybuses operating between Holloway depot and Parliament Hill Fields had to use this thoroughfare. Opponents to trolleybuses at Parliament Hill Fields cited that cars descending West Hill at high speed would be endangered by the trolley vehicle turning circle. The police were to deal with the matter of the speeding cars and the turn was to be supervised by the conductor or duty regulator. At the inspection, Colonel A.C. Trench commented that a number of trees had necessarily been cut down in Pemberton Gardens (by Holloway depot) in order to accommodate the trolleybuses; he said it would be a pity if the tree outside 16 Pemberton Gardens should suffer the same fate and arrangements were made to add white painted letters to it. It is not known what the letters said.

Initially, standard vehicles were allocated to the routes but were soon replaced by B2 short-wheelbase vehicles which were sufficient for the patronage. Consequently, the 517/617 around the Holborn loop had to be adjusted to increase the morning peak service inwards via Grays Inn Road, and outwards via Grays Inn Road in the evening peak at the expense of the service via Farringdon Road. As early as March 1939 the General Manager referred to the absence of improvement in earnings on these routes; in February 1950, loadings taken on routes 513/613 showed that the all-day loadings north of Kings Cross averaged 24 per bus and only 16 per bus on the Holborn sections. Despite being unimportant trolleybus routes they nevertheless passed the main line stations at Kings Cross and St Pancras. Beyond here the trolleybuses operated through the most dismal surroundings on the network as they passed along Pancras Road, creeping furtively under a number of railway bridges which carried the tracks out of St Pancras; the wiring between two of these bridges was connected by long metal runners and was normal practice for such needs.

Top and Centre **Pancras Road Kings Cross, 22nd September 1952. The B2 class were the main allocation on these routes until 1952 when they were replaced by C1s; 116 is seen shortly before withdrawal. No. 132, the first of the C1s, still retains its sidelights between decks; the destination blind erroneously describes Farringdon Rd as Farringdon St**. Both Alan Cross

Left **No. 1439 had been a native of east London for almost 20 years, being transferred to Highgate depot in April 1960. Even in January 1961, when this photo was taken, the area around Kings Cross Station was still sett-paved.** Tony Belton

On Sundays from 17th November 1940, route 513 operated from Hampstead Heath to Holborn Circus and back to Hampstead Heath, remaining in this form on this day of the week thereafter with route 613 being withdrawn on Sundays. Retained, though, were a few Sunday morning 613 journeys from Parliament Hill Fields to Holborn and back although one returned to Hampstead, On Bank Holidays until 1958, route 613 operated but on these occasions 513/613 worked as weekdays, although some 613s started and finished at Parliament Hill Fields, some travelling via Grays Inn Road and some via Farringdon Road. From Bank Holidays 1959, route 613 only operated a small number of early journeys with the rest of the work being left to the 513. An odd working on Bank Holidays until 1958 was a trolleybus travelling direct from Hampstead Heath to Parliament Hill Fields. A time card note instructed the conductor to display FORTESS WALK until this was reached; PARLIAMENT HILL FIELDS being displayed from there. Supplementary vehicles were put on routes 513, 615 and 639 over the Easter periods of 1959 and 1960 by when, generally speaking, supplementary Easter services had ceased.

On Bank Holidays, Hampstead Heath and Parliament Hill Fields became focal points for Londoners, due to the attractions of the fair and the heath itself, with both locations giving access to Hampstead Heath. London Transport catered for these needs by operat-

No. 1378 at Swains Lane, Parliament Hill Fields; the short workings to Windsor Terrace at busy times gave day trippers a frequent service from 'Angel' Islington. The 'fairy lights' for assisting drivers at night can be seen. Don Thompson

ing supplementary trolleybuses not only then, but also on summer Sundays, with these running from the very earliest days. Taking Easter Monday 1946 as an example, there were 55 departures an hour at busy times, made up of forty-five 639s and ten 513s; on August Holiday Monday 1958, forty 639s and ten 513s were still needed. Generally speaking, the 615 had supplementaries working to Kings Cross and Windsor Terrace, City Road with the 639 operating supplemen-

taries to Windsor Terrace and Moorgate. These were the only times that the routes were really busy. The short working facility at Windsor Terrace had a restriction for summer Sundays and Bank Holidays and was the only such restriction. The turn could also be used for emergency purposes.

Just as all four routes were introduced together so were they all withdrawn together in stage nine, their last operating day being Tuesday 31st January 1961.

No. 1002 is about to cross the 'Angel' Islington junction. London Transport seem to have little faith in the ability of their drivers to negotiate this junction without dewiring, as there are two separate banks of guard wires which will attempt to arrest flaying booms from going through the upstairs windows of the Pearl Assurance Company. Michael Dryhurst

1358 ascends Highgate Hill whilst in the background another 611 descends. The trolleybuses were the speediest passenger transport vehicle up the hill and have never been bettered. Fred Ivey

HIGHGATE HILL

London Transport's penultimate tram to trolleybus conversion was of tram route 11, whose suburban terminus at Highgate Village was at the very top of Highgate High Street, a location not suitable for turning trolleybuses. It had been intended to replace the trams on 4th September 1938 as stage four of the North London Trolleybus conversion programme, but London Transport experienced considerable frustration in that there had been protracted negotiations with local authorities to find a suitable turning point. It was not until Sunday 10th December 1939 that route 611 first ran; it worked daily from Moorgate to Highgate Village and operated out of Holloway depot. The Highgate Village terminus was only a few yards short of the tram terminus and was at the junction of South Grove and Highgate High Street on land purchased by London Transport. In 1938 London Transport had been empowered to

extend the 611 to a point on North Road approximately 60 yards north of Castle Yard; presumably a turning location was considered here but the powers were not acted upon. These powers were only available until 31st December 1940 and were the only instance of temporary powers being granted; agreement on a turning circle was made after the passing of the 1938 Act. (Powers were also sought for the use of Castle Yard and Southwood Lane which would have been a most feasible routeing).

In September 1937, consideration was given to extending the 611 via North Hill to North Finchley and powers were to be sought for this. If this had happened, the 517/617 would have been consolidated with some other service, but would not have run to North Finchley. Plans for this and the routeing via Castle Yard and Southwood Lane were thwarted by local objections by Highgate

School, Hornsey Borough Council and Middlesex County Council, with hazards for schoolchildren being quoted. Highgate School made the point that there had been no public transport down North Hill for 100 years and there was no need for it now. An agreement was reached whereby London Transport abandoned their plans for operating down North Hill in return for opposition being dropped to what was to become the Highgate Village turning circle. The L1s were delivered by May 1939, so the scheme could have taken place any time after that; that the vehicles were ordered and delivered implies that there was confidence in the idea coming to fruition. A Sunday daytime 611EX service operated from Highgate Village to Islington Green until July 1941 with also a couple of late night Saturday journeys.

Highgate Hill was steep enough at 1 in 10 to cause the J3 and L1 class trolleybuses used

It is the last day of trams in north London, 5th April 1952, and E1 class car 199 is one of two tramcars hired by the Light Railway Transport League that day and is seen just north of the Archway Tavern; on the right is TD 5 on route 210. No.1037 squeezes between these two fine passenger carrying vehicles and is about to pass beneath an overhead feeder. Plastered on traction standards are details of bus routes replacing tram routes. Jack Wyse

on the route being required by the Ministry of Transport to be fitted with special braking equipment. They were given electric braking apparatus and experiments took place on the hill before opening to determine the descending speed. On ascending the hill, a run-back preventer operated automatically in the event of a trolleybus commencing to run back due to power failure or a circuit breaker tripping, and limited the speed to 2mph. On descending the hill, a coasting brake, pre-set by the driver, automatically controlled the speed to approximately 16mph maximised at 19mph. This procedure was operated by a special lever, but any additional braking was done with the footbrake. Special instructions were in force for vehicles descending the hill: on leaving the terminus a compulsory stop was made at pole 514 (at night, even in wartime, it carried an illuminated compulsory stop sign) where the coasting brake was put

into operation. The vehicle was used in this manner with a compulsory stop being made at Waterlow Park; at the compulsory stop at pole 487 the trolleybus was again brought to a standstill and the coasting brake switched out after which the trolleybus was driven in the normal way. Originally, passengers were allowed to stand when vehicles were ascending the hill but were not allowed to stand when descending until pole 487 was reached; this was amended in January 1942 when six passengers were allowed to stand throughout the descent. An MoT order instructed conductors to supervise the turn at Baring Street and signal the driver on to the main road.

Route 611 was one of great contrasts. Commencing at the important 'City' terminus of Moorgate, it soon passed through the drab areas of Hoxton and Canonbury before reaching Highbury Corner. After the 'Nags Head' junction, it embarked upon a steady climb to

Archway, where it parted company with other routes, to climb Highgate Hill to the select Highgate Village. It was one of London's less inspiring routes but was always busy and on Bank Holidays a supplementary service operated between Highgate Village and Baring Street, New North Road. The intensive service meant that people had easy access to Highgate Village from where they could walk to Parliament Hill Fields, Hampstead Heath or Kenwood. Many such trips per duty were performed by the crews, but were not popular due to having to swing the trolleys at Baring Street and having to pull six frogs every journey.

The 611 carried intermediate two-way traffic through the Highbury, Holloway and Highgate areas and was consistently one of the highest earning trolleybus routes. There were more specially-equipped vehicles for this route than necessary and the surplus was

used on other routes from Highgate depot; therefore, in the event of a vehicle developing a fault and needing to be changed, there was the possibility of a J3/L1 being unavailable. London Transport were meticulous about the Highgate Hill MoT stipulation and any standard vehicle used in these circumstances was not permitted to run beyond Archway Station. The only known instance of a non 'Highgate Hill' trolleybus operating on Highgate Hill was in 1950 when vehicle 1768 carrying some experimental equipment was used. Vehicles 489-493 and 1379 were also fitted with coasting and run-back brake equipment, so it is conceivable that they could have operated on the 611. On icy mornings, a 'Cub' breakdown vehicle would take men to Highgate Hill where salt was placed on the road to give the trolleybuses adhesion.

In 1957, London Transport engineers looked into the possibility of using the 611 as a test bed for the Routemaster bus; the idea was not proceeded with as it would have meant too long a period of dual motorbus/ trolleybus operation at Highgate depot. In the very earliest plans which were formulated for the trolleybus conversion, dated 28th May 1954, route 611 was grouped with the main Highgate conversion which was to take place on 1st January 1960. On 2nd June 1954, a revision saw route 611 advanced to be converted on 1st January 1959 along with routes 557, 623 and 625; at this time it was stated that the staging programme should take into account "special types of vehicles in certain areas", so this may have been one reason why the 611 was removed from the main Highgate conversion. Another reason would seem to be to even out the number of replacement buses needed for each stage and the 611, being a self contained route, was ideal for this. Matters were to change yet again and the 611 was grouped with routes 626, 628 and 630 at conversion stage seven. On Tuesday 19th July 1960 the route ran for the last time and a flag bedecked trolleybus operated for the day. The vehicle concerned, 1360, made the last trip down Highgate Hill and when it entered Highgate depot, closed route 611.

Top **The four overhead crossings at Old Street Station were the most heavily used individual items of special work on the entire system — they were each used by 1961 trolley heads each Monday to Friday at the peak of trolleybus operation. 1362 crosses Old Street at City Road.** Don Thompson

Centre **An unusual visitor to route 611 is K2 class 1335 seen on the approach to 'Nags Head'. As this class was not fitted with the special braking systems for this route, 1335 will turn at the Archway Station loop and pick up its timing on the next southbound trip.** Sid Hagarty

Right **Two trolleybuses could stand round the traffic island at Highgate Village terminus, it being 1049 and 1363 on this occasion. Apart from the removal of the trolleybus infrastructure, this location remains unchanged today.** Fred Ivey

THE FINCHLEY ROUTES

The first trolleybus routes to penetrate the City of London, 521, 617, 621, did so on Sunday 6th March 1938; the 617 operated daily from North Finchley to Holborn Circus via Farringdon Road with the 517 commencing on Monday 7th March 1938 and working from North Finchley to Holborn Circus via Grays Inn Road. The 517/617 operated out of Holloway depot and worked via Archway. Upon introduction these four routes linked via High Holborn, two separate tram termini which had been situated in Grays Inn Road and Farringdon Road, thus forming what was known as the Holborn Loop. On 1st June 1938, routes 517/617 were reallocated to Finchley depot but returned to Holloway on 29th October 1941. On 8th January 1939 the 517 began operating daily, replacing the 617 on Sundays; on 29th October 1944 the 617

was reinstated on Sundays. Commencing on 28th March 1954, the 517 was curtailed on Sundays to operate only to Kings Cross although two early morning journeys operated to Holborn Circus. At the same time the 617 was withdrawn on Sundays, last operating on 21st March 1954. On August Bank Holiday 1938, routes 517/617 were extended to Barnet (this had no connection with Barnet fair). This was repeated on Christmas Days 1938/39 and the facility was retained on fare charts until 1950; route 645 tickets were issued on the Barnet section at these times.

It was originally anticipated that route numbers 617 and 621 would be used in both directions round the Holborn loop; a further recommendation entailed the 617 operating via Farringdon Road and the 621 via Grays Inn Road. The terminal workings via Grays

Inn Road and Farringdon Road loop were considered to be efficient in that congestion was minimised and assisted the efficient regulation of the services. Holborn terminus was at an intermediate point in the central area between the City and West End, setting down passengers within a reasonable walking distance of their work and all routes operating there served the Clerkenwell industrial zone. Holborn was one of only three termini in the City of London, the others being Liverpool Street and Aldgate.

Above **21st June 1938 and trolleybus 976 turns from Farringdon Road into Charterhouse Street. At that time 'Archway Tavern' was displayed on the destination blinds before giving way to 'Archway Station'. Smithfield Market is in the background.** London Transport Museum U27411

No stand time was allowed in Charterhouse Street generally speaking, but vehicles tended to lay over to adjust their timings. Conductors were instructed that the route number shown on the up journey (to the City) was to be retained until the suburban terminus. Many in-town termini were difficult to photograph in sunlight, due to the presence of high buildings; one such location was in Charterhouse Street, but 317 obliges on this occasion. The conductor has perfectly positioned the blinds for the return trip to North Finchley. In the background, the new Daily Mirror building nears completion. There was no predominant class of vehicles on routes 521/621. Don Thompson

From the MoT inspecting officer's report it can be deduced that London Transport considered that the clockwise routeing at Kings Cross should take a left turn from Caledonian Road into Pentonville Road for Kings Cross Road, but as this turn was very sharp and traffic much congested, the routeing hitherto adopted by the trams was retained, via Grays Inn Road. All trolleybus services from Kings Cross in the 500 series travelled via Grays Inn Road, High Holborn, Charterhouse Street, Farringdon Road and Kings Cross Road while those in the 600 series travelled via Swinton Street, Kings Cross Road, Farringdon Road,

Charterhouse Street, High Holborn and Grays Inn Road. The inspecting officer was informed that Prince Consort's statue was to be removed. It presented a difficult turn from Charterhouse Street into High Holborn in that a reverse curve was made. However, the statue was not removed and remains to this day. There was no stopping place in High Holborn, although in the interests of passengers, the inspecting officer suggested that there should be reconsideration on this point by the City police authorities after a few months. High Holborn never received a trolleybus stop.

For many years the ways in which the Holborn loop was traversed was highlighted on the destination blinds at many depots. No.754, the solitary X4 class member, is in Kingsway, North Finchley whilst 951 passes through New Southgate. *V. C. Jones/Don Thompson*

The 521 and 621 worked daily and operated out of Finchley depot. They ran from North Finchley to Holborn Circus via Wood Green and Finsbury Park with the 521 going round the Holborn Loop via Grays Inn Road and the 621 operating via Farringdon Road. The Saturday afternoon and evening service was cut back to Kings Cross on 19th March 1955. Outside Friern Barnet Mental Hospital, the traction poles were fitted with spikes to prevent patients climbing out. The correct terminology for them was 'anti-climb guards' but they were known colloquially as 'lunatic spikes'. These routes suffered in later years from traffic congestion and in Monday to Friday evening peaks from May 1956 a localised section was operated from North Finchley to Wood Green to provide a more regular service at that end of the route. There were always particularly early journeys on the 521 with the first Monday to Saturday journey on the trolleybus system being a 521 leaving Finchley depot at 2.56am for Holborn Circus, catering for press and market workers. This journey held the record for longevity, for it worked from 7th March 1938 to 7th November 1961; it replaced the 3.14am Monday to Saturday, Wood Green to Holborn 21 tram.

With the last arrival of the traffic day on a Saturday, a 628 into Hammersmith depot at 2.35am (2.16am Monday to Friday), the system was open for daytime trolleybuses for almost 24 hours, but these very late journeys were withdrawn in November/December 1940. There were also very early journeys on the 621 on Sundays to cater for press workers. Also served in this locality was Mount Pleasant sorting office and the Union of Post Office Workers were granted many requests to cater for postmen when their night shifts ended. As an example, a Monday to Saturday 517 arrived at Rosebery Avenue after 6am from 1st

July 1938; it meant that a single 517 journey was made 1½ hours before any others and it was a facility that was retained for many years.

On Sunday 6th March 1938, route 609 was also introduced; worked by Holloway depot it operated daily between Barnet and Moorgate. Even in that age, the Board's officers arranged with the police for unauthorised car parking to be stopped in Finsbury Square (Moorgate) where trolleybuses were required to stand between trips. At Holloway Station Bridge, one of the piers projected into the carriageway and for the benefit of trolleybus drivers, the Islington Borough Council surveyor undertook to provide reflectors on it. Finchley depot first worked the 609 on August Bank Holiday Monday 1938; on 26th/27th December 1938, they again worked the 609 between North Finchley and Islington Green (quoted in the Traffic Circular as 609EX). There were examples in earlier years of routes having regular EX allocations and these could be found daily. From 14th May 1938, they were given a permanent Sunday afternoon allocation thus increasing the number of vehicles on Sundays by 50%. On 29th October 1941 the 609 was transferred to Finchley depot in exchange for their 517/617 workings; by 1942 passenger traffic on Mondays to Saturdays required a 50% increase in vehicles. The Monday to Saturday service on routes 521/621 was cut by 25% in August 1939 and the initial service frequency was never restored. Highgate depot returned to the 609 on Sundays from 9th November 1952. Highgate usually used L2s on its 609 allocation because these vehicles and those at Colindale and Finchley had heavier tensioning on their booms for negotiating Barnet Bridge where the booms were brought down to almost roof level. Drivers on routes 609 and 645 were not considered to be fully-fledged trolleybus drivers until they had dewired at this location!

Originally, powers were obtained for a loop to be constructed at Barnet via Wood Street, Union Street and High Street. The powers were never exercised and the 609 and 645 terminated opposite Barnet Church in the same place as the tram terminus. Initially only one trolleybus was allowed on the stand here, due to the intervention of the Barnet Safety First Council. This was later altered and two trolleybuses were allowed on the stand simultaneously despite the fact that there were many occasions when three vehicles were scheduled together. To prevent three vehicles being on the stand at the same time, a skate and signal system operated. When two vehicles were on the stand, a light shone in a box attached to a traction standard and was visible from the stop prior to the terminus; the light was extinguished when a trolleybus passed a skate in the overhead as it left the terminus. Passengers were not allowed to be carried between North Finchley terminus and Finchley depot but were allowed to travel to Holloway depot in the earlier years. The northbound frog at Islington Green where routes diverged for 609/679 to proceed to Holloway was unique in that it was the only semi-automatic frog apparatus supported by a wall rosette.

The terminus at Moorgate was a short distance north of the tram terminus and short of Moorgate itself, but was within half a mile of the Bank, and City workers were set down within reasonable walking distance of their places of work. The terminus was very good, for there was adequate space for standing vehicles and passenger queues and the terminating routes were also well clear of the worst bottlenecks of City traffic congestion.

There were regular bombing incidents in the Farringdon area and these affected the Holborn routes. Services were diverted early in the war in both directions via temporary wiring around the back of Mount Pleasant

sorting office as the top part of Farringdon Road could not be used. It is thought that this diversion was in use for about a year (from March 1941 to February 1942). During the war, an emergency turning circle was constructed at Vine Street Bridge; it meant that two circles, one from either direction, were strung in the same street. Of interest was the fact that a traction standard on the Clerkenwell Green circle supported a span wire for two separate circles, Vine Street Bridge and Clerkenwell Green, and as such was unique on the system.

All these routes traversed the trolleybus station at North Finchley (the only other trolleybus station was at Aldgate). It was a public highway which had been commandeered by London Transport for its trams and trolleybuses and is still a public road to this day. The terminus had been specially constructed in tram days and was considered efficient, for it was situated at a main road junction and in a shopping area which was an important local traffic objective; it was the only location on the system where routes from three directions had a common terminal. An oversight occurred at North Finchley in that Nether Street and the parallel Kingsway were not authorised for trolleybuses upon their introduction in 1936 and the Parliamentary powers were not granted until 1937!

The routes to Holborn operated via Caledonian Road, passing Pentonville prison on the way; no doubt the last view of freedom that some inmates saw were the trolleybuses. When major work was being carried out on the railway bridge in Caledonian Road on Sunday 8th February 1959, northbound vehicles were towed in service past the bridge. Southbound vehicles passed by means of battery or gravity power with booms being lowered or not lowered as circumstances dictated; for safety reasons the power was cut off over the affected section. To save continual

1519's positive boom is about to touch the contact skate on the approach to Barnet terminus; to the driver's left is the traction standard mounted signal box that gives him clearance to the stand at the top of the hill. An MoT instruction that conductors were to give a clear warning to following traffic when a turn was about to be made here, may have been observed at the start of the trolleybus services, but it was not being carried out in 1961. Brian Pask

No.948 passes under the extraordinarily high Archway Bridge. Viewed from the top of the bridge, the trolleybuses seemed the size of the 'Matchbox' trolleybus model that became available. All classes of trolleybus at Finchley depot were used on route 609. Don Thompson

1478, followed by 1323, turns into Finsbury Square, Moorgate. At this corner the overhead is supported by rosettes (an attachment holding a span wire to a building). Ron Lunn

Highgate depot's 1427, on their small Sunday allocation on the 609, is due to make one of their few journeys to Barnet. It heads a line up of seven vehicles in Finsbury Square. As many of the vehicles behind are probably not in departure order, the loop wire will be used to enable the correct departure sequence to be kept. If seven vehicles could be seen on a Sunday in latter days, how many trolleybuses could have been seen in the late 1940s in peak hours at this location? Michael Dryhurst

handling of the front valances many vehicles ran without them, giving them a rather ragged look. At Clerkenwell Junction, route 521 trolleybus conductors became very agile in that they pulled the semi-automatic frog from the platform without the vehicle stopping in the process.

There was little interchanging from one route to the other; 517 to 617 and vice versa at North Finchley and 521 to 621 and vice versa at North Finchley with a solitary 621 becoming a 609 at North Finchley on a Sunday morning. Routes 521/621 had one scheduled journey per year for a number of years to Turnpike Lane Station. This was on Christmas Day and it was only in later years that it was added to the destination blinds. The 517/617 were interworked with the 609 between North Finchley and 'Nags Head'. Between North Finchley and 'Nags Head' it was quicker to travel via 517, 609 and 617 than via 521/621.

These five routes were not considered as some of the busiest of the trunk trolleybus routes because they were competing with each other and with other trolleybus routes. The only section where they were on their own was between North Finchley and Wood Green on the 521/621. However they still provided frequent services, gave good links to the places they passed en route and gave a direct service to the fringes of the City areas. There were major trolleybus complexes at North Finchley, Wood Green, Manor House, 'Nags Head' Holloway and 'Angel' Islington, all of which were traffic objectives. As with so many trolleybus routes, they served many shopping areas and Underground stations.

Top With matching registration and route number, 1521 pauses at the bottom of Grays Inn Road. Little did the photographer realise that this quite ordinary vehicle would close the London trolleybus system some months later. Peter Moore

Centre The trolley arms of 939 are being lowered to enable another trolleybus to pass in Nether Street during the resurfacing of the North Finchley terminus. Temporary wiring was constructed and was in use for six weeks from mid-September 1956; Finchley's 320 waits on the innermost of the two wires that existed here. Don Thompson

Right North Finchley trolleybus station was the only place on the system where routes from three different directions immediately confronted each other and then terminated simultaneously. Leyland 1267 is flanked by two AECs, 565 and 938. Norman Rayfield

Routes 517 and 617 last operated on Tuesday 31st January 1961 as part of conversion stage nine. As Highgate depot was losing its last trolleybuses on 25th April 1961, their 609 Sunday workings were supplied by RMs from 30th April until 5th November that year. It had been planned to keep route 609 operating until January 1962, but it was found possible to include it at conversion stage 12 along with routes 521/621. This was due to route 629 being pushed up the conversion process by two stages and the 609 was put in its place. Thus routes 521, 609 and 621 last operated on Tuesday 7th November 1961. Along with route 641 they were the last trolleybus routes to run over the former London County Council Tramways area and the last routes to operate over former conduit-equipped tram routes. They were also the last routes to run into the heart of the City just as routes 521, 609 and 621 had been among the first. The honour of being the last trolleybus away from the City of London fell to 1464 as a 521 from Holborn which strangely enough had been Poplar depot's last service trolleybus. The last trolleybus away from a 'City' terminus was 1456 from Moorgate.

Above Right **There were no scheduled turns at East Finchley Station; judging by the early hour, it is probably wise to assume that a member of staff was late arriving for work, thus causing 996 to turn short.** Fred Ivey

1545B on the 617 approaches East Finchley, heading a line of vehicles which would now be collectors items; no specific classes were allocated to routes 517/617. Fred Ivey

ROUTES 629 and 641

On Sunday 8th May 1938, just two days after the MoT inspection of the section to Enfield, two very important routes were added to the trolleybus network: route 629 working daily between Enfield and Tottenham Court Road and route 641 running daily between Winchmore Hill and Moorgate. Both were worked by Wood Green depot. This was a significant stage in the tram to trolleybus conversion for it marked the time when trolleybus mileage became greater than tram mileage. There were still almost twice as many trams scheduled at this time, though, reflecting the fact that the 'light' services were converted first. The number of scheduled trolleybuses did not exceed the number of scheduled trams until June 1939.

The 629 and 641 were ideal for trolleybus operation, for they required speedy, efficient and high-frequency services for which the trolleybus was ideal. Working together from

Winchmore Hill through Wood Green and Turnpike Lane, they parted company at Manor House. The 641 followed Green Lanes in its entirety, which was from Winchmore Hill to Newington Green. The routes served a number of bus and Underground interchange points and shopping areas with the shopping area between Wood Green and Turnpike Lane being particularly popular. The 629 was the first trolleybus route to run to Tottenham Court Road. London Transport hoped to extend it to Bedford Square, but this was successfully opposed by local authorities and local wealthy residents. A further proposal to turn via Francis Street, Huntley Street and University Street was declined by the Minister of Transport because of disturbance to patients and staff of University College Hospital, so the turning loop round Fitzroy Street had to suffice. There were two separate loops here, the anti-clockwise one via Whitfield

Street being a police requirement, for they were worried about the congestion factor. To give an equal service on the section from Winchmore Hill to Manor House, routes 629 and 641 had their timings interworked. Between Wood Green and Manor House the 521/621 joined forces to create an intensive service on that section. The 629 and bus route 29 overlapped on the section from Palmers Green to Tottenham Court Road. To save costs in the war, bus route 39 (Southfields to Turnpike Lane), which paralleled the 629, was withdrawn between Camden Town and Turnpike Lane outside peak hours from 15th November 1939. There were regular suggestions from staff and passengers to extend the 641 to Enfield but this only happened when a gap occurred on the 629. Route 629 was one of a number of routes where only one frog pull (Manor House northbound) was required on a round journey.

A few operational aspects are of interest. Upon inception, route 629 did not finish its traffic day until about 2am daily; late finishes such as this were common, but these late journeys were withdrawn early in the war. On Saturday evenings in the early years, vehicles from Moorgate, Enfield and Palmers Green would congregate in Redvers Road, Wood Green on 'foreign service' to provide late night journeys on route 625 to Tottenham Hale. Between 1938 and 1952 there was joint tramway conduit and trolleybus operation between Manor House and Balls Pond Road on route 641 with a similar operation from Archway to Bloomsbury. The normal service coped with speedway and greyhound racing at Harringay Stadium, although extras were run for big events.

Large numbers of people had to be transported to and from Moorgate which was only about half a mile short of the Bank and about 85 trolleybuses an hour arrived and left here in the morning and evening peak hours, the 641 being the most frequent.

Powers were held by London Transport to operate to Alexandra Palace and the use of trolleybuses in Alexandra Park was discussed between the Park trustees and London Transport on 28th December 1934. The £1,400 per year subsidy which was offered by the trustees was not deemed sufficient by London Transport; the scheme was dropped and the powers to operate along Turnpike Lane and Priory Road, to terminate at the southern entrance of the Park, expired on 2nd August 1940. London Transport also held powers for the section from Enfield Town to Ponders End but they were not exercised either.

For the war effort, 'foreign stabling' took place, cutting out some unnecessary mileage. A number of routes were involved and it entailed parking at distant depots in off-peak hours. Rubber was saved on tyres and less electricity was used, although there was no saving on crew costs as staff were fully utilised in a day's work. At Holloway depot in off-peak hours, vehicles from routes 609, 629, 659 and 679 parked in this way.

If it was necessary to cover gaps in service, 641s were extended to Enfield and curtailed at Baring Street on return. Similarly, route 629 sometimes found itself working to North Finchley (a display was on the blinds). In later years the 629 suffered from traffic congestion at the London end to the detriment of the service to Enfield and a localised 629 evening peak service was introduced between Enfield and Wood Green to alleviate the problem. The 629 on Bank Holidays ran a supplementary service from Redvers Road to variously Mornington Crescent Station or Tottenham Court Road.

There were a number of unusual journeys on the routes with the shortest one on the whole system being found on route 641. This was a journey 0.65 miles long on Monday to Friday evenings in the early post-war period and ran between Newington Green and Balls Pond Road, a three-minute journey!

Facing Page **1145 and 1210 have travelled from Winchmore Hill, probably within sight of each other for most of the way; they now part company on the setts at Manor House.** Tony Belton

Left **The Tottenham Court Road terminus was situated in Maple Street. No.981, a J2 pushed into Wood Green depot to enable the conversion to take place on time, stands.** Charles Klapper

Routes 629 and 641 are best remembered for their long association with the H1 class. Most of Wood Green depot's allocation were withdrawn between April 1959 and April 1960 to be replaced by K classes but 816 survived and here works to Newington Green only; it is hustled along by 1302 at Baring Street. Tony Belton

Occasionally route 641 trolleybuses operated to Finsbury Park Station; if a vehicle was too late to be curtailed at Balls Pond Road, recourse was made to this loop. Some vehicles operated in service to Finsbury Park whilst others ran light from Manor House. On this occasion the crew were happy to carry passengers to Finsbury Park. Peter Moore

At Enfield the terminal loop was via Cecil Road and Sydney Road with return being via The Town and London Road. No.1254 passes RT 1004 as the K2 turns from Cecil Road into Sydney Road which became a one-way street upon the introduction of trolleybuses; in early years the Enfield terminus was known as the 'Country end'. Fred Ivey

There was a 641 which left the depot and travelled via Bruce Grove to Moorgate, having to battery around the corner at Manor House, 623 being shown until Manor House where the route number was changed. A similar manouevre had to be carried out by a Moorgate-bound 641 that had come from Epping Forest via route 623 and a further derivative 641 ran from Epping Forest to Moorgate via Wood Green (these journeys were operating in the early post-war period). There were instances of working on routes 623 and 625 before taking up as 641 and an evening 641 journey ran from Winchmore Hill to Woodford and return although 625 was displayed. Also there were 623s working from Manor House to Tottenham Hale where they had a short stand time before becoming a 625

to Winchmore Hill and then operating as a 641. All these odd journeys were withdrawn by 1951. On Christmas Days until 1959, two 641s worked directly from Winchmore Hill to Tottenham Hale before returning to depot and on Christmas Day 1960, the former 625 Enfield journeys were covered by route 629 working to Finsbury Park or Turnpike Lane. At the latter location a double battery manoeuvre was required. It was originally planned that some 641 journeys would operate from Moorgate to Enfield on this particular day, two northbound and three southbound, but none did. As many of the Christmas Day 625 EXTRAS, as they were known, had only worked to Tottenham Hale it was surprising that these special 629 Enfield journeys did not operate there.

Changing from one route to the other took place as follows:

641 to 629 at Palmers Green

629 to 641 at Palmers Green

627 to 629 at Finsbury Park

629 to 641 at Winchmore Hill

641 to 629 at Winchmore Hill

It was planned that both routes would be withdrawn together, but due to the London Traffic Management Unit introducing a one-way system at Tottenham Court Road, route 629 was moved up two stages in the conversion programme and last operated on Tuesday 25th April 1961 as part of stage 10. Route 641 continued to run until stage 12 and was withdrawn after operations on Tuesday 7th November 1961.

1323 is about to take on a new driver at the crew changeover point at Wood Green; RT 3227 on a 715 relief passes by. The pavements on both sides of the road are full of activity. Before the introduction of route 641 it was suggested that 'Moorgate' be described as 'Finsbury Square' on the destination blinds. This did not occur as passengers were familiar with MOORGATE, which had been used on the trams.
Sid Hagarty

Originally vehicles from the north entered Wood Green depot by overhead wire; before long though, they entered from this direction by a combination of battery and gravity power. 777's crew will be unaware that this is its final movement in active service for on the date that the photograph was taken, 26th April 1960, it was replaced by a K class vehicle ousted from Walthamstow depot at stage six of the trolleybus conversion programme.
Denis Battams

Below Left For a few days in June 1960, the irregularly used loop at Tottenham Court Road was used due to a fire; 1352 turns into Whitfield Street. Michael Dryhurst

Below 1059 was the highest numbered trolleybus to receive a wire grille, and is seen passing through Winchmore Hill. 'Fairy lights' and guard wires imply that this is a curve to be treated with caution by trolleybus drivers.

ROUTE 653

Introduced on Sunday 5th March 1939, route 653 operated daily between Aldgate and Tottenham Court Road via Stamford Hill. A pattern in previous conversions was maintained with this one, in that reduced running time was given when compared to the tram running time. The 653 was always worked by Holloway depot save for some operations by Stamford Hill depot on Easter and Whit Mondays 1940. It was a very important and extremely busy service which was mainly due to the fact that for much of the way there was no parallel service; many of the areas that it served, Whitechapel, Bethnal Green, Hackney and Stamford Hill were always seething with activity and the trolleybuses were well loaded. There was a far more intensive service daily between Aldgate and Finsbury Park than over the section from Aldgate to Tottenham Court Road, due to the fact that other services were joined at Amhurst Junction and Manor House. The 653 secured good two-way traffic and at Maple Street, Tottenham Court Road terminus, queues formed during peak hours for trolleybuses on routes 627, 629 and 653. All three services were so heavily pressed that it was necessary to turn short some vehicles on all routes at Mornington Crescent

Station, so as to clear Camden Town passenger traffic which would otherwise have had very long waits.

The tram to trolleybus conversions provided many new facilities for the travelling public, although in a few cases links were withdrawn. Many routes gained earlier and later journeys with the latter being particularly pertinent to routes 628 and 653. The London Transport of its day made great efforts to accommodate the public and in the 653's infancy there was a connection on Saturday nights at Stamford Hill at 1.21am for a 643 from Holborn and a 649 from Ponders End to connect with the last but one 653 to Hackney at 1.23am. However, the outbreak of war brought restrictions and in November /December 1940 every trolleybus schedule was changed. This was necessary as last departure times were brought forward on all routes; exceptions were made for war workers, and special munition journeys were laid on, some at night and some in the morning. Most routes had reduced allocations on Mondays to Saturdays, although a few had increases, but the vehicle requirement stayed about the same; Sunday services were also reduced, resulting in 20% fewer vehicles

being required. As the war progressed, augmentation was necessary and by the time it ceased, about 100 more trolleybuses were required on Mondays to Fridays (about 40 more on Saturdays) than had been the case before the war; in the immediate post-war period, Sunday services were restored to their pre-war level. Last finishing times were reinstated between February and April 1946, but many did not reach their pre-war times; the prime example was the last 659 from Holborn, which left shortly after 11pm in contrast to a 1.00am departure pre-war.

Above **1138 negotiates the five items of special work that it has to cross at 'Nags Head', Holloway. 1154 passes in the other direction to Enfield and four other trolleybuses are in view.** Ken Blacker

Facing Page **Trolleybuses of most classes allocated to Highgate depot operated on route 653. 1524 heads for Finsbury Park while RT 1916 heads for Ilford one wet Sunday morning in January 1961. Until August 1959, routes 661 and 663 connected with the 653 here at Mile End Gate.** Tony Belton

Route 653 was the first trolleybus service to use Minories trolleybus station. An early idea for Minories was for three sets of wires to be constructed to allow overtaking, but just two sets were erected and vehicles normally found this adequate. When planning this trolleybus terminal in 1936, much thought was given to its use by all traffic in conjunction with a one-way scheme. The 653 operated in a horseshoe formation and few passengers travelled the full length of the route as bus routes 23 and 25 were far quicker. The schedule for Sunday 5th March 1939 shows that route 653 was operating a three-minute headway with route 629 from Tottenham Court Road from 9.37am to 12.55pm. From then until the finish of the day it worked a six-minute headway with a four-minute headway on route 629, such was London Transport's desire for operating efficiency. London Transport took notice of its passengers' requirements, for a letter from Mrs C. Compitts-Harris in 1950 produced a journey from Euston six minutes later on Saturdays. This was the last bus, but in fact the last three trolleybuses had to be altered.

Route 653 was the most frequent of the services between Manor House and Finsbury Park, which was the most heavily trolleybus-trafficked section on the system, although Stratford Broadway and Canning Town Broadway came close behind. At the height of the Monday to Friday morning peak hour in 1947, 154 southbound trolleybuses per hour were scheduled on this section, while in the evening peak, 145 vehicles per hour were scheduled in the opposite direction; 1,631 vehicles used this section each way during a traffic day at this time. Between 1939 and 1948 route 653 grew in stature with the number of vehicles being gradually increased.

Throughout its weekday life the 653 had a very early start to its day with the first journey leaving the depot at 3.37am for Hackney; in the route's infancy the last arrival at the depot was at 2.22am from Hackney on a Saturday night. On Bank Holiday Mondays, there were even earlier starts (the reason for these is not known), with the first vehicle leaving the depot at 3.05am; this worked to Hackney Station before making two return trips to Stamford Hill. On its third trip from Hackney, it went to Manor House and then back to Hackney before making a journey to Tottenham Court Road. All of this occurred before 6.25am and required the conductor to pull 19 frogs and perform two trolley swings. The turn at Stamford Hill was the most arduous on the system for a conductor, in that four 'pull and hold' frog pulls were required in addition to a trolley swing. Despite being arduous, such an operation was just considered to be 'part and parcel' of the job for the trolleybus staff. The frog from Clapton Common for this working was the only one on the system where the wiring led into a dead-end on the nearside and these two turns each Bank Holiday Monday gave this manoeuvre a total of six scheduled workings each year! It was a common sight to see vehicles on routes 627/653 parked in Warlters Road ('Nags Head' short working) without a crew. This location was one of only two that had a time restriction; vehicles were officially only allowed to turn here before 7.30am and after 7pm and in emergency; presumably London Transport considered Christmas Day scheduled workings here were emergencies! Of interest was the frog operation at the junction of Warlters Road and Parkhurst Road for its supporting traction pole was set in private property and the lever was therefore cantilevered; it was one of only two such devices on the system.

Having replaced an awkward tram terminal stub in Whitechapel High Street, the Minories trolleybus terminus at Aldgate was very convenient; route 653 was both the first and last route to use this complex. Seen with other motorbuses and trolleybuses in the last days of route 653, trolleybus 1425 leaves this inner London terminus. It later became the last trolleybus to leave Hammersmith trolleybus terminus on 8th May 1962. Derek Norman

The route was unfortunately subject to considerable traffic delays, resulting in curtailments. There were many turning points on this route with most of them being used over the years for scheduling purposes; it was common to see most of them used in the course of a day due to passenger and traffic density. Turns could be made from both directions at closely spaced Hackney Station, Kenninghall Road and Stamford Hill with the turns at Stamford Hill both requiring a trolley swing. Turns at these places from the Aldgate direction meant that destination displays showed via points from the opposite direction. Major junctions were passed at Gardiners Corner, Stamford Hill, Manor House and 'Nags Head'; 627s changed to 653s at Finsbury Park and Tottenham Court Road.

A number of interesting aspects about the route are worthy of note: 653 was carried on Hackney depot blinds and would be used on a substitute vehicle if a vehicle from Holloway depot was run in with a defect. A few journeys on the 627 schedule operated to Stamford Hill and Aldgate and Sunday 653 Extras had their

crew relief in Stamford Hill depot. An oddity for the route was its operation from Archway Station to Smithfield every Christmas Day from 1939 with a first departure of 4.23am from the depot (at Christmas 1938 these journeys operated as 679). In many instances, Christmas Day schedules stayed the same with changes only being made in later years; (munitions journeys were another example of unnecessary workings being left on schedules). These 653 journeys continued until 1960 despite the fact that Smithfield Market had been closed on Christmas Day for some years. The lone trolleybus that worked these journeys carried little else but the crew and fresh air in later years: the last journey operated directly from Smithfield to Aldgate. For many years there was the need to transport workers home in the early hours of Christmas morning and the trolleybus staff had to work some very unsocial hours; the earliest day journey was the 3.26am departure from Holloway depot to Holborn Circus on route 513, which was the same time as the first weekday vehicle.

The figures below relate to the Monday to Friday November 1947 schedule. Aldgate trolleybus station was by far the busiest terminus on the system; an astounding 124 trolleybuses left here between 7.30 and 8.30am — a rate of more than two a minute! This is broken down as:
31 vehicles on routes 567/569
27 vehicles on route 653
2 vehicles on route 627 (operating as 653)
26 vehicles on route 661
40 vehicles on route 663

The total for the whole day was 1,358 movements, made up by:
323 departures on routes 567/569
2 departures on route 627 (operating as 653)
369 departures on route 653
292 departures on route 661
372 departures on route 663

The first trolleybus away was a 663 at 4am with the last departure being a 653 at the surprisingly early hour of 11.34pm. Duty inspectors here had to be astute to ensure good arrival and departure times so that the trolleybus station was not overwhelmed.

1054 is gleaming after its last overhaul in April 1958 and is seen loading in Amhurst Road, Hackney. It was to meet a rather sad end under the Kentish Town West railway bridge; it is thought that this was the only such mishap. Fred Ivey

The nearby Gardiners Corner at this time was the busiest junction on the trolleybus network; 372 movements per hour were made at the height of the morning peak hour, (including 80 from the east on the Commercial Road services) meaning that a trolleybus passed through less than every ten seconds! Also astounding was the fact that 4,002 trolleybuses passed through in a day. This was made up by:

1406 movements on 565/567/569/665

16 movements on night route 665

4 movements on route 627 (operating as 653)

510 movements on route 647

738 movements on route 653

584 movements on route 661

744 movements on route 663

The second busiest junction at peak hours at this time was Old Street Junction followed by 'Nags Head'; in the course of a day 'Nags Head' had the second highest number of trolley heads (3,985) clattering over its overhead with Old Street Junction in third place. Manor House, though, was the location where the largest number of vehicles could be seen in a day; 3,878 trolleybuses used the main junction while 209 vehicles on the 623 turned at the circle and two 641s battery manoeuvred, totalling 4,089.

By 1955 however, 'Nags Head' was the busiest junction in the course of a traffic day with about 450 more trolleybuses than Gardiners Corner. In fact, Gardiners Corner had now slipped to fourth position behind Manor House and Old Street. The 1947 position of more trolleybuses being able to be seen at Manor House than at any other single location still prevailed though. Route 653 became the last trolleybus route to serve Aldgate, in conversion stage nine, and on Tuesday 31st January 1961 it operated for the last time; the 653 wires were still to see some use, for London Transport sold most of the Q1 type trolleybuses to Spain in early 1961. Some of them had already travelled to Aldgate via the 653 from where they were towed to Poplar garage for storage prior to shipment. A large batch was withdrawn on 31st January and, between 1st and 9th February, route 653 wires were kept live to enable the Q1s to travel to Aldgate under their own power before they, too, were towed to Poplar. These journeys were made during the late evening but no doubt caused some confusion to would-be passengers who knew that the 653 trolleybus was now history.

THE KINGSLAND ROAD ROUTES

Trolleybus services started running along the Kingsland Road on Sunday 5th February 1939 when route 647 was introduced daily from Stamford Hill to London Docks and route 649 gained a lengthy southward extension to Liverpool Street. It now became Ponders End to Liverpool Street Station daily, restoring the link across Stamford Hill which had been broken the previous October by partly converting tram 49; the possibility of a common terminus for bus and trolleybus routes at Liverpool Street was looked into but unsuccessfully.

On Monday 6th February 1939, routes 643 and 683 first operated; route 683 worked between Stamford Hill and Moorgate on Mondays to Saturdays. Only on Saturdays was a late evening service provided and this did not last beyond summer 1944. The route never operated on Bank Holidays. Route 643 worked on Mondays to Saturdays from Wood Green Station to Holborn Circus and was a big improvement on the 43 tram that had only run from Holborn to Stamford Hill; it absorbed the 625 'shorts' that had been operating between Wood Green and Tottenham Hale in Monday to Saturday peak hours. The clockwise and anti-clockwise workings around the Holborn Loop were numbered 643 despite differentiating numbers being allocated to routes already working round the loop; from Friday 7th April 1939, route 543 was shown when operating via Grays Inn Road. An instruction for route 643 stated that the destination blinds when running up via Farringdon Road were to be turned between Clerkenwell Road and Farringdon Street Station and when running up via Grays Inn Road were to be turned between Holborn Hall and Holborn, Grays Inn Road. From inception there were no late Monday to Friday evening journeys via Grays Inn Road. On Sundays there were a few very early morning 643 journeys between Stamford Hill and Holborn Circus which were variously allocated to 647, 649 and 649A over the years. Routes 543, 643, 647, 649A and 683 operated out of Stamford Hill depot. STAMFORD HILL Amhurst Park/ AMHURST PARK STAMFORD HILL blind displays were used on depot journeys and indicated to pointsmen at Stamford Hill Broadway that the 'frog' did not require to be pulled; passengers were not allowed to be carried along Egerton Road to the depot.

Above **1152 is the second of five trolleybuses approaching Dalston Junction. Bunching of trolleybuses such as this was not an infrequent sight on these services.** Denis Battams

Right **1198 on route 683, waits on the stand at Stamford Hill. As can be seen it is attracting little custom and the lack of patronage was the reason for its withdrawal in January 1959.** Michael Dryhurst

1227 is being driven onto one of the two traversers in Stamford Hill depot. On the platform, a tram type controller moves the traverser, and resting against the guard rail is a bamboo pole covered in insulating tape. Behind is 1307 which has run in on one of the few 649 journeys operated to Liverpool Street by this depot. John Aldridge

Commencing on Sunday 12th May 1940, route 649 operated a section from Liverpool Street to Wood Green; this gave a similar service to the 543/643 on weekdays and in November 1940 it enabled the 625 Sunday 'shorts' from Wood Green to Tottenham Hale to be withdrawn. Stamford Hill depot operated this section which on 17th April 1949 was renumbered 649A and became the only route to carry a suffix on the blinds (these were known at times as 543 Extras). On Bank Holidays the 543 operated rather than the 649A; this was due to the closure of markets near to Liverpool Street on these days. From Bank Holidays in 1959 the 649A operated as opposed to 543.

Route 683 was never a money-spinner and bus route 76 paralleled it for most of its length; in fact the 683 would not have come into being if the Metropolitan Traffic Commissioner had allowed motorbuses on route 76 to turn at Finsbury Square. From Wednesday 17th October 1956 the 683 operated in Monday to Saturday peak hours only. It suffered an early demise when, as part of London Transport's service cuts following the 1958 bus strike, it was withdrawn after operations on Tuesday 6th January 1959 without replacement. Despite being one of the least important trolleybus routes, the 683 was involved with 'compensated frogs' which were located southbound at Dalston Junction and

northbound at Mildmay Park; all routes that used this apparatus were involved. 'Compensated frogs', which were operated by the conductor, meant that points stayed in the position for which they were last set. They were instituted so that drivers would take more notice of illuminated frog signals than had been the case hitherto, for many dewirements took place due to drivers neglecting them. With 'compensated frogs' they were forced to observe them. This certainly had the desired effect, for dewirements at these locations became infrequent, but strangely enough this apparatus was not perpetuated throughout the system. They were instituted in 1939 but it is not known when they were removed. Rather oddly, the 683 was detailed to be able to be curtailed at Downham Road, Kingsland Road which it did not pass, but not at Mildmay Park, which it did. Route 543 was withdrawn on Saturday afternoons and evenings between Holborn and Shoreditch in April 1949; from January 1959 the Saturday evening 643 service was similarly cut back.

Route 647 was a very consistent route, not sustaining any change whatsoever save for a few journeys working to Liverpool Street; it was the only route to serve the London Docks and passed near to the Royal Mint. It was the first and last route to cross the busy Gardiners Corner and in later years was prone to delays in Commercial Street due to lorries wanting access to warehouses. The routes that served the central area found it difficult to maintain schedule times in later years and curtailments were frequent. Route 647 drivers had to negotiate three major junctions each way in quick succession: Gardiners Corner, Bishopsgate and Shoreditch; in early years, some 647s were scheduled to Liverpool Street. A warehouse fire at London Docks during the war forced trolleybuses to turn on battery power at Cable Street, about 200 yards north of the terminus.

To the frustration of the supervisory staff, most of the short workings on these routes were available from the wrong direction: Downham Road (which had a restriction of 6 to 9.20am and 6 to 8pm and emergency use), Shacklewell Lane and Stoke Newington. Inspectors at Stamford Hill, where most service adjustments were made, were not aware of late running vehicles until they had passed these points, it being curtailment points to the south that were required. Shacklewell Lane (Crossway) was the most infrequently used of these turns; not only in later years did it require a double trolley swing, but the presence of parked vehicles on the loop made it a difficult manouevre. It was only used when absolutely necessary, with such use seeing much sparking from the green oxidised traction wires. It was wired clockwise but was the only location on the system that was detailed as being available from both directions when the layout dictated otherwise. To overcome the lack of curtailment points, an agreement was made with the staff to operate an unclassified curtailment point. By using the wiring from Dalston Junction along Balls Pond Road, the Kingsland Road services were able to gain access to the wiring in Dove Road, the short working at Mildmay Park. The wiring along Balls Pond Road, whose services were withdrawn in April 1959, was retained for more than two years to accommodate the Kingsland Road services. Another unofficial use concerned routes 543/643 which upon curtailment could be turned at Tottenham, Snells Park which was off line of route. Due to congestion, the short working facility at Shoreditch, at the junction of Old Street with Great Eastern Street, was altered in January 1959; Curtain Road was used, thus shortening the time required to make this frequently used turn. This was the last new construction work that was undertaken on the trolleybus system and this rather obscure road became the last resting place in London for some of the Q1s. They were parked here for onward towing to Poplar garage before shipment to Spain.

There was always plenty of trolleybus activity at Stamford Hill, which was one of a number of places on the system where vehicles could turn from north, south, east and west. It was the main changeover point for staff on the Kingsland Road services and it was not unusual to see numbers of vehicles in the vicinity, poles under hooks, waiting for staff who had been delayed by late meal reliefs to take them over. It was common practice that when vehicles were delayed by crews' late reliefs, that they were parked out of the way – this entailed parking them in depots, side streets or in places along main roads where they would not cause an obstruction. The K classes were the main types to be seen on these routes apart from a few Hs and Ps from Edmonton depot.

1337 has plenty of customers at the main northbound stop at Stamford Hill. In the background a 647 turns. Tony Belton

Below 1130 on route 647 turns outside the 'Blue Anchor' pub at London Docks. An MoT special instruction stated that the turning movement here was to be carried out under the supervision of an official or the conductor — this never seemed to happen though! Peter Moore

Bottom 1137 waits at the traffic lights at Dalston Junction, a window cleaner goes about his daily business and a number of items of street furniture of the day can be seen on the right of the picture. 1137 is running late and has been curtailed at Clerkenwell Green. Tony Belton

The Kingsland Road services ran to frequent headways and were always well patronised for they passed through the heavily populated areas of Stoke Newington, Dalston and Shoreditch serving shops, markets, cinemas, Underground and British Rail stations and crossed many bus and other trolleybus services. Routes 543/625/643 carried good station feeder traffic to the Piccadilly Line at Wood Green from the Lordship Lane area; the Seven Sisters Corner trolleybus junction was encountered en route with the service on the section from there to Bruce Grove being one of the most frequent on the system. Even when passenger demand declined in the 1950s, there was still an intensive trolleybus service along the Kingsland Road.

Throughout the system, vehicles changed from one route to the other while in the depots; the earliest was a night 543 arriving at Stamford Hill depot at 5.02am on a Sunday morning and departing as a 649 at 5.12am. In practice the vehicle was left in Egerton Road. Changing from one route to another occurred with 543 changing to 643 at Wood Green and vice versa. A 543 and 643 operated from Wood Green to London Docks although there was a two-minute wait at Stamford Hill where the blinds were changed to 647; Stamford Hill was to be shown as far as this point. At Stamford Hill Circle a 643 night bus became a 643 day bus and 649s became 647s. 649s became 647 and 649A at Egerton Road in the same fashion as described above; such workings led to battery manoeuvres at Stamford Hill Broadway. Vehicles should have turned within the depot confines, but due to there being a lack of space to turn in the early hours of Sunday morning, the vehicles were left with poles down in Egerton Road before taking up service via Clapton Common.

Route 649A last operated on Sunday 16th July 1961 with routes 543, 643, 647 and 649 all operating for the last time on Tuesday 18th July 1961; they formed conversion stage eleven.

Top **1131** approaches Clerkenwell Junction and as a 643 will work around the Holborn Loop in a clockwise manner. As a safety precaution, 1131's conductor waits until all platform movements are finished before pulling the semi-automatic frog handle; if he had pulled it while these movements were still occurring, the changed signal light may have misled the driver into thinking that the platform was clear and he may have moved forward. Robert Jowitt

Centre **1125** and **1314** head up Egerton Road, the wiring link to Stamford Hill depot. Both are working the Sunday 649A and are going to the two termini of the route. Denis Battams

Left **1151** is seen on one of the few Stamford Hill Sunday 649 journeys; it has just turned at Liverpool Street Station and the two separate turning circles that were eventually constructed here can be seen. That nearest the camera seemed only to be used for trolleybus photographers' whims. The turning circle was reputed to be the sharpest at which a trolleybus could turn. There was also a siding wire at the trolleybus stand. Peter Moore

Left **Opposite the TROLLEY BUS CAFE at the top of Tramway Avenue, 1347 and 1231 wait for crews to take them over. Drivers are wearing two licence badges so the photo can be dated between April and July 1961. The heavy overhead crossings show up almost obtrusively in this view.**
R.F. Mack courtesy John Fozard

Below **The TROLLEY BUS CAFE was naturally frequented by trolleybus crews. If the signwriter had consulted a dictionary he would have spelt 'TROLLEYBUS' correctly.**
John Gillham

THE HERTFORD ROAD ROUTES

There were a number of routes or groups of routes that could best be considered as main arteries of the London trolleybus network and the routes that operated on the Hertford Road certainly fell into this category. The most northerly point on the trolleybus system was reached on Sunday 16th October 1938 when trolleybuses first ran to Waltham Cross, routes 649, 659 and 679 being introduced on a daily basis. It had first been planned that this conversion would take place on 7th March 1938. Route 659 operated from Waltham Cross to Holborn Circus with Edmonton depot being given the whole allocation. Route 679 operated from Ponders End to Smithfield on Mondays to Saturdays with Waltham Cross being the northern terminus on Sundays. Initially Holloway depot operated the 679 but from 14th December 1938 a small Monday to Saturday allocation was given to Edmonton depot; the route was extended to Waltham Cross during Monday to Friday peak hours and all day Saturday at this time. Commencing on Sunday 5th February 1939, Edmonton depot took over the whole 679 allocation, which worked to Waltham Cross daily from the same time.

Route 649 from Edmonton depot was introduced at the same time, running from Ponders End to Stamford Hill. On 5th February 1939 it was extended daily to Liverpool Street Station with Stamford Hill depot gaining a small allocation; on Sundays from 14th May 1939 it was extended to Waltham Cross as on Easter Monday 1939. By July 1942 two late evening journeys were working to Waltham Cross on Mondays to Saturdays. Stamford Hill depot always played a minor role in operating route 649, being confined to a few Monday to Friday morning peak hour journeys from Stamford Hill to Liverpool Street and some very early Sunday morning runs to Waltham Cross. On many Bank Holidays until 1958 though, they had a large allocation to the route which had by now gained an extension at both ends, albeit in a piecemeal fashion. From Wednesday 5th May 1948 the 649 was extended to Waltham Cross on Mondays to Saturdays and meant that routes 649, 659 and 679 were now operating to Waltham Cross daily. On Sunday 6th November 1938, route 627 was introduced daily from Edmonton depot and worked between Edmonton Town Hall and Tottenham Court Road. It had been anticipated that this conversion would occur on 4th December 1938. From Sunday 5th February 1939, Holloway depot replaced Edmonton depot on Sundays and from the next day the Monday to Saturday work was operated by Edmonton, Holloway and Wood Green depots. In May 1940 a few Monday to Friday peak hour journeys were extended to Ponders End and from November 1940 some Saturday morning journeys were operating here also, with afternoon runs being added from May 1948. The 627 was extended yet again on Wednesday 19th May 1954 when it reached Waltham Cross on weekdays. Between November 1940 and May 1948, Edmonton depot did not contribute 627s on Saturdays. From October 1943 Sunday work was confined to early morning journeys on the Tottenham Court Road to Edmonton Town Hall section. However, route 627 worked Bank Holidays from at least Whitsun 1944 but only on the Ponders End to Tottenham Court Road section; these were only worked by Edmonton depot. In the interests of rationalisation, the parallel bus route 69 was withdrawn between Wormley and Tottenham in 1938/39.

From Monday 7th November 1938, a Monday to Saturday (also Good Friday) 627 very early morning service was introduced between Archway Station and Smithfield. Worked by Holloway depot, they were for Smithfield Market staff. They were more appropriately transferred officially to the 679 from 22nd October 1952 although it was normal practice to display 627. Some odd journeys emanated from this bifurcation and resulted in a Highgate depot 679 journey from Smithfield to Ponders End and 627 journeys from Archway Station to Edmonton Town Hall/Waltham Cross. Within the last two years of operation, consideration was given to

1149 turns into Seven Sisters Road at 'Nags Head'. It was the last standard trolleybus to be overhauled but due to depot allocation vagaries, was not one of the last survivors. Tony Belton

1695 turns at Smithfield; this was the last trolleybus to leave Edmonton depot two days after the depot's final conversion. Lyndon Rowe

Allocated to Holloway depot was X5 class 1379. Seen outside the ivy clad Manor House offices, it is without front adverts.
F.G. Reynolds

1364 has become so delayed that it has had to be curtailed at an off-route short working point, Stamford Hill. The running number has incorrectly been placed in the depot code position.
Fred Ivey

working these journeys from Edmonton depot. This involved turning the vehicles at Finsbury Park Station as opposed to Archway, which would have meant a part battery manoeuvre. Amazingly, the first journey from Edmonton depot would only have had to leave at 3.26am, a mere 16 minutes difference from the first departure from Holloway depot which had to travel to Salisbury Road (Archway terminus) initially. When extra running time was given due to the blackout, route 679 had ten minutes extra (74 minutes/64 minutes) allowed between Smithfield and Waltham Cross, this being the highest such increase on the system.

At Smithfield, originally, a curved line of studs was set in the roadway as a guide to trolleybus drivers and a watch was to be kept on the parking of cars and vans at this point to keep the trolleybus path clear. At the MoT inspection it was stated that drivers were to exercise caution when approaching the playground exits of the National School and St James' Church School at Ponders End, where playgrounds opened directly onto the route. The inspecting officer instituted a 10mph speed limit when passing below the railway bridge at South Tottenham Station. There were many such examples, but London Transport's rulebook stipulated that 5mph was not to be exceeded under bridges.

Wood Green depot, for an unspecified reason, were not allowed to work further north than Edmonton Town Hall despite Waltham Cross being included on the blinds, but such workings did occur to cover passenger requirements. Operation from Wood Green depot was confined to Mondays to Saturdays. Their depot workings were of interest, for on leaving the depot some worked via route 629 to Tottenham Court Road while others travelled via Lordship Lane to Bruce Grove to pick up the line of route which was via Tottenham Hale to approach Edmonton Town Hall. Running into depot was usually from Edmonton Town Hall via Tottenham Hale and Lordship Lane, but there were occasions when they ran direct to depot via Turnpike Lane. An interesting provision on Wood Green blinds was a BRUCE CASTLE display. Its use was thus: if a 627 from the Tottenham Court Road direction was running late it could be sent to Wood Green depot direct from Bruce Grove without going to Edmonton Town Hall and Tottenham Hale. To avoid confusion to intending passengers on the Tottenham Court Road to Manor House section who may have assumed that it was going via Turnpike Lane, this display was used. Such workings were uncommon, but in the rainy evening peak hour of route 627's last day, a knowledgeable inspector sent vehicle 1258 back to Wood Green depot this way, using the 'Bruce Castle' display for the last time. In earlier years, 627s operating from Finsbury Park to Redvers Road, Wood Green showed this; they then operated to Tottenham Hale as 625s before returning to Wood Green depot and are prime examples of the flexibility of trolleybus operation.

Trolleybus 1167 and RT1132 pass at the Queen Eleanor statue at Waltham Cross. K types predominated on these routes; the only others to be seen this far north, were from the many classes of vehicle that Highgate depot put out on route 627. Ron Lunn

Waltham Cross was used as a wartime dispersal point with a few vehicles being parked overnight; a lay-by was specially constructed for terminating trolleybuses here. During the war, the RSA gunpowder factory at Powder Mill Lane, Waltham Cross had a shift that finished at midnight and munition trolleybuses were laid on for this, despite the normally early finish to services generally. A Sunday to Friday 679 'slept overnight' at Enfield bus garage, arriving at 1.42am and departing at 3.37am as a 649. Its stabling was in fact a lengthy stand time, although in practice the crew returned the trolleybus to Edmonton depot for their break where they used the sofa in the ladies' rest room. This working had started during the war and was the only instance of this type of operation on the trolleybus system. The Sunday 659 allocation was increased from 17 to 42 between 1940 and 1953 although it suffered a heavy retrenchment in 1955 when it was cut in one sweep to 30. In 1955 all routes except 603, 639, 659 and 679 suffered allocation cuts. The 679 was the only route to gain an increase when the Sunday and Monday to Friday allocation was boosted (the Saturday allocation stayed the same).

Of all the groups of routes detailed in this book, the Hertford Road services were the most intensive, which was due in no small measure to the lack of parallel motorbus routes. There were occasions in post-war years when 150 vehicles were needed in the Monday to Friday evening peak hours, with 152 being required on Saturdays and 95 on Sundays. As late as October 1955, 150 vehicles were required on Saturdays. On Christmas Day 1947, 148 crew duties were operated from Edmonton depot; they worked 288 duties on Saturdays in 1949. On top of these Saturday duties were the many extras that were laid on when Tottenham Hotspur FC were playing at home.

987 passing through Finsbury Park is only going to Spurs' Ground. In this instance, the loop is being used to correct late running rather than a 'Spurs Special'. In the background, railway signal semaphore arms are in abundance. Fred Ivey

These four trunk routes to central London were busy and many journeys were scheduled to turn back at Ponders End to cater for the build-up of service density along the Hertford Road between here and Edmonton. At Edmonton Town Hall many other vehicles turned back, thus giving a more frequent service from here. They were required to give another build up to the through service from Waltham Cross and Ponders End as they passed southwards through Bruce Grove and Tottenham to cater for a further increase in the density of population on the southern section. The 'City' termini all had workings from Waltham Cross and although this last section of the route was less busy, the combined routes gave a high-frequency service over the common section from Waltham Cross to Tottenham. Edmonton and Tottenham were busy shopping areas with large numbers of passengers as a result. More passengers came from the various British Rail and Underground stations that were passed on the way. At the height of the morning peak for the Monday to Friday November 1947 schedule, 91 trolleybuses on the Hertford Road services passed Seven Sisters Corner on

the journey south with 71 vehicles going north at the height of the evening peak hour, such were passenger requirements for these routes. Even in 1961 there were 68 vehicles passing south and 74 vehicles passing north at the height of the peak hour. Saturdays were always busy and even until 1959, Sunday trolleybuses were well laden after 10am. Major junctions were passed at Seven Sisters Corner, Manor House and 'Nags Head' where the 627, 659 and 679 went their different ways.

The Tottenham Hale wiring was retained after trolleybus conversion stage six to enable trolleybuses from Hertford Road to turn; Chesnut Road was traversed regularly by scheduled trolleybuses but the wiring in Broad Lane was left up for emergencies. Shortly before conversion stage ten, a fire in Tottenham High Road brought this wiring into use; it was not 'frogged-in' by now and although northbound vehicles were having their trolleys swung to the appropriate wire, it had been overlooked that the southbound wire needed a trolley swing procedure to take place too. Vehicle after vehicle came to grief with a dewirement. This diversion via Broad Lane, Tottenham Hale and Chesnut Road was also used on Sunday 7th May 1961 when the victorious FA Cup-winning Spurs team toured the Tottenham area in an open-top bus, culminating in a celebration at Tottenham Town Hall. This was over a week after trolleybus conversion stage ten, so in theory the power should have been cut off. Either an oversight had occurred or the power was switched back. A further instalment of the Tottenham Hale saga was that the early morning Monday to Friday 649 working from here at 4.36am was cut out at stage ten but not the Saturday one. Either a trolleybus on this working or a vehicle curtailed by an

inspector who was unaware that Tottenham Hale had been deleted from the system after stage ten, came to grief just beyond the feeder pillar in Chesnut Road and was stranded. It had to be towed to Tottenham Hale and back to regain live wires. Another diversion in January 1959 involved routes 623, 627, 659 and 679 when a new railway bridge was being rolled in at Seven Sisters Road. The section from Amhurst Junction to Seven Sisters Corner not being available, the routes were diverted via Stamford Hill. Journeys northbound had an easy path as they used the 653 short working facility and inspectors were positioned with bamboo poles to swing trolley booms. Journeys southbound however, had to travel via the outside of Stamford Hill depot and Clapton Common to gain the 653 wires which led to their own tracks. This diversion also occurred during the war when southbound vehicles turned via Stamford Hill Broadway and then used batteries into Amhurst Park.

Changing of vehicles, one route to the other occurred as;

649 to 659 at Waltham Cross
649 to 679 at Waltham Cross
659 to 649 at Waltham Cross
679 to 649 at Waltham Cross
659 to 679 at Waltham Cross
679 to 659 at Waltham Cross
679 to 649 at Ponders End
679 to 659 at Holloway depot
679 to 627 at 'Nags Head'

There were some 659/679 journeys to and from Stamford Hill and a 679 worked from Smithfield to Holloway depot where it became a 659 to Kings Cross (see above); the display NAGS HEAD HOLLOWAY was used as 'Holloway depot' was not on Edmonton's blinds. The

most complex derivative schedule was the 627 Monday to Friday one for May 1954: at Wood Green six 625s and two 641s worked onto the route while one 627 worked onto 629: at Highgate two 679s (one at 'Nags Head') and four 653s worked onto the route (at Tottenham Court Road) while four 627s worked onto 653 and four worked onto 517/617: at Edmonton seven worked onto 679 and two worked onto 659; the changeovers occurred in the depot apart from those noted above. For the war effort, some Edmonton 649s foreign stabled in Stamford Hill depot in off-peak hours. Passengers were not allowed to travel down Tramway Avenue to and from Edmonton depot.

Routes 627, 659 and 679 operated for the last time on Tuesday 25th April 1961 when they were withdrawn in stage ten of the conversion programme. Route 649 was retained for a further twelve weeks until stage eleven of the conversion programme and last operated on Tuesday 18th July 1961.

Facing Page Upper **1678 is about to negotiate two overhead crossovers in quick succession at 'Angel' Islington, so the driver is about to take his left foot off the power pedal. The front blinds have become mixed and the modern paper route blind seems rather incongruous with the old style linen one. The 679 always ran less frequently than its partners on the Hertford Road routes.** Michael Dryhurst

Facing Page Lower **The last K3, 1696, leaves Enfield bus garage for a journey to Kings Cross. This was the only instance on the system where a motorbus garage was used by trolleybuses; two other trolleybuses, one on each of the lay-by wires, wait for departure time.** Lyndon Rowe

Below **1380 was the only trolleybus to carry an FXF registration and is seen here just about to pass the crossover leading out of Warlters Road, the short working point for 'Nags Head' Holloway.** Michael Dryhurst

THE HACKNEY ROUTES

Trolleybus routes 555 and 581 first operated on Sunday 11th June 1939. The 555 worked from Leyton depot and ran between Bloomsbury and Leyton, Downsell Road via Cambridge Heath on Mondays to Saturdays; it restored the link to Downsell Road that had disappeared in June 1937 when much of the local tram network was withdrawn. On Sundays it worked between Bloomsbury and Leyton Green with Leyton being known as the 'Country' terminal on early schedules. Hackney depot worked on the route for a short time from 21st June but was given regular daily work from 10th December 1939. It was necessary to make new arrangements for trolleybuses at Bloomsbury terminus, the stand being situated in Red Lion Square. Vehicles were not allowed to stand in the square, but they did so on the offside of Red Lion Square. Upon the diversion of tram route 31 to Islington on 10th December 1939, the 555 was increased by almost 50% daily; from 11th December 1939, journeys to Downsell Road became peak hours only with this service being shortened to Leyton Green in May 1940. The Downsell Road section was restored in June 1949 when it returned in Monday to Friday peak hours; in May 1950 it was restored there all day on Saturdays, although from October 1956 it was only during shop-ping hours. The 555 had three curtailment points in the same direction within a space of half a mile at Shoreditch: Columbia Road, Pitfield Street and Tabernacle Square.

On Sunday 12th May 1940, the 555 was extended on Sunday middays to Woodford, 'Napier Arms'; it had previously operated here on 6th and 7th July 1939 and on Easter Monday 1940. Woodford journeys were withdrawn in November 1948 but were restored on Sunday afternoons on 11th October 1953 (there was also one early morning journey); this compensated for a 40% reduction on the 581. Thirteen journeys were provided at 20-minute intervals but they were gradually whittled down until in 1959 there were just six journeys at 30-minute intervals, spread over two hours. On Christmas Days from 1939 and Bank Holidays from 1954, both 555 and 581 worked to Woodford. Leyton's contribution since their withdrawal from the main 555 allocation in April 1946 were a few very early daily journeys which continued until withdrawal. Even these operated under the guise of 581.

Route 581 worked daily from Woodford, 'Napier Arms' to Bloomsbury via Essex Road; part of the Monday to Saturday service always terminated at Leyton Green. It was operated by Walthamstow and Hackney depots on Mondays to Saturdays and by Hackney only on Sundays; journeys to Walthamstow depot were in service. From 8th May 1940, Leyton depot replaced the Walthamstow allocation although Leyton had operated on the 581 in a minor capacity in July/August 1939. From 12th May 1940 the 581 was withdrawn on Sundays, being restored each summer from 1942 to 1946, with the route operating on Sundays all year round thereafter. The 581 Sunday allocation was cut back from 17 to 7 between 1952 and 1959, a reduction of 60%.

Above **1145 passes beneath the overhead outside Lea Bridge depot. Two N1s on route 661 are terminating at the depot; the 661 service was the last to regularly use the depot wiring here.** Lyndon Rowe

Facing Page **1123A passes through Hackney on its way to Shoreditch Church. Many of the Weymann rebodied vehicles were withdrawn before the conversion period due to their poor body condition. However, 1123A survived until conversion stage two. At Hackney, well turned out vehicles from Clapton and Lea Bridge depots rubbed shoulders with grubby trolleybuses placed on route 653 by Highgate depot.** Fred Ivey

It was originally anticipated that route 555 would operate as service 671 and work from Hackney and Holloway depots – hence the inclusion of 671 on the Holloway route blinds. Route 581 was originally planned to have worked as service 681. (Further details on route numbering policy are on page 162).

Route 677 from Hackney depot first worked on Sunday 10th September 1939 and ran from Smithfield to West India Docks daily. It operated in a horseshoe formation,

was always busy and carried a good two-way traffic across Hackney and Dalston. Islington was another main area to be served by the route. Tram 77 had run to Aldersgate but London Transport could not find a suitable turning circle there (powers were obtained to operate to Fann Street, the Aldersgate tram terminus). Discussions were held with the MoT about the possibility of a roundabout at the junction of Goswell Road and Clerkenwell Road but nothing came of the matter and the

new trolleybus service was diverted to Smithfield. On Sundays and Bank Holidays, only part of the service ran through to Smithfield due to the closure of the market and much of the service ran as far as Mildmay Park only. An interesting arrangement was in force at Hackney bus garage where the electric supply was from a feed from the trolleybus overhead. The arched railway bridge in Burdett Road on route 677 required two sets of illuminated lamps at night for the guidance of drivers.

It was noted at the onset of war, that although economies would have accrued by closing Leyton depot, it was worth sacrificing these as Hackney depot was in a vulnerable area and it was considered undesirable to have more vehicles than was necessary under one roof. Not all of the combined requirements of routes 555/581/677 could have been housed at Hackney, so part of the 677 would have worked from the always under-utilised Poplar depot - hence the inclusion of 677 on Poplar blinds. From October 1950, Leyton submitted the smallest number of vehicles for service each day.

From its introduction, there were always very early journeys on route 555 with the earliest being a weekday 3.09am departure (3.06am during the war) from Leyton depot to Bloomsbury, going first to Leyton Green. This journey replaced the 3.20am 55 tram from Bloomsbury to Kenninghall Road. It came to London Transport's notice that a 'pirate' lorry fitted with seats was operating 'early 555 journeys' on Sunday mornings. Steps were taken to eradicate this and in November 1948 a journey to Bloomsbury left the depot at 3.12am, this being the earliest Sunday departure on the system. These early journeys catered for press workers with the first 555 on Sundays having time card instructions that read: 3.54am from Bloomsbury to be maintained at 4am at Farringdon Road for press workers. This particular journey had to connect with the 699 staff bus due at 'Bakers Arms' at 4.32am to Chingford. Throughout the system, many specific instructions were made on schedules and notes were made on time cards for connections to be made with train, tube, bus, tram and other trolleybus services and were most prolific on these routes. Routes 555 and 677 had instances of specific vehicles having to make three timed connections. This was surpassed by a 677 that had to make five time card connections, although some were on staff journeys; the schedule form with the highest number of

Top **A surprise allocation to Lea Bridge depot, between late 1955 and late 1957, was P1 class 1720 which is seen here turning into Graham Road, Hackney. It also had a spell at Clapton depot in June 1956.** Ron Lunn

Above **The main terminus for route 555 was outside Leyton bus garage and 1245 awaits its next trip to Bloomsbury; vehicles often parked on the other side of this road. Apart from Walthamstow's early allocation on the 581, the K classes were generally the only ones to be seen on this set of routes.** Don Thompson

Below **1305 leaves Clapton depot on a short working to Clerkenwell Green. The bus spotter is collecting trolleybus numbers and is no doubt aware that Clapton's days as a trolleybus depot are numbered, for the depot reconstructor's nameplate is exhibited on the depot wall.** Denis Battams

connections to be made to other vehicles was on route 677 where eight were required. Throughout its life the first Monday to Saturday 677 from Hackney depot to Smithfield was at about 3.30am for Smithfield Market workers. It was the main route to operate to Smithfield, but despite the large number of vehicles turning, no passing loop was provided. The 567s often arrived out of turn and much boom lowering had to take place on routes 677/679.

The only interchanges were 555 to 581 at Leyton Green and Woodford. For most of its life, one weekday 555 worked from Bloomsbury to Woodford. In spring 1953, due to tram track removal in Rosebery Avenue, westbound 581s were diverted via Farringdon Road and Clerkenwell Road and a special curve was inserted in the overhead at Clerkenwell Junction; battery was used at Theobalds Road. During a schedules dispute, 40 lorries driven by Royal Army Corps personnel worked routes 555, 581 and 677 on 21st and 22nd April 1944.

This set of routes passed major overhead junctions at Leyton, 'Bakers Arms', 'Angel' Islington, Dalston Junction, Mildmay Park and the junction at Clerkenwell Road/ St John Street. Routes 555 and 581 had motorbus and other trolleybus routes paralleling them and bus route 38A did the same for most of the way. Route 581 carried an extremely heavy peak traffic but routes 38/38A had the advantage in reaching the central area traffic objectives, so that the 581 carried very little normal hour traffic. There were few things of note about these two routes and they went into gradual decline. A more intensive service was operated nearer to the London terminal and the 555 always had short workings from Bloomsbury to Hackney Station/Kenninghall Road in Monday to Friday peak hours with a number of vehicles turning at these times at Clerkenwell Green. From November 1948, the 581 on Mondays to Fridays, apart from evenings, had a more extensive service from Bloomsbury to Kenninghall Road. Special provision was made on the 581 for a small number of evening peak journeys to turn at Rosebery Avenue, Green Terrace to cater for Water Board staff who worked nearby. Both routes had sparse Sunday services in their later lives and operated at 15-minute headways for much of the day. Despite travelling through well-populated areas, both routes gave links for only a small percentage of passengers and produced poor receipts; the 581 operated at a heavy loss and it was decided to advance the route in the conversion programme.

As these three routes were planned to be converted simultaneously, routes 555 and 677 met an earlier-than-planned demise. Before this happened, route 555 had its evening service withdrawn in June 1958 on Mondays to Saturdays, with all the vehicles being in the depot by 8pm. They ran for the last time on Tuesday 14th April 1959 in stage two of the conversion programme.

ROUTE 557

When London Transport introduced trolley-buses to the Chingford area on Sunday 6th June 1937, it was necessary to curtail tram route 57 (Chingford Mount to Liverpool Street Station) at 'Bakers Arms' Leyton; London Transport did not want to continue running trams on a single route to Chingford for a further two years, nor were they yet ready for trolleybuses to penetrate the fringe areas of central London. The splitting of the tram route caused inconvenience to passengers, as many people used the direct service; it was not until Sunday 11th June 1939 that the through service was restored with the introduction of trolleybus route 557 operating daily between Chingford Mount and Liverpool Street Station. It was originally planned to operate this service with the 673 route number. The 687 was simultaneously withdrawn between Chingford Mount and Leyton Depot. Walthamstow depot provided the whole allocation; the only time that another depot assisted was between November 1940 and April 1943 when Leyton depot had a small Monday to Friday daytime off-peak al-

location on the section from Chingford Mount to Leyton Green. A requirement at Liverpool Street meant that an inspector was on duty at all times and movements were controlled by a policeman; a white semi-circle was painted in the roadway here initially to assist drivers. There were ultimately two sets of loops that could be used; one gave an alternative turn in Bishopsgate and a siding existed at the actual terminal point.

The 557 provided some important and useful links as it passed through the busy areas of Walthamstow, Leyton and Hackney on its southward run to its City terminal. It was a very straightforward route and only a few short workings ever existed; a single Monday to Friday morning peak hour journey ran from Liverpool Street to King Edwards Road, Hackney with some going to Kenninghall Road. On Saturday evenings a few journeys operated from Chingford Mount to Leyton Green. The 557 had the only scheduled working to Hoe Street, Grove Road for a short time in the early post-war period, when a single Monday to Friday evening peak journey ter-

minated there. It is believed that the wiring was specially erected in order that there would be a short working facility to the north of 'Bakers Arms' in the event of the junction sustaining war damage. It was constructed early in 1941 and completed a north, south, east, west turning configuration near the 'Bakers Arms'. Later, the wiring was tied off from the main running wires but was still energised and was used occasionally by service trolleybuses. It always received the attention of the overhead line staff. Hoe Street, Uxbridge Station and Fulham Palace Road, Edgarley Terrace (pre-1951) were the only wired turns that did not appear on destination blinds.

Above **During the course of a day, there were many classes of trolleybus to be found on route 557 as Walthamstow depot did not discriminate classes to routes. Allocated to the depot from October 1958 to January 1959 was the first of the N1 class, AEC 1555 which had been transferred in from Ilford depot. It is seen here approaching Bell Junction, Walthamstow.** Alan Cross

There was little passenger traffic to be picked up by each trolleybus between Cambridge Heath and Shoreditch on routes 555 and 557 as shown by D2 class Leyland 483 in Hackney Road. If the plans for south London trolleybuses had come to fruition this factor would have been accentuated, as proposed route 631 would also have operated along this road. Fred Ivey

All services along the Lea Bridge Road provided for the build up of passenger requirements for transport towards central London. The 557 with the other trolleybus services along the Lea Bridge Road passed near the Clapton greyhound racecourse, but the normal service catered for this. However, extra trolleybuses were laid on for dog racing at Walthamstow Stadium with Hackney and Leyton depots providing these extras, which parked in Walthamstow depot during the event; 557 details were available on their blinds with the vehicles mainly making journeys to Hackney and Leyton. An instance is related of a minor diversion on the 557 at 'Bakers Arms'; there was a problem with the overhead at the left turn towards Chingford

and vehicles had to make a right turn and travel down to Leyton Green to pick up wiring which would bring them back to line of route. Vehicles were foreign stabled at Hackney depot in off-peaks as part of the war effort and, because of bomb damage, motorbuses had to be used on the route on an occasion during the war.

Liverpool Street Station, an important main line terminal, was the only British Railways station where London trolleybuses turned outside. Moorgate and Liverpool Street were the most prestigious London termini and the 557 always ran frequently; in the immediate post-war period there was a three-minute service on Saturdays and a four-minute service on Sundays,

while on Mondays to Fridays a three-minute peak hour service and a five-minute off-peak hour service operated. The route was busy on Bank Holidays and a three-minute service ran in the afternoon and evening. Route 557 shared its wires with other trolleybus services throughout; the 697 and 699 to 'Bakers Arms', the 555 and 581 to Hackney and the 555 to Shoreditch, where it linked up with the 649 (and 649A on Sundays) for the final leg to Liverpool Street. These services detracted from the 557's potential earning capacity but despite this it did not undergo any drastic pruning such as occurred to other services operating in similar circumstances. It was withdrawn on Tuesday 2nd February 1960 in stage five of the conversion programme.

An unadvertised service that 'locals' got to know about operated between Leyton, Downsell Road and Chingford Mount to accommodate punters for Walthamstow greyhound racing. The crew are working this duty as a piece of overtime. 1335 heads north in Leyton High Road; the via points on the destination blind are misleading but perforce, sufficed. Most of the extras ran into Walthamstow depot whilst events were occurring. Some staff, however, would park their vehicles at the 'Crooked Billet' poles down, and would spend their break in the Dog Stadium. David Packer

THE FOREST ROAD ROUTES

Trolleybuses were introduced to Forest Road on Sunday 18th October 1936 when route 623 commenced operating daily between Woodford, 'Napier Arms' and Manor House Station. This early tram to trolleybus conversion was an event of double significance. It was the first trolleybus route to use roads previously unserved by trams where London Transport was the instigating body (it was also the third instance of trolleybuses operating over roads previously unserved by trams) and was the first incursion of trolleybuses into the heart of north London; route 623 was to remain a sole intruder into heavily occupied tramway territory until May 1938. Tram route 23 had run from 'Napier Arms' to the 'Ferry Boat Inn' so the 623 gave vastly improved facilities. The section from the 'Ferry Boat Inn' to Seven Sisters Corner was new to electric street traction. At Woodford, a turning circle for trolleybuses only was specially constructed on ground handed over to London Transport by the Conservators of Epping Forest. At Manor House, it was agreed with the Ministry of Transport that for an experimental period of four months, trolleybuses should turn in the wide main road. Any misgivings about its suitability were swiftly allayed, as this means of turning remained until its last day.

Initially in Monday to Friday peak hours and all day on Saturdays, a six-minute service operated on the section from Woodford to Tottenham Hale with a six-minute service to Manor House. Of historical significance is the fact that the section from the 'Ferry Boat Inn' to Wood Green tramway depot was included in the Metropolitan Electric Tramways (Railless Traction) Act of 1913 authorising the use of trolleybuses.

Route 625 started on Sunday 8th May 1938, running from Woodford, 'Napier Arms' to Wood Green daily, being extended on Mondays to Saturdays to Winchmore Hill from Wednesday 12th October 1938. Route 625, like its companion 623, gave improved facilities. The 625 extension to Winchmore Hill came about because of the number of vehicles that would have had to be accommodated at the Redvers Road (Wood Green) terminus upon the 643 conversion, as only four vehicles were allowed to stand here. For the same reason some 641s were run only as far as Newington Green/Turnpike Lane Station. London Transport was concerned about the number of complaints that would arise and decided to reduce the expected number by making these revisions. The 625 also served Chesnut Road, previously unused by trams,

which was the seventh and final such instance on the system. Walthamstow depot participated in all five London Transport instigated trolleybus extensions over roads previously unserved by trams – the other three being on the 685 at Higham Hill, Church Road Leyton and Silvertown Way. The 625 swallowed up the 623 'shorts' which were extended from Tottenham Hale. Lordship Lane now became devoid of trams. The Saturday evening service only ran to Wood Green and from December 1939 this became the terminus on Monday to Friday evenings. In November 1940 the Winchmore Hill extension became Monday to Saturday peak hours only, for with the re-location of the terminus of bus route 233 into Wood Green depot, more space became available for the 625 in Redvers Road. In April 1950, Saturday Winchmore Hill journeys were withdrawn altogether. Route 625 was curtailed at Walthamstow, Beacontree Avenue in Monday to Saturday peaks from October 1938 with the Monday to Friday evening service following suit in May 1940; from May 1950 it was curtailed here all day on Saturdays. The Saturday all day service returned to Woodford from 15th September 1951, due to pressure from the staff, who stated that 'makeshift' toilet arrange-

For much of 1938, trolleybus 435 was allocated to Walthamstow depot; from here it was transferred to Bexleyheath where it was destroyed by bomb damage in June 1944. It is seen here at 'Bell Junction' turning into Forest Road and is using the unusual centre wire arrangement, whereby trolleybuses from either direction used the same traction wires in a few instances, principally depot workings. This practice economised on overhead equipment but due to sparks caused by pole changing during the war the practice ceased. 435 is working an EXTRA on Forest Road. Charles Klapper

Left 1077 passes through Epping Forest on the final leg of its journey to Woodford. All classes at Walthamstow depot were used on all of their routes, so this sylvan scene through which 1077 is passing is a far cry from the dockland areas in which it might be working the following day. 1077 survived to run on the last day of trolleybuses in London. Fred Ivey

Below The cat's-cradle of overhead wires at Walthamstow 'Bell Junction' will not see trolleybuses for many more days as the 'Buses for Trolleybuses' notices are in place. 1098, carrying Charlton blinds in its front boxes, negotiates the junction. Denis Battams

ments at Beacontree Avenue were no longer acceptable (it was only three minutes running time from Woodford). Woodford was always reached on Sundays and Bank Holidays. Passenger traffic beyond Beacontree Avenue was light, so route 623 generally sufficed on the Woodford section. From November 1947 a number of 623 Monday to Friday evening peak journeys turned here with some morning peak journeys following in September 1951. A few journeys however did operate on the 625 in both directions, Woodford to Winchmore Hill. There were regular meetings between staff and management about routes 623/625 and a regularly discussed topic was running time. The staff described the routes as a 'race track' and claimed that the running time did not allow conductors enough time to collect all the fares.

London Transport obtained powers to operate to Woodford Green but they were not exercised due to objections by the Conservators of Epping Forest and Woodford Council; regret was expressed about this by Walthamstow Corporation. The terminus at 'Napier Arms' was operationally convenient but was still considered as a false terminus, as it was on the fringe of Woodford itself. London Transport also anticipated operating route 623 to Tottenham Court Road; their planning was so advanced that the destination was included on early Walthamstow blinds despite the fact that trolleybuses did not reach Tottenham Court Road until 1938. The extension was not proceeded with due to other routes running there from Manor House. One change that did take place was the terminal arrangement at Redvers Road, Wood Green, which changed from clockwise to anti-clockwise formation in 1954. This was to have been of a temporary nature due to road works and for a time it meant that Wood Green depot had to be used for vehicles from Green Lanes turning from the south.

Initially Walthamstow depot operated route 623 but from March 1939 until May 1954, Wood Green depot ran a few journeys. From the beginning, route 625 was operated by Walthamstow and Wood Green depots. Sunday work was solely by Walthamstow, although Wood Green had a few journeys from February to December 1939. Leyton depot worked a trolleybus on the 623 and 625 on Monday to Friday middays from April to October 1944. Wood Green always played a minor role in the operation of the 625 with their Saturday work finishing in 1948. From 1951 they were confined to working in Monday to Friday morning peak hours. Operation by Wood Green depot to Woodford was rare in later years and was confined to Bank Holidays. On the few occasions when vehicles ran into Walthamstow depot from Woodford (Christmas Day or when there was no relieving crew), the trolley poles would be pulled down at Bell Junction and the vehicle would run all the way to the depot under a combination of battery and gravity power before sweeping into the depot yard.

379 glides to a halt just before the Epping Forest loop. It is not brand new as the vehicle has been rebuilt to a full width cab. It appears that the finial on the traction standard across the road has been knocked off by a dewired trolley boom. Terry Cooper collection

Left **Bruce Grove is a hive of activity as 1282 passes through. A bamboo pole hangs from a traction standard for easy access, implying that drivers travelling north on the Hertford Road services are passing through the junction more quickly than is wise.** Fred Ivey

The Forest Road wires hosted more unusual journeys than any other group of routes mentioned in this book. Many of these had started in the earlier part of the war and were to remain for some years after the end of hostilities. Route 623 journeys for mentally deficient schoolchildren were run at midday from Walthamstow depot to Woodford, then running to Markhouse Road, Lea Bridge Road; they travelled via Forest Road and turned left at Standard Junction to proceed via route 685. The return journey necessitated a battery manouevre at Standard Junction on the way to the depot. An afternoon journey ran similarly but returned to the depot via 'Crooked Billet'. These journeys survived until 1951. For a number of years, two very early morning weekday journeys operated from Walthamstow depot to Lea Bridge Road via Forest Road and Standard Junction. On return they ran via 'Crooked Billet', one to Wood Green and the other to Manor House, crossing back on themselves at Standard Junction. The official timetable shows them as direct journeys from 'Crooked Billet' to Manor House/Wood Green. The Saturday journeys continued until 1959 with the Wood Green one surviving until the 685's demise.

The 625 operated journeys from Beacontree Avenue to Enfield on Christmas Days from 1939. Postal deliveries were made on Christmas Day and transport was needed for workers to Enfield sorting office. For operating expediency route 625 was extended to Enfield rather than run 629s, although on Christmas Day 1960 the 629 provided these journeys; all were worked by Wood Green depot. Other 625 Enfield journeys commenced early in the war for munitions purposes when a regular early Sunday morning service operated between Enfield and Beacontree Avenue. After the war they became known as 'fishermens journeys' as they took anglers from Enfield and Winchmore Hill to the River Lea; some only ran as far as Tottenham Hale. They continued until March 1954, after which the early Enfield journeys ran as ordinary 629s. The fare chart for route 625 gave direct fares from Walthamstow depot and Woodford to Enfield but the former was superfluous as Walthamstow depot never operated beyond Winchmore Hill. Enfield to Woodford journeys were also unknown. 625s working for most of the day on the 629/641 schedule were known as 'foreign service' and other Forest Road derivatives are found in the chapter detailing route 641.

The most difficult place to obtain a good photograph of a trolleybus at a terminus was at Woodford, for trolley arms tended to get 'lost' in the branches of the trees. 1280 with linen destination blinds in its boxes awaits departure on the specially constructed turning circle. Fred Ivey

Routes 623 and 625 were interworked so as to give a regular headway along Forest Road. Between them they operated a very frequent service along this road and were always important members of the trolleybus network. There were a number of interchange points: Bell Junction, Standard Junction, Tottenham Hale, Bruce Grove and Seven Sisters Corner, giving passengers easy transfers to other routes. Wood Green and Manor House Underground stations were also important interchanges with the 623 catering for a very heavy station feeder traffic from the Walthamstow and Tottenham areas to the Piccadilly Line at Manor House. Operating at high frequencies, these routes also served the factories along Forest Road, many of which were involved in war work, and the trolleybuses played an important part in transporting their workers. Specials ran also to the Lebus factory at Tottenham Hale. The routes brought day trippers to the terminus at Woodford which was on the edge of Epping Forest, with the trolleybuses coming into sylvan surroundings for the last leg of the route. The short working point at Beacontree Avenue was considered important enough to have an inspector on duty at times.

Operating expediencies saw vehicles changing from one route to another:
623 to 625 at Woodford
625 to 623 at Woodford
623 to 625 at Epping Forest
625 to 623 at Epping Forest
625 to 641 at Palmers Green
641 to 625 at Winchmore Hill
625 to 641 at Winchmore Hill
625 to 641 at Redvers Road
641 to 625 at Redvers Road
625 to 629 at Redvers Road
629 to 625 at Redvers Road
627 to 625 at Redvers Road
623 to 625 at Tottenham Hale
625 to 623 at Tottenham Hale
625 to 629 at Enfield (journey commenced at Epping Forest).

Both routes figured in stage six of the trolleybus to bus conversion programme and ran for the last time on Tuesday 26th April 1960. However, on Wednesday 27th April 1960, passengers in Lordship Lane were confronted with route 625 trolleybuses and the replacing motorbus route simultaneously: route 625 was to have a rather ghostly exist-

ence for another year. Wood Green depot operated some Monday to Saturday peak hour 627 journeys which returned to the depot via Tottenham Hale. The more conscientious conductors would wind up route 625 on the route and side blinds and this continued after conversion to motorbus. A notice was exhibited in Wood Green depot shortly after the 625 conversion, instructing conductors to show blank route and side blinds on these journeys. When matters are brought to the staff's notice, they sometimes have a tendency to have the opposite effect and the instructions are often disobeyed. Most vehicles showed 627, the odd vehicle would show blank but still route 625 continued to be shown. Upon route 627's conversion to motorbus on 26th April 1961, route 625 was finally buried.

Above **933 was a late addition to Walthamstow's fleet and is seen at Seven Sisters Corner. Upon abandonment of route 623 the wiring along Broad Lane, for which 933 is now heading, was retained for emergency purposes; 1133 on route 643 waits at the traffic lights. Fred Ivey**

In the latter days of the Forest Road and Lea Bridge Road trolleybuses, it was necessary to divert short sections of track around roadworks; coming out of the Forest Road diversion is 1253 which was chosen to represent a standard London Transport trolleybus in its museum fleet. Today it is on view in the London Transport Museum at Covent Garden. Fred Ivey

Due to the frequent service offered on routes 623 and 625 it was common for trolleybuses to travel together. At the 'parting of the ways' at Tottenham Hale, 1099 heads for Wood Green whilst 935 makes tracks for Manor House on the final Saturday of operation, 23rd April 1960. Ray Golds

Even as far north as Edmonton Town Hall, the 625 route number was displayed. While 1181 heads for Waltham Cross, 814 makes a journey to Wood Green depot but first must travel via Tottenham Hale. This area today has changed out of all recognition. Fred Ivey

THE BOW ROAD ROUTES

The tramcars operating on the Mile End Road/Bow Road routes were extremely busy; the replacing trolleybuses proved likewise when they commenced on Sunday 5th November 1939. Two daily routes were introduced that day; the 661 from Aldgate to Leyton Depot and the 663 from Aldgate to Ilford Broadway with both being allocated to Bow depot. Between April 1944 and May 1948, Leyton depot operated three trolleybuses in Monday to Friday peak hours on the 661. (Evidence suggests that Leyton's contribution to routes 623, 625, 661, 685 and 697 may have commenced in December 1943). At the MoT inspection, the inspecting officer noted that much heavy traffic passed over two weak bridges of the London Midland & Scottish Railway at Bow Station. It had been promised

a year previously that they would be reconstructed, but as there appeared to be no prospect of this happening under what were now wartime conditions, and as also the inspecting officer was satisfied that the passage of trolley vehicles at low speed would not cause any additional risk of failure, trolleybuses were allowed to use the bridge subject to a speed limit of 10mph; a further restriction was that not more than one trolley vehicle should be on either of the bridge roadways at one time. The turning circle at Finden Road, Green Street was brought into use at this time and the inspecting officer said that care would need to be taken here to avoid tree branches, as it would be regrettable if the trees had to be lopped extensively.

Above **1607** passes the junction of Green Street with Romford Road. Vehicles operating from Bow depot always looked smart and 1607 is no exception. Don Thompson

Above Right **1591** enters Whipps Cross roundabout; M and N classes were originally allocated to Bow depot, but it was the N class, of which 1591 was a member, that were associated with these routes throughout their lives. Only Ks from Leyton depot's short-lived allocation broke their monopoly. Norman Rayfield

Left **1602 enters Hainault Street
from Ley Street whilst on a
diversion involving routes 663
and 693; this was probably
when a fire had occurred in
Ilford High Road. Two bamboo
poles hang on a traction
standard signifying that this is a
known dewirement spot.**
Fred Ivey

On Wednesday 29th October 1941, London's last new trolleybus route was introduced. This was route 695 which operated from Bow Church to Chadwell Heath and provided an east to west trolleybus link route over Ilford Broadway, restoring the mileage of the 86 bus route which had been withdrawn from Limehouse to Chadwell Heath on 18th October 1939. It ran on Mondays to Saturdays and was operated by Bow depot, but from 10th November 1948 Ilford depot gained some Monday to Saturday work on the route; their Saturday work was lost in November 1951. This gave the SA class the opportunity to work west of Ilford and these vehicles looked very strange indeed in the areas around Stratford and Bow; the 695 operated on Bank Holidays. Eastbound facilities along the Romford Road had to be built up from Bow to deal with heavy industrial traffic in the vicinity and at Stratford Broadway and this was a main attribute of route 695.

Some paperwork implies that the 695 and short working 661s terminated in Bow depot prior to November 1947, while other paperwork describes them as turning at Bow Church. Early fare charts state that passengers were allowed to travel along Fairfield Road so the actual original terminus for the 695 is unclear; from November 1947, short working 661s and 695s turned in the depot. The 663 and 695 were busy between Stratford and Ilford along the Romford Road but beyond Ilford Broadway the 693 made life easier for the 695. The 661, 663 and 695 timings were interworked; the frequency was so good that there was a continual flow of trolleybuses. There was a battery turn at Colchester Avenue on the Romford Road which would not have been available for Ilford depot 695s which used SA class vehicles with no traction batteries.

Of the three routes the 663 was the busiest despite being paralleled by the 25 group bus routes for its entire length; the 86/A covered it for most of the way, too. The 661 and 663 travelled together from Aldgate, through Mile End and Bow, where the 695 was joined, to Stratford; here the quieter 661 worked via Leytonstone and the rural Whipps Cross to Leyton while the 663 and 695 continued to Ilford. For most of its life the 663 terminated here while the 695 joined forces with the 693 to Chadwell Heath. The number of passenger-carrying vehicles on the road from Stratford to Aldgate was huge and on the trolleybus services alone there were 67 vehicles arriving at Aldgate between 7.30 and 8.30am on the November 1947 schedule.

From November 1951, during Monday to Friday off-peaks and evenings and all day Saturdays, alternate 661s terminated at Bow depot on journeys from Leyton. This was due to bus routes 10 and 96 paralleling it from Leytonstone to Aldgate. At Stratford the 661 joined forces with the 25 and 663 thus further draining its use; however, route 661 provided an essential link between Leytonstone and Leyton via Whipps Cross. Route 661 made

Bow and Ilford depots shared the 695 allocation from 1948-1959. Trolleybus 1740 approaches Stratford Broadway whilst 1580 is in Stratford Broadway itself. The extension of the Central Line caused reductions on route 691 and the vehicles displaced were utilised by giving an allocation on route 695 to Ilford depot. Fred Ivey

special provision for visitors to Whipps Cross hospital; on Bank Holidays a supplementary service operated between Whipps Cross and Stratford Broadway. The 61 tram service had terminated very awkwardly at the 'Bakers Arms' junction but the 661 conveniently turned in the forecourt of Leyton depot. When this depot was closed at stage two of the trolleybus conversion programme, the 661 became almost its sole user. During the war, a few of Bow's 661s foreign stabled at Leyton depot in the off-peak hour. Tram 63 had terminated awkwardly too, just short of Ilford Broadway at Ilford Hill, but the 663 was extended over Ilford Station Bridge into Ley Street to turn in Thorold Road for its terminus. The 663 always had an early start with

the first vehicle on the road at about 3.30am on weekdays to Aldgate; on leaving the depot towards Aldgate, trolleybuses had to circle Bow Church to get to line of route a very generous six minutes being allowed for this. Although described as the Bow Road services, this thoroughfare was only part of their routeing; the Mile End Road was traversed by routes 661 and 663 with the 663 and 695 running the length of the Romford Road. In 1948, the 661/691 services were reduced following the extension of the Central Line. At Leytonstone 'Green Man', 661s could turn from the Leyton direction; in doing so, three trolley swings would have been needed and this was the only such requirement on the system.

1601 basks in the sunshine at Aldgate terminus; the lack of a front bullseye was a short-lived unsuccessful experiment.
R.F. Mack courtesy Trolleybus Museum Company

Points of note were that latterly, passengers were not allowed to be carried on the section along Fairfield Road between Bow Church and Bow depot. Major overhead junctions were encountered at Gardiners Corner, Stratford Broadway, 'Princess Alice', Ilford Broadway, 'Thatched House' and 'Bakers Arms'. Route 663 was involved with two major diversions, the first of which occurred in the mid 1950s when all routes that used Aldgate trolleybus station, which was being re-surfaced, were curtailed at Gardiners Corner and turned at the nearby Whitechurch Lane, which was poled and wired for the purpose and as such acted as a temporary terminus. Secondly, due to the reconstruction of Ilford Station Bridge, terminating 663s from Ilford, Balfour Road were diverted via Hainault Street and Ilford High Road to Ilford Broadway on westbound journeys from 27th March 1958, a situation which continued until withdrawal.

Due to the factors of low passenger use and parallel services, route 663 lost almost a third of its Monday to Friday allocation between 1955 and 1958, 51 vehicles dropping to 35 in that short space of time. This was largely due to the electrification of the parallel British Railways service. Between 1952 and 1959, Bow depot lost a third of its allocation, down from 94 vehicles to 63 (In the same period Colindale depot lost almost 40% of its allocation: down from 39 vehicles to 23). The 695 also suffered cutbacks, with the Saturday allocation dropping from 22 vehicles to 9 between 1950 and 1956 – a drop of 60%. In many ways the 695 was a superfluous service, for bus route 86A operated over its entire length and the 25 group and 663 ran much of the way too. Following the 1958 bus strike, which brought about lower passenger use, the route was withdrawn after operations on Tuesday 6th January 1959. To compensate for this and to maintain the link across Ilford Broadway, route 663 was extended to Chadwell Heath on 7th January 1959 on Mondays to Fridays and in Saturday shopping hours, London Transport being able to do this with just one extra trolleybus on Mondays to Fridays and two on Saturdays; it was London Transport's last weekday trolleybus route extension. The 663 worked to Chadwell Heath on a number of other occasions also; from Aldgate on 10th August/30th November 1958 and 1st March 1959 when Ilford Bridge was closed for roadworks and on Easter, Whitsun and August Mondays 1959 when a supplementary 663 service operated from Bow depot to Chadwell Heath in addition to the main Aldgate to Ilford service. The 663 extension was short lived however, as the 661 and 663 were withdrawn after the close of services on Tuesday 18th August 1959.

1590 turns into the Trolleybus and Green Line Coach Station at Aldgate. Despite most of the routes being withdrawn in 1959, the sign continued in use until the end of trolleybuses here in 1961. Don Thompson

1625 on route 661 has been diverted through Hackney when a problem precluded the use of the normal routeing. The route number blind has been turned to show blank. Bow trolleybus drivers are unlikely to have travelled this way before; following the Lea Bridge Road wires to Kenninghall Road, they picked up the 653 wires here and followed them to Mile End Gate to find their line of route. Fred Ivey

Only two members of the SA1 class survived the service cuts of 1955-1959; the choice of 1727 and 1731 was due to their having later overhauls than the rest of the class. 1731 on route 693 joins the 691 diversion wires in Ilford High Road at Hainault Street. Extra poles, without finials, have been planted to take the extra weight of the overhead.
David Packer

THE ILFORD LOCALS

The trolleybuses allocated to Ilford depot are best remembered by the SA classes, but these were the third type of trolleybus allocated to the depot within about four years of opening. There was some doubt as to whether trolleybuses would work on the network of tram services of the erstwhile Ilford Council Tramways, for Ilford Council informed London Transport that they would rather have motorbuses as replacements. Having already declared the unsuitability of Ilford tram shed for conversion to a trolleybus depot and actively seeking a new site, London Transport gave favourable consideration to the Council's preference. However, such ideas were dropped and plans were made to introduce trolleybuses.

October 1937 was the original anticipated conversion date but it was delayed until Sunday 6th February 1938, when daily routes 691 and 693 first operated, working out of Ilford depot. Route 691 ran from Barking Broadway to Barkingside while route 693 ran from Barking Broadway to Chadwell Heath. There was an initial question mark about the viability of converting the Chadwell Heath service. The 691 was extended the length of Barkingside High Street, circling the roundabout at its top end; the tram terminus had

been at the junction of High Street with Tanners Lane. At Chadwell Heath, the 693 turned via Station Road to stand in Wangey Road. The original plan at Barking for these and the Barking Road services was for them to terminate at the junction of Heath Street and Axe Street. With the opening of the new London Road in 1936, vehicles from both directions made a circular turn using London Road, East Street and North Street with the terminus in London Road.

An MoT instruction stipulated that at the Perth Road entrance of Ilford depot, conductors were to direct drivers into the road. A later instruction was for conductors to direct buses from Perth Road into the main road. At Birkbeck Road (Newbury Park) conductors were to stand in the main road to supervise the turn and warn approaching traffic. Such instructions were not being adhered to in 1959! Trolleybuses were not allowed to pass in the narrow part of Horns Road between traction standards 107-111 and inward-bound buses had precedence until 12 noon and outward-bound buses after 12 noon. Consideration was given to a turning point at Seven Kings Station in the 1950s, but nothing came of it. Thought had also been given to using this point in original plans for the 693.

There were only two instances on the trolleybus system of 'end-on' termini acting in a dual capacity for routes from different directions. Hampton Court had connecting facilities and Barking Broadway saw routes crossing each other.

On Saturday 12th February 1938, route 692 was introduced, operating on Saturday afternoons and evenings between Chadwell Heath and Newbury Park 'Horns Tavern'. Working out of Ilford depot it ran for only 43 days, concluding on Saturday 3rd December 1938 due to the need to meet the growth in traffic on the 691 between Barkingside and Barking on Saturdays. The 691 and 693 were augmented in replacement. From inception the 691 worked only between Barkingside and Ilford (Balfour Road) after the evening peak hour on Mondays to Fridays. This gave cause for complaint that there was an unserved portion between Ilford Broadway and Ley Street at these times and from 8th December 1938 a through evening service was run. Introduced for an experimental period, it remained thereafter. There were many variations in fare scales on the trolleybus system, due to levels set within former tramway areas. The Ilford area gave the most generous rides.

The vehicles working these routes from the beginning were the stalwart E1 class, but in the early part of the war London Transport found itself short of all types of passenger vehicles, due to wartime losses and increased passenger demand. As new vehicles were not being built at the time, alternatives were sought. This resulted in 18 Bournemouth MS2 Sunbeam trolleybuses being borrowed and allocated to Ilford depot, which were the only Sunbeam trolleybuses operated in London. Their routes were entirely in suburbia and no hardship was caused to the public by using smaller-capacity 56-seat vehicles. Some E1s were reallocated when the Sunbeams entered service in December 1940. Nine Sunbeams were released in November 1941 and the other nine in September 1942. They were replaced because London Transport had secured 43 trolleybuses which were due be sent to South Africa. They could not be exported due to wartime restrictions and shipping difficulties, German U-boat activity, so an arrangement was made between the Ministry of War Transport and London Transport for them to be allocated to London. They entered service between November 1941 and June 1943, enabling the remaining E1s to be reallocated. The vehicles were classed as SA types; 25 Leylands had been destined for Durban and 18 AECs for Johannesburg. Special dispensation was obtained for their operation because they contravened the width and weight limits. They were completely different from other types of trolleybus. Their destination boxes, panelled-

No.587 has just turned out of the Newbury Park terminus at Birkbeck Road in 1938 and operates a short working on recently introduced route 692 to Ilford Broadway; the tramlines have been covered over. Charles Klapper

The tramlines have reappeared in the road surface during wartime as Bournemouth 72 makes a journey to Barking Broadway; these vehicles were nicknamed 'Yellow Perils' by the staff due to their doubtful braking performance. However they proved to be useful stop-gaps in the early part of the war. Charles Klapper

over or permanently locked front doors, leather seats, and darkened glass on the top window sections of the Durban vehicles were the most noticeable features. Traffic grew on both routes during the war, particularly the 691 and eventually the number of SAs fitted in well with the vehicle requirement.

Of the two routes, the 691 was the busiest and from its beginning there were always 'shorts' working from Barkingside to Ilford Broadway; these ran on Sundays until 1948 and until August 1959 worked all day, including evenings, on Mondays to Fridays and during Saturday shopping hours. There was often a two-minute service away from Barkingside with one going to Barking and the other to Ilford. At Chadwell Heath there were two separate stands for the trolleybuses at Wangey Road. One commenced at trolley pole 1 for two vehicles and the other at trolley pole 6 for a single vehicle. Should a fourth vehicle arrive then the first vehicle was to proceed on

Above **Apparent in this view of 1753 at Barkingside is the fact that the rear wheels (as on all SA classes) were inset of the body line, a matter of a 7ft 6ins chassis on an 8ft body. The front axle was modified to give a wider track more in line with the body. Although 1753 looks very sound, the SA classes had to undergo major rebuilding at Charlton works due to their inferior specification by their would-be South African owners. The SA classes had a central cream band below the windscreen and were fitted with towing eyes which were fitted in such a manner that the front valance did not have to be removed for towing as on standard vehicles.** Phil Tatt

Upper Left **SA class 1742 turns into Ilford Lane from Longbridge Road; the sliding exit door on the 'Durban' vehicles was permanently locked. The driver has both windscreens open and has discarded his jacket on what must have been a very hot day. Judging by the stance of the would-be passenger, he is well used to leaping aboard trolleybuses here.** Fred Ivey

Left **From March 1958, Barking bound 691s were diverted between Ley Street and Ilford Lane via Hainault Street and Ilford High Road. 1761 is about to turn onto the normal line of route at Ilford Broadway; it has just passed two semi automatic frogs in quick succession, having had to operate the first of them.** Fred Ivey

its journey. The 691 was particularly busy throughout because there were no parallel bus services; this was also the case along Ilford Lane between Barking and Ilford on both routes. One criticism of routes 693 and 695 was that they failed to reach the traffic objective of Romford. During the latter part of the war, suggestions were submitted by the Barking and Dagenham councils for the extension after the war of the trolleybus routes terminating at Barking Broadway and Chadwell Heath, to Becontree Heath and Dagenham respectively. These suggestions were put forward in the light of housing development, but London Transport did not pursue the matter. Ilford Broadway was the focal point of these routes and this junction had the largest number of pieces of overhead equipment on the system. There were 25 in all and the equipment was the nearest to being of grand union configuration whereby turns could be made to all directions from any given direction (the south to west side was missing); three tons of overhead equipment was held aloft here – all by flimsy-looking span wires and strain. The 691 had many customers for Plessey's factory in Ley Street and vehicles were bunched at factory starting and finishing times and at lunch breaks. Ilford football club had a considerable following during the routes' existence and extra trolleybuses operated to the ground in Ley Street before and after matches. Ilford crews travelled to Bow depot to pick up and later return standard vehicles for some of these workings. Bow vehicles used at Ilford depot were not used on scheduled 691 journeys to Ilford Broadway, as plain 'Ilford Broadway' was not given on Bow blinds.

The 691 and 693 did not lead colourful lives and it was only in the last 17 months of operation that there were any changes. Ilford Council embarked on a road improvement scheme in 1958 with the aim of reducing congestion at Ilford Broadway. The first phase included the widening of Station Bridge and on 27th March 1958, a one-way system came into operation: Barking-bound 691s, terminating 663s and 693 journeys from the depot were diverted via Hainault Street, which was wired and poled for the purpose. In April 1958 a new road, Balfour Approach, was opened with terminating 663s and short working 691s at Ilford Broadway using it. It was necessary to close Ilford Bridge on three Sundays, 10th August, 30th November 1958 and 1st March 1959, with special arrangements being made for trolleybus services on those days: the 691 operated from Barkingside to Thorold Road (Ilford Broadway turn) with an increased service on the 693 which operated normally. The 663 was extended to Chadwell Heath as Thorold Road was unattainable, and 693 depot workings and 691 staff journeys used Hainault Street, which was made two-way on these days, to gain Ley Street northbound. These journeys came in from both directions and caused some acutely-angled trolleyboom work at the junction of Ilford High Road and Hainault Street. They occurred at night time and it was not a good practice but as the SAs were not equipped with traction batteries there was no alternative. At the bottom of Hainault Street the vehicles moved by gravity into Ley Street. London Transport planned to re-open the wires across Ilford Bridge but this did not happen and the arrangements outlined above remained until the routes were withdrawn.

On Monday 16th March 1959, a disastrous fire burnt out Harrison Gibson's furniture shop in Ilford High Road and forcibly halted evening services on the 663 and 693. A number of vehicles became stranded on the Chadwell Heath section. Vehicles were towed via side roads to gain the wires, with some not returning to their depots until the early hours of the next morning. A local Boy Scout group assisted by pushing some of the SAs into position, but unfortunately this happened before bob-a-job week! The traction wires had either melted or been cut down, but were re-erected so that operations could start at 6.30am the next day. For some time this part of the High Road was effectively a trolleybus-only reservation. Fire appliances in the London area carried 'T' poles which, when attached to the running wires, cut off the current and may have been used in this instance.

A few operational aspects are of interest. A carnival was held at Barking each year and to prevent all the trolleybuses getting caught up in it, thereby disrupting the service, a tower wagon was positioned at Loxford Bridge to turn round some of the SAs here. (Standard vehicles used their batteries). Notes were made on time cards of the last 691

From the latter part of 1956 to the latter part of 1958, three standard trolleybuses were allocated to Ilford depot to cover for SA classes being overhauled; the vehicles concerned (899, 1399 and 1555) were fitted with specially made Ilford blinds. No.1399 at Barking Broadway shows the quaint FAIRLOP & BARKINGSIDE display. John Wills

Due to the withdrawal of five SA1s in January 1959, it was necessary from that time onwards for Bow depot to loan trolleybuses to Ilford depot on Saturdays when their allocation was higher than on Mondays to Fridays. They were normally to be seen on route 691, but in this instance 1556 is working on route 693 and is passing the now demolished 'The Hope Inn' pub at Ilford Broadway. Fred Ivey

1759 is the leader of four vehicles at Chadwell Heath which are entering Wangey Road from Station Road. The photograph can be dated as the summer of 1959 as the second vehicle is a 663 which was extended here upon route 695's withdrawal in January of that year. John Wills

The six inch width difference is very noticeable in this view of 1597 and 1759 at Thorold Road, Ilford. Despite being delivered more than three years after 1597, SA3 class 1759 will be withdrawn almost two and a half years before it, as there was no intention to re-allocate the SA classes after withdrawal of the routes from Ilford depot. Don Thompson

to Fairlop and the last 693 to Chadwell Heath to connect with a specific 663 at Ilford Broadway and right until 1959 there was a 691 time card note for a connection to be made with a 565 staff trolleybus at Barking, despite the 565's withdrawal almost three years previously! London Transport's short working list detailed battery turns on the 691 at Tanners Lane, Horns Road and on the 691/693 at Ilford Lane where vehicles were to reverse into St Luke's Avenue; without traction batteries, such short workings were unable to be carried out by the SAs. One icy morning an SA turned round in a narrow part of Tanners Lane where it was not normally possible to turn a trolleybus round. It turned completely round on the ice and the driver simply replaced the booms on the wires on the other side of the road and missed out the trip to Fairlop. An obscure Saturday operation in early years was the running of extras on the 691 and 693 for Dr Barnado's fetes. One day an SA became stuck on a dead section of wire and some policemen put their backs to the vehicle; it reached a live section of wire and all the policemen sat down hard in the road as the SA sped away!

The only interchange between the routes was of 691s to 693s at Barking Broadway with the only odd working being a 691 from Barkingside to Chadwell Heath on a Sunday morning. Working as a staff trolleybus to Ilford depot, it became a 693 once in Ley Street. For a number of years, on Saturdays leading up to Christmas, extra 693s ran between Chadwell Heath and Ilford Broadway. Route 691 and 693 timings were interworked but the 693 and 695 were unable to be so, because the 695 was interworked with the 661 and 663.

London Transport intended to retain routes 691 and 693 as an isolated network until July 1962 when, with the remnants of Colindale and Stonebridge depots, this outpost would have formed the last stage of the original conversion programme. Ilford depot was to be left until last to avoid transferring non-standard vehicles with the attendant difficulties this would have brought about. In the middle of 1958, when the need for economy became paramount, careful studies were made to see which garages/depots could be closed. It was decided that Ilford depot could be closed and so that immediate benefits could be realised, routes 691 and 693 were added to stage three of the conversion programme which occurred on Tuesday 18th August 1959.

On 13th August, it was reported that a buyer in South America had been found for the remaining 33 SA vehicles. Despite being held in store for a number of months they were sent to the scrapyard in early 1960. Even here, some lay untouched until September, for a number of them were put aside in the hope of finding a buyer. It was quoted to an intermediary, acting for Reus-Tarragona Trolleybuses in eastern Spain, that these vehicles were available at £1,200 each. Cohen's were being wildly optimistic about selling them at this price as London Transport were talking about selling Q1s for £500 at this time. No re-sale of any SAs took place.

The last daytime vehicle due into Ilford depot was 1758, a 693 from Chadwell Heath. However, 'last night gremlins' were at work, for 1763 sustained a puncture at Ilford Broadway just before midnight and arrived after 1758. There was one more planned piece of trolleybus activity that night though, so 1763 did not steal the 'honour' of being the last electric vehicle to enter Ilford depot. It was necessary for a trolleybus to take staff home after normal services had finished and 1756, performing this task, slipped unobtrusively into the now empty depot in the early hours of 19th August.

THE EAST HAM CIRCULARS

On Sunday 12th September 1937, two short east London tram routes which had run separately from Stratford Broadway to East Ham Town Hall and Upton Park 'Boleyn' were replaced by trolleybuses. They followed the same routeing as the trams but were extended via Barking Road to join each terminus, thereby creating a circular service around Plashet Grove, High Street North, Barking Road and Green Street. At High Street North, the Manor Park to Beckton trolleybus service would have joined them, but London Transport did not exercise the powers they held for this. Both routes, Stratford Broadway and East Ham Town Hall, were numbered 689 but despite having different via points on the destination blinds (via Green Street/via Plashet Grove) for journeys to East Ham Town Hall, it caused immediate confusion to the public and on Tuesday 14th December 1937 the anti-clockwise service was numbered 690. Originally, destination blinds were turned at Stratford and East

Ham but this practice soon ceased in favour of a 'lazy' display whereby one aperture sufficed for the round journey. In October 1937 approval was given for more running time due to difficulties in dealing with shopping traffic in the Green Street area. The 689/690 operated daily and were worked by West Ham depot.

The 689/690 brought passengers to the main interchange points of Stratford Broadway and the Barking Road, but despite passing through densely populated areas were never considered to be really busy except on Saturdays when throughout their lives an intensive five-minute service was run on both routes. This catered for heavy shopping traffic and meant that when West Ham FC were playing at home, the routes coped adequately in taking fans to and from the match at Upton

Park. A round trip on the 689 took just 34 minutes with 35 minutes being allowed for the 690; each trip required five frog pulls on both routes, averaging out at a frog pull every seven minutes. Lengthy in-service depot runs were necessary on both routes but no provision was made on the fare charts for them. The original terminal arrangements at Stratford Broadway for routes 669, 689 and 690 required them to operate anti-clockwise via Tramway Avenue and West Ham Lane; this was altered in the latter part of 1947 (operative on the schedules from 12th November) and they then circled the Broadway clockwise to stand outside the Church. Three minutes extra running time was given for this with the terminus now being situated at an important traffic interchange and in a busy shopping area. Routes 669, 689 and 690 had an out-

standing disadvantage in that they did not make direct contact with Stratford station (Central Line and Eastern Region British Railways lines).

A curtailment point for 689/690 was a battery reverse at Washington Road in Plashet Grove but its use was sporadic; the routes were so short, that when lost mileage occurred it was in the form of a complete journey. There was some changing from route 689 to 690 at Stratford Broadway and vice versa; 689 and 690 sometimes changed to 669 at Stratford Broadway; back at Stratford such 669s became 689 or 690 again. The routes were not major members of the trolleybus network and their passing at conversion stage five, after operation on Tuesday 2nd February 1960, went virtually unnoticed.

ROUTES 669 and 685

The first proposals for trolleybuses in Walthamstow were made in 1934 and entailed a route from Chingford Mount to the Barking Road at East Ham. It would have run via 'Crooked Billet' and Markhouse Road to Lea Bridge Road where the route would have split in two, one half going via Lea Bridge Road, 'Bakers Arms' and High Road Leyton with the other half via Church Road and Grange Park Road to High Road Leyton. It would then have run via Stratford and again the routes would have been split south of here, with one half following the eventual route 689 and the other half following the later route 690, thus obviating the need to turn trolleybuses at 'Boleyn' and East Ham Town Hall. Dual tram and trolleybus operation along Lea Bridge

Road and Barking Road would have occurred. A good case was put forward by the traffic department that new through facilities would have been made in many ways; a link would have been made from Walthamstow and Lea Bridge Road to Stratford and East Ham and to the residential areas of Church Road and Grange Park Road. It was emphasised that the portion of service that ran via 'Bakers Arms' would give a through connection from Markhouse Road to this busy shopping area. The department also noted that the two legs would link up with the local West Ham services and provide through facilities across Stratford Broadway, thus reducing the number of vehicles turning at this busy place. No action was taken on these proposals.

Route 685 was introduced on Sunday 17th January 1937, running daily between Walthamstow 'Crooked Billet' and Lea Bridge Road, Markhouse Road with the section from Higham Hill to 'Crooked Billet' using a road previously unserved by trams and becoming the fourth such instance on the system. The operating depot was Walthamstow. The wiring south of Markhouse Road enabled route 685 to gain a lengthy daily extension to Canning Town commencing on Sunday 12th September 1937; for the fifth time a road, Church Road Leyton, was used which had not previously been served by trams. West Ham depot now joined in working the 685 and provided the main allocation thereafter; Leyton depot contributed some workings from

Facing Page **Dismal surroundings made up much of route 685's southern end; 625 passes through Silvertown on a murky day, on its lengthy run to 'Crooked Billet', which was referred to by the staff as 'The Billet'. To cater for workers in this area, 685s were to be seen at odd times, late night on Mondays to Fridays and Sunday afternoons.** Fred Ivey

Left **On the wide Silvertown Way, 'Daisy Parsons' trolleybus 622 works south to North Woolwich as another 669 heads for Stratford Broadway. This type of overhead support was synonymous with Silvertown Way. Due to dock work, London Transport found it a perennial problem to make up crew schedules for the routes serving them.** David Packer

No.592 travels along Albert Road, Silvertown, working alongside the railway for some considerable way in this vicinity. The conductor of 592 has prematurely changed the blinds for the trip back to Stratford; it still has some considerable distance to travel before North Woolwich is reached, but it was common practice on the system, that once the last short working point had been passed, in this instance Silvertown Station, the blinds would be changed. Phil Tatt

April to October 1944, these being two vehicles which worked Monday to Friday midday from 'Crooked Billet' to Leyton, Downsell Road. From September 1937, Walthamstow depot were confined to operating a single Monday to Friday morning peak hour trolleybus from 'Crooked Billet' to Lea Bridge Road and from January 1938 until May 1940 they made no contribution at all to the route; until November 1947 Walthamstow again only worked as far south as Lea Bridge Road. On Thursday 4th August 1938 the route was extended in Monday to Saturday peak hours and Saturday daytime to Victoria Docks (Clyde Road) where vehicles turned by means of gravity / battery power. This arrangement continued until 1953, but was a most un-

satisfactory procedure during the blackout, when 46 vehicles needed to turn during the Monday to Friday evening peak hour. On Wednesday 24th May 1939 the route was further extended in Monday to Saturday peak hours to Silvertown Station, being extended here on Sunday afternoons and evenings from 17th November 1940. From Wednesday 8th May 1940, the route reached its greatest length when on Mondays to Saturdays a few peak hour journeys reached North Woolwich. This extension had been approved as far back as November 1938. In pre-LPTB days West Ham Corporation had proposed to operate a trolleybus service from Stratford to North Woolwich via Manor Road and Silvertown Way but the project was held in abeyance.

Walthamstow depot never worked beyond Silvertown Station, where the turning loop was via three minor roads and was the dingiest on the system. The extensions south of Canning Town provided good links for the many dock workers in the area and assisted with the inadequate (!) 669 service which was four minutes for most of Mondays to Fridays and for much of Saturdays and Sundays.

Always worked by West Ham depot, route 669 first operated on Sunday 6th June 1937, working daily between Stratford Broadway and Canning Town. On Sunday 6th February 1938 it was extended from Canning Town to North Woolwich over roads previously unserved by trams and was London Transport's sixth and longest such extension.

A peak hour leg on route 685 worked from North Woolwich to Upton Park 'Boleyn'; the illustrated blind display sufficed for the 'Boleyn' turn at Claughton Road for West Ham depot routes turning there. 602C is seen at North Woolwich on one of these journeys.
Lyndon Rowe

A number of C3s were allocated to Walthamstow depot from 1936 to 1959. 374 crosses the Lea Bridge Road at Markhouse Road and six overhead crossings are to immediate view. The fascia of Barclays Bank would be a museum piece today.
Don Thompson

From August 1938, there was continual augmentation to these routes due to the difficulties being experienced in handling passenger traffic on Silvertown Way in Monday to Friday peak hours (much of the extra traffic had come from the railways). It cannot be emphasised too much how important a part these routes played in transporting dockers to their places of employment during the war. Officials were located at strategic points so that each trolleybus went on its way with its prescribed load. So many vehicles were required that Poplar depot started to operate some 669 journeys towards the end of the war. Although many of these were short workings to such places as Plaistow Station, they did reach both ends of the route. To provide links for the dock workers, a number of Commercial Road derivatives and 669s worked from Upton Park 'Boleyn' to the Silvertown Way routes during the war and in later years there was a regular Monday to Friday peak hour 685 service from 'Boleyn' to North Woolwich. An odd journey that stayed on the schedule

from the war years until 1960 was a Monday to Friday 685 departure from North Woolwich at approximately 10pm; until April 1946 it had run on Saturdays and Sundays as well. Munitions trolleybuses ran on route 669 on Sundays until 1947 when they were replaced by factory journeys until 1952. To cope with increased work in the dock areas there was a heavy increase on the 669 service in April 1949, although there was a partial reduction of 685s to the area; 41 vehicles were required in the Monday to Friday morning peak hour on the 669 at this time. This extra work swallowed up the midday Poplar 669s running from Silvertown Station to Trinity Church, Canning Town which specifically took workers to Canning Town at lunchtime. It ended the Poplar involvement with the 669 but this facility continued until the end of trolleybus operation. Canning Town was always a hive of trolleybus activity; between 7 and 8am on Mondays to Fridays on the April 1949 schedule, the westbound track in Canning Town was served by 72 vehicles on

the 565 group, 44 vehicles on the 669 and 25 vehicles on the 685, totalling 141. This was bettered by 143 movements at Stratford Broadway eastbound in the evening peak.

The section between Canning Town and North Woolwich was always busy, for not only were many docks served but there were also numerous factories including the large Tate & Lyle sugar refinery. It seems incredible today that right until the trolleybus conversion, there were on each Monday to Friday morning between 7 and 8am, forty-two 669s and twenty-two 685s turning left from Barking Road into Silvertown Way, being joined by thirteen 569s from East India Dock Road, an astounding 77 trolleybuses in an hour. This meant a permanent procession of fully laden trolleybuses catering for the area's needs, though the requirement was not so heavy in the evening peak hour due to the staggering of workers' finishing times. However, between 5 and 6pm thirteen 569s, twenty-two 669s and twenty-one 685s made their way up Silvertown Way to Canning

Town. One of the delights of travelling on a fully laden trolleybus in the peak hour here was to gain the last seat on the top deck and to be met by a dense fog of smoke, so strong that the ceilings of the vehicles eventually turned a browny colour. It was no small wonder that West Ham depot allocated older E class vehicles to these routes! West Ham and Poplar depots were the last locations on the London Transport road service network to use the bell-punch and ticket rack system, which ended on Saturday 4th October 1958. Not long before, the author remembers seeing the now rare 1/4d olive green trolleybus tickets curling on their pack in a 685. The road was sett-paved between Silvertown and North Woolwich, with the road running alongside the railway; bowstring bracket arms were used due to the proximity of the railway and gave little space for bus stops. Silvertown By-pass and much of Silvertown Way are on viaducts and the support for the traction wires was by means of tubular gantry poles attached to the traction standards so as to reduce the strain on the pole foundations.

The 685 was an extremely busy route and hard work for conductors. Not only did it run through the dock areas, but also through the busy shopping areas of Canning Town, Green Street and Leyton, with football traffic being catered for when West Ham FC were playing at their ground at Upton Park. If Leyton Orient FC were holding a big match at their Brisbane Road ground, extras were run between 'Crooked Billet' and Lea Bridge Road. When West Ham played at Tottenham Hotspur FC, extras were run on the 685 between Canning Town and 'Crooked Billet'. Fans had to change at Standard Junction to the 625, for no direct journeys were made to Tottenham as London Transport did not like vehicles working on 'foreign wires'. On Saturdays there were short workings at both ends of the route to cater for shoppers, with vehicles running to Finden Road or Wanstead Flats from the south, while from the north there was a shuttle service, known to the crews as 'the shoot', from 'Crooked Billet' to Lea Bridge Road. It was named thus because only 17 minutes were allowed for this journey and the vehicles literally had to shoot there and back! Routes 685/687 efficiently served the highly populated area of west Walthamstow and the Blackhorse Lane factory area and 685 workings on 'the shoot' assisted in carrying this traffic. These operated daily over the years, although from January 1952 the Monday to Friday peak hour workings were extended to Leyton, Downsell Road. On Bank Holidays, Wanstead Fair took place and a supplementary 685 service operated from Canning Town to either Downsell Road or Wanstead Flats, with a similar service operating from the Docks to Wanstead Flats on route 687.

Above **1523 passes north up Cannhall Road, Wanstead. Had fate not intervened, 1523 would have been withdrawn at conversion stage nine. The sale of the Q1s led to it being despatched from Highgate depot to Fulwell depot on 31st January 1961 where it would remain in service until the last day of trolleybuses in London.**
Norman Rayfield

There were very few 685 journeys that worked the whole length of the route from 'Crooked Billet' to North Woolwich – four southern trips and two northern trips each Monday to Friday; these journeys commenced in January 1952. North Woolwich was not served by the route on Mondays to Fridays between April 1949 and January 1952 apart from the single 10pm journey, with the North Woolwich trips on Saturdays being withdrawn after 26th January 1952. An interesting manoeuvre that routes 685 and 687 had to undertake from time to time was at Walthamstow, Sinnott Road. This was done by batterying into Blackhorse Lane and then proceeding by gravity with the trolleys bouncing strongly under their retaining hooks. On one occasion a Walthamstow 685 was curtailed here and when it reached the main road found a West Ham vehicle stranded; during road works a trench had been dug across the road and both vehicles had to be towed out!

The only instances of vehicles working from one route to another concerned 685s becoming 687s at 'Crooked Billet', enabling them to return to West Ham depot earlier than going via line of route, and a 669 which became a 685 at North Woolwich. West Ham 685s and Commercial Road depot runs from the east worked into the depot from Canning Town due to wiring constraints at 'Greengate'. Only on Christmas Days did 685s battery manoeuvre from the north into the depot. On the system, vehicles changed from one route to another while standing in the depot during the day - the highest number from one route to another being on Mondays to Fridays in the fifties on route 669: six worked to 565 group, seven to 697/699, two to 685 and one to 689/690 (one also worked off 689/690). The highest number of vehicles to work off a single route was on Saturdays in the fifties when eight 669s changed to 685. During the war some West Ham 685s foreign stabled at Walthamstow depot in off-peaks.

These routes were typical of the east London trolleybus; they were hard working and, were very much part of the scene for 23 years. The vehicles coped admirably and shortly before the 685 conversion, the author recalls a replacement Commercial Road RM pulling up alongside a 685 at traffic lights on the Barking Road near Canning Town with the bus driver intending to show who had the better vehicle. The elderly E class pulled away from the lights showing a clean pair of heels to the RM which was still, embarrassingly, trying to clear the traffic light area.

The order of the conversion programme was dictated by the need to remove trolleybuses from the East End first; this was because there were a number of manually operated substations in the area which were expensive to run and it was thought wise to dispense with these at the earliest opportunity. These routes were included in stage five and on Tuesday 2nd February 1960 they ran for the last time.

Facing Page Top **1406 leaves the 'Crooked Billet' terminus for the long run down to Canning Town. In the background is the 'Crooked Billet' Public House: it was the only pub that was detailed as the main terminus on destination blinds.** Don Thompson

Facing Page Centre **The Wanstead Flats short working point at Dames Road has a rather dismal background; the occupant of one of the railway arches is 'Forest Gate Garage (Mark 2)!' 969's driver gives a hand signal, a feature of trolleybus drivers.** Fred Ivey

Facing Page Bottom **The E3 class did not last the course due to their general bad body condition. No.648 is on the dead-end wire at Canning Town and is a typical instance of the E classes use on the Docks routes.** Alan Cross

Above Left **At Canning Town, two 685 route trolleybuses, 621A and 1524, head for their home depot of West Ham after peak hour working on the route. 621A was a member of West Ham's fleet for its post-war years.** Fred Ivey

Left **In this vista of Stratford Broadway, seven trolleybuses are to be seen; 1640 leads four others with all of them being on either the Bow Road or Docks routes. 643C stands level with 1640.** Don Thompson

THE DOCKS

Mrs Daisy Parsons became the first lady mayor of West Ham and in this capacity she was asked to inaugurate trolleybus services in the Borough on Sunday 6th June 1937. She was issued with a special licence which enabled her to drive the first vehicle from West Ham depot to the 'Greengate' Hotel at Barking Road (it appears to have been driven on its batteries but with its poles on the wires). This took place at 6.43am, being the first 699 departure. The vehicle concerned was 622 which was fitted with a special plaque on the lower deck bulkhead, recording that Alderman Mrs Daisy Parsons J.P. had inaugurated trolleybus services in the Borough of West Ham. Three trolleybus routes commenced that day to serve the Royal Victoria and Royal Albert Docks (DOCKS on the destination blinds). Route 687 operated between Docks and Chingford Mount via Custom House and Forest Gate; route 697 between Docks and Chingford Mount via Custom House and Stratford, and route 699 between Docks and Chingford Mount via Prince Regent Lane and Stratford. The three routes ran daily and were worked by West Ham and Walthamstow depots, sharing common wiring between

'Thatched House' Leyton and Chingford Mount. The Docks terminus was at Connaught Road and it was proposed that a turntable would be constructed on a bridge over the stream which flowed here. The possibility of extending the route southwards was investigated, but as there were several level crossings and a swing bridge over the Dock, this could not be proceeded with and a special turning place on a raised platform was constructed. Greengate Street had been the site of trolleybus trials by West Ham Corporation in connection with a Tramways conference for about a week in September 1912.

The MoT inspection on the section from Chingford Mount to Walthamstow depot took place on 15th January 1937, with the section from 'Crooked Billet' to Chingford Mount being used only for training drivers. This was the only such instance of a section of wiring being so used for a considerable length of time. The section of wiring from Walthamstow 'Crooked Billet' to Walthamstow depot meant that passengers on 685 depot journeys could be conveyed between these points if they so desired stated Lieutenant Colonel E. Woodhouse in his report. He inspected the

section from Walthamstow depot to Connaught Road, Docks via routes 687, 697 and 699 on 1st June 1937 and stated he had been informed that "It will be necessary to run a few trams at peak periods for a time between Barking Road and Victoria Docks terminus via Freemasons Road and Prince Regent Lane, but this will cease when additional trolleybuses are delivered". It is assumed that this did occur but should not be confused with the tram service that continued to run to West Ham Stadium.

Above **1663 is at the head of four trolleybuses that have shunted onto the siding wire at Connaught Road terminus, thus allowing any vehicles that should precede their departure time, to pass. At the rear is an EXTRA working on a West Ham Stadium special.** Terry Russell

1406 pauses at the traffic lights at Leyton, 'Bakers Arms'; the junction carried one of the major overhead layouts on the system. C. Carter

Below 591 crosses the 'Princess Alice' overhead complex on its way to CROOKED BILLET while another 687 passes by on its way to DOCKS. Vehicles of all classes allocated to West Ham and Walthamstow depots worked on this group of routes. John Gillham

It was also necessary at this time for the narrow section of a hundred yards in Plaistow High Street to be controlled by signals which were worked by trolley wire contacts. The light signals were provided at either end of Plaistow High Street and trams and trolleybuses were not allowed to pass. The lights were originally arranged with red and green lenses but lights did not burn unless a vehicle was in the section. An entering vehicle lit the red signal at the remote end of the section while a green one lit the one which faced the driver. The lights were extinguished when a vehicle left the section. The Board's regulations laid down that a vehicle was not to enter the section if the driver found the signal was against him, but was to wait until the light was extinguished; trams and trolleybuses were not to run under the operating skate or follow another vehicle through until the preceding vehicle had cleared the line. The arrangements were satisfactory but the inspecting officer considered that the red and green lights might prove confusing to other road users. He discussed this with the Board's officers and they agreed to substitute the

coloured light signals with white lights (probably in the form of vertical and horizontal white arrows). This apparatus remained until Plaistow High Street was widened. The inspecting officers continually referred to tram tracks being removed as soon as possible after abandonment, but as the tracks were left down until 1942/43 it is conceivable that this apparatus survived until then. Reference was made at this time to the delay in completing sub-stations. Many delays occurred in the East End and these were a contributing factor in delaying tramway abandonment notifications and consequently tram to trolleybus conversions.

There were only two allocation variances on the routes; the 697 had a few Saturday journeys operating between Chingford and Stratford from April to October 1944 which were worked by Leyton depot; it was planned for this depot to provide some Saturday duties leading up to Christmas 1954 but it is not known if this happened. Walthamstow depot was withdrawn from the 687 by April 1944 and a schedule note at that time stated that it was not to operate on the route at any time.

On Sunday June 11th 1939, the Liverpool Street to Chingford Mount facility was restored with the introduction of route 557 (the 687 had replaced the 57 tram to Chingford in 1937). Route 687 was therefore cut back from Chingford Mount to Leyton Depot daily. On Wednesday 29th July 1942, it was revised in peak hours and diverted at Leyton High Road via Markhouse Road and Billet Road to 'Crooked Billet'. The Monday to Saturday off-peak service turned variously at Leyton Depot or Leyton, Downsell Road until Wednesday 5th May 1948, when the whole Monday to Friday service was operated to 'Crooked Billet'. From Saturday 6th May 1950, the route worked there all day on Saturdays, with the Sunday service following from 7th May 1950. The route now became Docks to 'Crooked Billet' via Markhouse Road daily; over the years, some 687s operated to and from Docks and Leyton via Stratford. Bus route 34 was withdrawn between 'Crooked Billet' and Leyton Green on 1st November 1939 as part of the policy during the war to withdraw bus routes that paralleled trolleybus routes. It had suffered a prior re-

Facing Page **Walthamstow depot's 971 stands in Willis Road, Plaistow, on the Plaistow Station short working loop. Dingy back streets for short working points for trolleybuses were commonplace in the East End.** Fred Ivey

Above **963 was transferred into West Ham depot in January 1959 and worked there for just over a year. Little do the two East End girls, arm in arm in Plaistow High Street, realise that 963 has but two more days of life left in her after this, for it is 31st January 1960. Beyond is the junction at Clegg Street which seemed to have more than its fair share of trolley arm collisions.** Norman Rayfield

trenchment on 17th February 1937, when as part of the Walthamstow trolleybus scheme which was planned for the following month (but which was delayed until June), it was withdrawn between Stratford and Leyton Green. A shuttle service of supplementary trams was put on for the gap in the service that would have otherwise existed – a case of trams replacing buses!

If any set of routes was to epitomise the east London trolleybus then it was this one. Known to the staff as 'The Docks Road', the trolleybuses carried huge numbers of dockers away from the docks, wending their way through the narrow cobbled streets of Plaistow. So many dockers were carried that conductors describe working on the 699 as being similar to 'working in a madhouse' for they had to be quick to collect all the fares between the Docks and Barking Road where many people alighted. Timekeeping was very important and any slight delay caused a bunching in the service. At Plaistow, Clegg Street the manual frog was set in favour of the 687 as it turned right; the main service, 697/699, required the frog to be pulled and

1443's conductor pulls the hand frog from the platform at the junction of Connaught Road and Prince Regent Lane; he is able to do this as the handle is cantilevered due to the supporting pole being set in railway property.
A.G. Newman

1382 turns from Prince Regent Lane into Connaught Road for the last run up to the terminus. It was at this location that Tommy Steele admitted throwing fireworks onto 699 trolleybus platforms. Travel by pushbike seems to be popular in this area, although two cyclists appear to wonder what is being photographed; in fact one of them seems so intent with looking at the photographer that he will ride into a traction pole if he doesn't turn his head in the corect direction fairly soon. Don Thompson

even the most rotund of conductresses would run for the frog handle, pull it and let go in one fell swoop without the vehicle stopping. Because so many people wanted to be transported from Plaistow to the Docks, peak hours saw many vehicles working to and from Bull Road, Plaistow to accommodate them. This turn was specially wired for this purpose in August 1941 with vehicles turning there on Mondays to Saturdays from 27th August. Prior to this, vehicles displaying EXTRA (avoiding the need to change blinds) worked from Docks to Plaistow Broadway via Prince Regent Lane to return via Custom House, with others working in the reverse direction. Known as 'Docks and Plaistow Broadway Circle' journeys, those working from 699 to return via 697 required a trolley swing at Plaistow Broadway; this was most unusual in that such manoeuvres were normally confined to short workings. Even on Sunday mornings in later years, short workings on route 699 from the Docks terminus to West Ham depot and Bull Road occurred to accommodate the dockers. Large numbers of passengers from the east would congregate in Prince Regent Lane by Barking Road for a 699, with those from the west transferring at 'Abbey Arms' for a 687/697 – the Commercial Road services fed these three routes.

The 687 was the quietest of these routes with the 697 and 699 receiving heavy

loadings through Stratford, Leyton and Walthamstow. Extra 699s operated from Chingford to Stratford to cater for shoppers at busy times. The 697 and 699 alternated between the two termini and an intensive service always operated. Until May 1948, trolleybuses were arriving and leaving the Docks at the height of the Monday to Friday peak hour at the rate of about one a minute. Between 7 and 8am on Mondays to Fridays until 1960 there were 35 vehicles leaving Bull Road on routes *669*, 697 and 699 for the dock areas; as time progressed though, the number of vehicles to the Docks declined. From May 1948 the 697/699 operated peak hour journeys from Chingford to Leyton, Downsell Road due to heavy loadings on the northern section. On Bank Holidays, supplementary 699s operated between Docks and Stratford Broadway.

A greyhound and speedway stadium was situated in Prince Regent Lane and extra trolleybuses operating from Bow, Poplar, West Ham and Walthamstow depots served them. Some vehicles parked in Prince Regent Lane during these events, ready for departure when the crowd turned out, while others parked in West Ham depot and returned at the appropriate time; vehicles mainly operated to and from Plaistow Station, Stratford Broadway and Downsell Road. From June 1937 a tram service with a number of open-

balcony former West Ham Corporation trams, especially retained for the purpose, operated these specials, but commencing on 3rd August 1938 this service was taken over by motorbuses; this went on until the conversion of the Commercial Road trams to trolleybuses in June 1940, when enough vehicles could be drawn from local depots to meet this need. Understandably, London Transport were unwilling to license 12 new trolleybuses solely for this purpose from June 1937 to June 1940. Extra vehicles were also provided for bigger matches played at Leyton Orient football ground.

There was changing, one route to the other as follows:

699 to 697 at Chingford Mount
697 to 699 at Chingford Mount
699 to 697 at Bull Road
697 to 699 at Bull Road
687 to 697 at Downsell Road
697 to 687 at Downsell Road
699 to 697 at Docks
697 to 699 at Docks
697 to 687 at Docks
697 to 687 at Leyton depot
697 to 699 at Leyton depot
697 to 699 at Stratford Broadway

A West Ham 697 became a 699 in Walthamstow depot each Sunday between February and April 1960; it operated here rather than Chingford Mount to allow ve-

hicles to reposition themselves there. During the war, Walthamstow 699s foreign stabled at West Ham depot during the off-peaks, returning to service as 697s and routes 687, 697 and 699 were some of a number of routes that operated factory and munition journeys at this time. On Christmas Day 1938 routes 697 and 699 worked journeys from 'Crooked Billet' to Lea Bridge Road. At Chingford Mount the stand was for five vehicles although only three were allowed after 11pm, but if a sixth vehicle were to arrive or a fourth after 11pm then the first one was to leave early. West Ham depot used a variety of classes on these routes, but there were always some E class vehicles to be seen; Walthamstow depot used all of their classes.

Major trolleybus junctions were at Stratford Broadway, Leyton 'Bakers Arms', Walthamstow 'Bell', 'Greengate', 'Thatched House' and 'Princess Alice'. These routes were extremely important and linked many parts of east London; consequently there was supervision at a number of points to ensure that a good service was given throughout. These routes played a very important part in transporting dock workers to their places of employment during the war. West Ham depot was bombed twice in eight days in the war and many vehicles ran without glass.

All three routes figured in stage six of the trolleybus to bus conversion programme and last operated on Tuesday 26th April 1960. Both the last 697 and the last 699 from the Docks were due into West Ham depot at 12.12am but the last 699 of all was one due in to Walthamstow depot from Chingford Mount at 12.13am. London Transport had decreed for trolleybus 622, that 'The first shall be last' and she was retained in service for a further 12 weeks after conversion stage five after all her remaining fellow E class vehicles had gone for scrap. This was so that she would operate the last journey in the Borough just as she had worked the first journey those many years before. The crews had nicknamed 622 'Daisy' for as long as anyone could remember. The staff at West Ham depot completely decorated her and she was exhibited in the depot forecourt for much of the last day. Unfortunately the plaque was stolen sometime prior to the end of January 1960 and a handwritten notice was put in its place for the day. Trolleybus 622 did indeed operate the last journey on the 699 into West Ham depot, but the delay was so great that it arrived at the depot far later than the last 699 into Walthamstow depot. The largest crowd seen so far in the conversion programme amassed to see 622 home and it was given a send-off that only East Enders could give. East London and dockland were seeing their last trolleybus, but defiantly 622, with her last seconds ticking away, dewired as she entered the depot from Greengate Street. In the drama of the event no-one had thought about pulling the frog handle! Acting as conductor on the last journey was the then Lady Mayor of West Ham, Mrs Violet Ayres.

643C on route 699 and 1283 on route 557 at Chingford Mount trolleybus terminus, where today virtually no red London buses serve; an overtaking wire facilitates trolleybus movements here.
Martin Brown

1390 passes the crew relief point at Plaistow Broadway. The 'used car show' advert dates the photograph as April 1960. Soon 1390 will move to Highgate depot and later to Fulwell where it will survive until the very last day of trolleybus operation in London.
Fred Ivey

No.622 leaves West Ham depot on its ceremonial run on 26th April 1960; on its return to the depot, trolleybus operation in the East End came to a conclusion.
Michael Dryhurst

THE COMMERCIAL ROAD

London Transport's last tram to trolleybus conversion took place on Sunday 9th June 1940. It was the 28th conversion from trams to trolleybuses and finally eliminated trams in east London. The entire programme had cost nearly £12 million. This conversion was much delayed for it was hoped to introduce trolleybuses to the Commercial Road on 14th January 1940. Two routes were introduced that day. The 567 operated Mondays to Saturdays from West Ham, Green Street to Aldgate, with the Saturday evening service being extended to Barking Broadway; on Sundays it worked from Poplar to Smithfield.

Route 665 worked daily between Barking Broadway and Bloomsbury. On Monday 10th June 1940, route 565 was introduced and operated in Monday to Saturday peak hours from East Ham Town Hall to Holborn Circus via Grays Inn Road. All three routes were operated jointly by Poplar and West Ham depots, although Poplar always had the lion's share of the allocation. On Mondays to Saturdays a two-minute service operated on the 565 and made it the most frequent of these routes for the first year of operation. Not only did the routes traverse all of the Commercial Road but also the entire length of East India

Dock Road and Barking Road. Main locations served were Poplar, Canning Town, West Ham and East Ham. The 567 route number was allotted in order to distinguish Aldgate operations in spite of its consolidation with the 665. It was originally planned to operate the Commercial Road services under one route number, 665, whether the journeys were to Aldgate, Bloomsbury or Smithfield; a service to Holborn Circus was an afterthought. As the 500 series of route numbers was now being used on the 'north side' it was possible to use the 500 series for this set of routes.

Opposite **1654(WH)** and **1431(PR)**, both 567s, arrive at Gardiners Corner together. 1654 will proceed down Commercial Street to Smithfield while 1431 will turn into Whitechapel High Street for Aldgate. 1431 was one of a small number of trolleybuses to operate on 9th May 1962; in fact it was allocated to the last running of all but was usurped by 1521. Early in the route's life, between June and December 1940, the Sunday 567 Smithfield journeys had worked with the 665 route number. Fred Ivey

For most of its life, trolleybus 1482 worked along the Commercial Road; in this instance it has been curtailed at the rather posh sounding Arbour Square, and leads two other 665s through Canning Town. Fred Ivey

West Ham depot mainly used M and N classes on the Commercial Road services although there are recorded instances of E and J classes working thereon. 1533 is seen in Barking Road, Upton Park; the driver seems pleased about his photograph being taken, but his trolleybus driving days are numbered as the 'Buses for Trolleybuses' notices are pasted on traction poles. Fred Ivey

Poplar depot always used L3 vehicles; 1439 works a 565 journey to Poplar depot and negotiates the facing frog at Blair Street/Aberfeldy Street; Blair Street was the eastern terminus of night 665 route. Although routes 565 and 665 worked in parallel formation along the Commercial Road, they did not both operate around the Holborn loop. This remained a unique anomaly. David Chapman

On Wednesday 23rd July 1941, a new route commenced when the 569 began operating between Aldgate and Silvertown Station in Monday to Saturday peak hours. It was introduced to give new links for those working in the dock areas and, by replacing bus route 106 between Canning Town and Victoria Dock, it saved on imported fuel. Silvertown Way was now left to trolleybuses. On Wednesday 29th October 1941 the 569 was extended to North Woolwich. Starting in November 1944, four Sunday morning trips were made from Aldgate to North Woolwich and in doing so the route operated daily. This was increased to six journeys in February 1946 and remained so thereafter; corresponding journeys were depot runs. From time to time these journeys were referred to as 567 and 665; detailed as 567 on Good Fridays, 569 was displayed to avoid confusing the public. The 569 operated a few early journeys on Bank Holidays as the docks were open every day throughout the year, apart from Christmas Day and Boxing Day. Due to the building trade working on Good Fridays, boosted services, as opposed to Sunday services, were run on a number of routes. The 569 was worked mainly by Poplar depot but a few journeys were operated by West Ham depot, though they ceased to do this after April 1949. The 565 was extended to Barking in Monday to Saturday peak hours from 23rd July 1941.

Upper Left **X6 class trolleybus 1670 was always allocated to West Ham depot and could be seen on any of its routes; on this occasion it is seen on route 665 at the Barking terminus. Its front valance had fewer flutes than standard trolleybuses.** Martin Brown

Left **1465 waits in Pier Road, North Woolwich before the final approach to the terminus. The driver has left the cab to visit the adjacent WC, leaving the passengers to await his return!** Norman Rayfield

Above **Until the mid-1950s there were a small number of P1s at West Ham depot. 1713 is seen in Commercial Street; just in front of it is a feeder pillar, and its associated wiring is mounted the height of the traction standard and out to the overhead wires.** Martin Brown

Right **It will have been necessary for 1483's driver to have learnt his trade well to take it over the complex overhead layout at Gardiners Corner without getting stuck on a 'dead' section. 1483 is about to take the second of six items of overhead special work at this location, four being in quick succession as seen in this view.** Don Thompson

Many changes occurred to the Barking section of route 567. Part of the Monday to Friday service was extended there in October 1941; it was increased piecemeal, becoming an all-day working in November 1945. The Saturday service was gradually increased until it became all-day in April 1942. The Sunday service ran there regularly from 6th May 1945, having worked there intermittently from July 1941. In April 1949, the 567 was extended to Smithfield in Monday to Friday peak hours and all day on Saturdays; such journeys were in essence short workings of route 665, but the peak hour journeys were required to accommodate the build-up of passenger traffic in Clerkenwell Road between Goswell Road and Old Street. Bus route 5 was withdrawn over most of its length on 5th February 1942 and embraced the section from Upton Park to Aldgate which paralleled these trolleybus routes, it being policy at the time to withdraw such operations to save fuel. Commencing in 1943 was a daily Plaistow, Bull Road and North Woolwich section which over the years operated as 567, 569 and 665; Sundays-only from April 1949 (the weekday workings were placed with the 669s), it continued until October 1951. Also working on Mondays to Saturdays was a West Ham, Green Street to Silvertown Station section which operated in Monday to Friday peak hours from October 1943 and in Saturday morning peak hours from April 1944. Working as 567/569, these ceased in April 1949. Both of these bifurcations were laid on for the war effort as were two unusual journeys that ran on Sunday afternoons and operated from Poplar depot. They operated as 565 Extras and worked to Silvertown Station on leaving the depot. They then worked to East Ham Town Hall before running to North Woolwich. From here they went to Stratford Broadway before working to Canning Town and the depot. London

Transport maps for 1949-1952 show that the 565 worked from Holborn to East Ham only but the schedules show it operating from Holborn to Barking during this time. On the 1952/53 maps, route 565 is shown as running to Holborn Circus via Grays Inn Road and Farringdon Road when only one option was open to it. The 565 was withdrawn on Saturdays after 9th April 1949.

Barking Road, at East Ham, was impassable at some stage in the war due to bomb damage. Reports are sketchy, but it is believed that Katherine Road and Wakefield Street were poled and wired in both directions; High Street North was also used. This diversion was used by the Commercial Road services.

These routes were of a very complex nature, but had settled down by 1952 to operate as: 565 Barking to Holborn in Monday to Friday peak hours; 567 Barking to Aldgate with daily projections to Smithfield, although such Monday to Friday journeys were peak-hours; 569 North Woolwich to Aldgate, Monday to Saturday peaks with a few Sunday journeys; 665 Barking to Bloomsbury daily, although alternate vehicles on Mondays to Fridays turned at Clerkenwell Green. They were busy services, operating along a main arterial and passenger thoroughfare, serving many shopping areas and giving useful links to trolleybus routes serving the dock areas. They also provided services to the edge of the City area at Aldgate and Bloomsbury. Working alongside the Commercial Road trolleybuses were bus routes 15, 23 and 40 and Green Line coaches, such was the passenger requirement on this thoroughfare. There was heavy traffic along Commercial Road of vehicles making for the docks and Thames tunnels and trolleybuses were regularly curtailed in later years. When West Ham FC played at home, large crowds were carried to Upton Park. On Sundays the markets near

Aldgate were served by trolleybuses on many routes, with the 567 working journeys from Aldgate to Poplar in the mornings and at midday. For the last few months of operation, for an unknown reason, many of these 'shorts' operated between Trinity Church, Canning Town and Arbour Square, which was about the same mileage. These routes went past dowdy shops in Limehouse and Stepney although by the late fifties, modern flats had started to appear in Limehouse and Poplar; it was not until Barking was reached that more pleasant surroundings were encountered.

So intensive were these routes, that it is worthwhile elaborating:

Between 7.30 and 8.30am on the Monday to Friday schedule commencing in April 1949, seventy-five trolleybuses passed through Gardiners Corner from the east (143 vehicles between 6.45 and 8.45am) with 79 passing from the west between 5 and 6pm. Inevitably, some vehicles were simultaneously timed and at Gardiners Corner, four arrived together at 7.51am: the 7.15am 567 Barking to Smithfield, the 7.15am 567 Barking to Aldgate, the 7.16am 569 North Woolwich to Aldgate and the 7.21am 569 Silvertown to Aldgate. This also occurred many times in the evening peak hour with vehicles from Holborn, Smithfield and Aldgate arriving together and travelling on the same timing to Canning Town. As an example, two went to Barking and one to North Woolwich. On the November 1947 schedule there were two 569 departures at 7.39am from Aldgate to North Woolwich. During the latter part of the war, 134 vehicles were required for Monday to Friday morning peak hours. This included 90 from Poplar and 44 from West Ham, with 131 vehicles being required in the evening peak. This heavy peak demand made the routes expensive to operate and, apart from those included in stage two of the conversion programme, they were the highest loss-makers.

There were many overhead junctions to be negotiated by the Commercial Road trolleybus routes. At West Ham 'Greengate', 1447 passes through on a journey to Smithfield with an RTW behind on route 15 to East Acton. Norman Rayfield

Journeys to and from Poplar depot were made empty. Powers were obtained to operate round the side of the depot to Poplar wharf. These were the only 'wharf' powers and no doubt were due to everything in the area being embraced in 'blanket' powers – no wiring was constructed. Poplar depot had a very intensive run-out in 1947-49; between 6 and 7am fifty-five vehicles left the depot, being 64% of the total run-out.

In 1953 the Borough of Holborn suggested new terminal arrangements at Bloomsbury which entailed a slight shortening of the loop, with vehicles using Drake Street. However, delays prevented introduction, even though it had been tested for clearances in March 1953;

by the time that all parties had agreed to the new routeing, the conversion programme was so near as to not make it worthwhile implementing. Back in the nineteen-thirties, Parliament rejected a proposal to operate to the end of Oxford Street via Hart Street (now Bloomsbury Way), New Oxford Street and Bury Street. By using Commercial Street, Great Eastern Street, Old Street and Clerkenwell Road, the trolleybus routes involved were the only ones (with the 679 in St John Street) until 1950 operating on inner London roads that were not served by motorbuses.

Demand for these services did decline however. The 565 had decreased to a 14-

minute service by 1956 with the number of passengers travelling to and from Holborn Circus being very small and it operated for the last time on Tuesday 16th October 1956. Despite this, a one-minute service ran in the peak hours afterwards on the combination of the other routes.

Interchanging from one route to the other occurred as:

665 night journey to 665 day journey at Poplar (on the road).
665 to 567 at Barking
567 to 665 at Barking
567 to 565 at Barking
565 to 665 at Barking
665 to 565 at Barking
565 to 567 at Barking
567 to 665 at West India Docks
565 to 567 at West India Docks
665 to 567 at West India Docks
565 to 665 at West India Docks/Clerkenwell Green (whichever suited conductor)
665 to 565 at West India Docks
567 to 665 at East Ham Town Hall
565 to 567 at East Ham Town Hall
665 to 567 at East Ham Town Hall
567 to 565 at East Ham Town Hall
565 to 665 at East Ham Town Hall
569 to 567 at Aldgate
567 to 569 at Aldgate
565 to 567 at West Ham, Greengate Street.

A 569 ran from North Woolwich to Bloomsbury; also a 569 from North Woolwich turned at Trinity Church, Canning Town where it had a short layover before going to Bloomsbury. The reason for not working direct was to prevent two vehicles travelling from Canning Town to Bloomsbury on the same timing.

A facet of trolleybus operation was the utilisation of crews and vehicles to operate on more than one route during the course of a day's work. An example was a West Ham running that worked on routes 565, 567, 665 and 687 during its working day. There were instances of staff working on four routes in a day (645, 660, 662, 666); for this reason, bell-punch tickets often listed some or all of the routes operated by a particular depot on the front of the ticket. When paper-ticket issuing machines became the norm, 000 was displayed in the route number box for the same reason, although there were instances where a route number was given.

On 7th September 1958, eastbound trolleybus services were diverted at the Blackwall Tunnel due to a second bore being made under the River Thames. They were diverted from East India Dock Road and travelled via Blair Street to line of route. This also affected depot workings and much new wiring had to be put up for all of this; in fact, it was all in situ when routes 567, 569 and 665 were withdrawn at stage four of the conversion programme. They last operated on Tuesday 10th November 1959.

Poplar's 1484 passes the old northern entrance to the Blackwall Tunnel. This location has changed beyond all recognition in today's London. Fred Ivey

FOOTBALL SPECIALS

TOTTENHAM, SATURDAY 16TH OCTOBER 1948.
Tottenham Hotspur have played Queens Park Rangers and the crowds need to get home. An unidentified L class trolleybus (left) from Holloway depot takes on its complement of passengers at White Hart Lane, while Edmonton depot's 888 (above) similarly takes supporters home; as can be seen, trolleybuses had almost a complete monopoly at these times. *LTMuseum*

London Transport have always had a very professional approach to handling supporters to various sporting events in the capital, the most popular of these being Association Football. A number of London clubs had grounds in the vicinity of trolleybus routes and are mentioned in the relevant chapters of this book. Fortunes for these clubs varied over the years and in many cases the supporters were catered for by little or no augmentation. Brentford was at one time a first division club, while West Ham was normally resident in the second division; trolleybus provision therefore depended on the success of the clubs.

London Transport's greatest single challenge has been in the provision of catering for supporters to and from football matches at Wembley Stadium. The British Rail and Underground stations at Wembley transported the bulk of the them, but the stadium was close to trolleybus route 662 and large numbers of spectators were thus accommodated. The biggest event to be catered for was the FA Cup Final first held at Wembley in 1923 when Bolton Wanderers beat West Ham United 2-0. In the trolleybus era, 100,000 spectators would attend these matches and the transport planners would be aware of the number of people to be moved.

The FA Cup Final was always held on a Saturday and was followed the next Saturday by the Amateur Cup Final which began to be played here in the post-war years. They also were attended by near-capacity crowds and teams such as Bishop Auckland, Crook Town, Pegasus (the combined Oxford and Cambridge Universities teams) and Walthamstow Avenue were regular participants. Home and foreign Internationals were also held here either on a weekday or a Saturday afternoon, due to the fact that floodlighting was not then available.

Careful study by the traffic planners estimated that in the instance of the Cup Final, forward traffic could be carried by the normal service and 22 extras with the return traffic needing the normal service and 40 extras. As there were no other parallel trolleybus services, the extras religiously displayed EXTRA in the route blind box. The operation commenced at Friday midnight when the extras, driven by men from the rolling stock department and traffic drivers, left various depots on their journeys through the silent streets to Stonebridge depot where further reinforcements converged after the morning peak hour on Saturday. Vehicles were fitted with Stonebridge destination blinds at the front

although generally speaking, other blinds were not changed, which led to side panels such as 607 being displayed. A supplementary schedule was operated between Paddington/Scrubs Lane and Wembley and when the work was completed before the match, the extras would park in Stonebridge depot. When the match was nearing its close, the vehicles would leave the depot and go to Sudbury where they turned and ran back to Wembley Hill Road. The first four were parked on the lay-by wire specially installed here, which enabled service buses to run through normally; the other extras were lined up west of Wembley Hill Road with booms down. As soon as the game was over, the spectators swarmed out and the first two buses were full; a bang on the side from the inspectors in charge of loading and they were away. The next two would move up to load and their places would be taken by two signalled down by the district superintendent. They coasted downhill into the lay-by with their poles down; while they awaited their move to

the loading stop, up went the poles and soon it was their turn to depart. It took 90 seconds to fill a trolleybus and the loading of 60 buses an hour was easily maintained. Queues rarely formed, for as the crowds arrived, so they were loaded. This procedure was the one adopted in the early post-war years, but all the extras turned at Wembley Hill Road for the last few years of operation.

London Transport had to provide most of the public transport to get football supporters to Tottenham Hotspur FC's ground at White Hart Lane, Tottenham. For much of the trolleybus era they were a first division side and as with all home football matches the games were fortnightly. There was no Underground station to take the majority of the crowd and motorbus services in the area were scant, so the trolleybusmen were virtually on their own. The task was considered greater than that at Wembley where there was a nearby Underground station. In 1948 as many as 46 extra vehicles were used on the north-south services and the nearby cross

routes; there were also 70 vehicles an hour on the normal services. Vehicles not only came from Edmonton, Stamford Hill, Holloway, Wood Green (which borrowed vehicles from Clapton in addition to using their own) and Walthamstow depots but, also from east London depots such as Bow and Poplar with extras being run before and after the match. It was a far easier proposition to transport the fans before the match for their arrival was over a longer period. While the match was being played, vehicles would park either in Edmonton depot, at Town Hall Circle, at Manor House or near to Spurs' ground. A special siding was wired up right outside the ground to hold some of the vehicles which were to take the supporters home. When the match was over vehicles had to arrive one by one so that a continuous stream of trolleybuses could be sent on their way. The siding was not long enough to take all the required extras, so those that could not be accommodated here would be parked on the opposite side of the road with booms lowered, giving

272 on the ordinary 662 service has been curtailed at Stadium, Wembley Hill Road on Cup Final Day 1957; Aston Villa are playing Manchester United and their supporters make their way to the match. Fred Ivey

service vehicles a free passage. On inspectors' instructions the booms would be raised and the vehicles would turn round the Snells Park loop to take up their positions with the ordinary services taking up their share too. The extra vehicles were sent to destinations south from the football ground and usually displayed a route number, due to the many trolleybus routes operating in the vicinity. Upon inspectors instructions, they were sent to various destinations. 'Foreign' vehicles showed EXTRA with a blank destination blind. Queue control was difficult due to the size of the crowd, which could be over 70,000 dispersing at the same time, but the whole procedure was carried out within an hour of the final whistle. Even the ordinary schedule was amended to accommodate the supporters; 627s turning at Finsbury Park were extended to Tottenham Court Road.

In the 1950s the football supporters were turning to alternative means of transport and, coupled with the staff shortage, the number of extra trolleybuses declined; this was exacerbated with the onset of the trolleybus conversion scheme, for vehicles from the East End depots were no longer available. However, from December 1955 routes 659 and 679 had some Finsbury Park to Snells Park journeys built into the schedule before the match; other vehicles could be noted working from Manor House to Snells Park under inspectors' instructions, having been taken off mainline work. In the 1960/61 football season, Spurs were enjoying a very successful season and were receiving great support; in fact they became the first football club this century to win the FA Cup and League Championship in a season. On Cup Final day one Edmonton trolleybus was displaying a Spurs rosette in the cab. By Easter the crescendo was being reached and on Good Friday, 31st March 1961, when Spurs beat Chelsea 4-2 in front of a 65,032 crowd and on Easter Saturday 1961 when they beat Preston North End 5-0 in front of a 46,325 crowd, a supplementary schedule was drawn up; three 649s from Stamford Hill depot working from Dalston Junction to Snells Park (this being the only recorded instance of an unofficial turn 'Dalston Stoke' being used officially) with seven Stamford Hill 649s and five Edmonton depot 649s working from Stamford Hill to Snells Park. Twelve 659s were to run between Manor House and Snells Park. Whether they all ran is not known, as such work was covered on voluntary overtime. As part of the general provision over the years, Wood Green depot operated extra 625s from Bruce Castle, with the supporters having to make their way there so that they could be carried to Wood Green. If these vehicles had been parked outside the ground they would have had to have travelled via Tottenham Hale, which would have taken a long time due to the crowd milling about. To a lesser degree, the trolleybus services brought football supporters to Finsbury Park for the nearby Arsenal FC matches but the proximity of Arsenal Underground station made these matches less important from the point of view of trolleybus provision.

Stonebridge's 199 works as an EXTRA whilst 312 and 313 from Finchley depot are parked ready to take up service with home-going crowds. 312 and 313 will have worked light to Sudbury and back and await calling down by an inspector. Fred Ivey

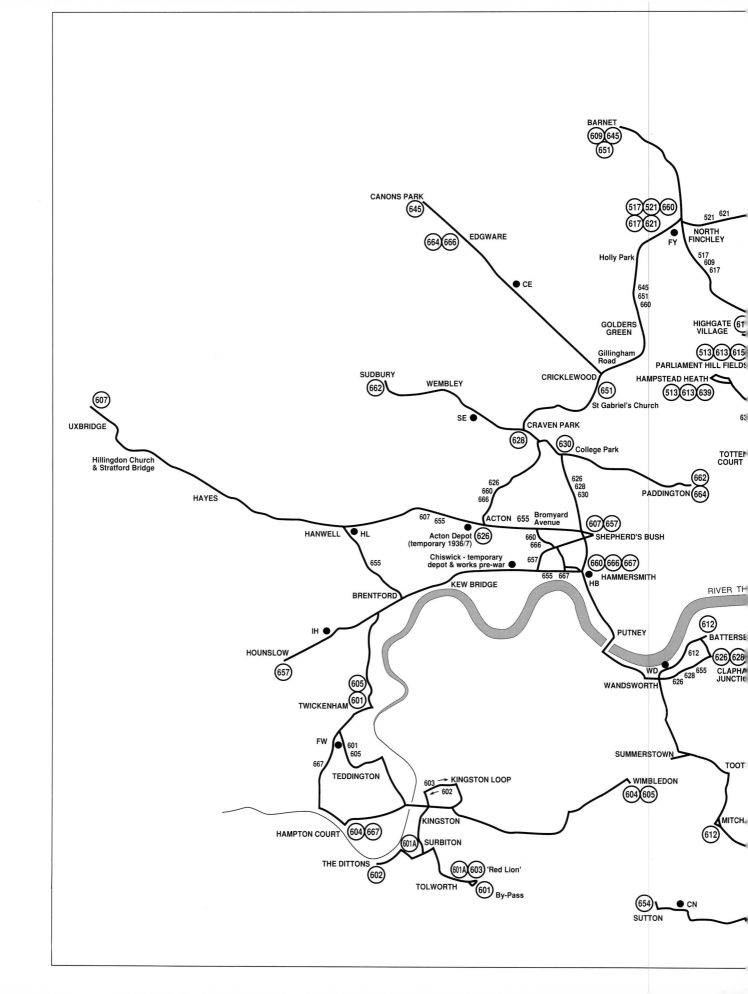

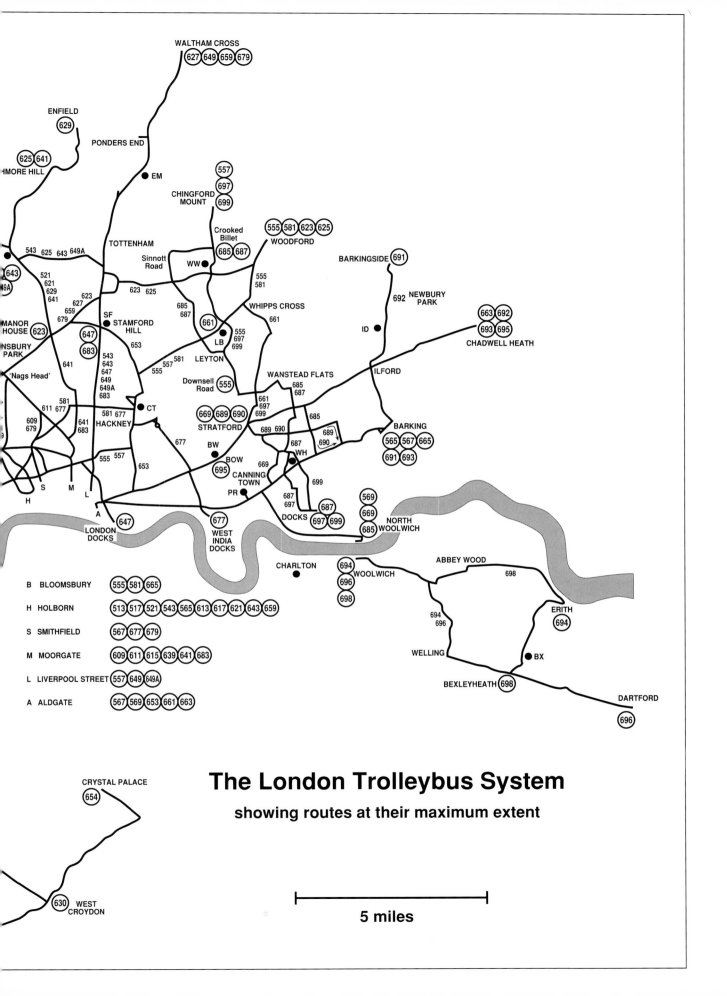

The London Trolleybus System

showing routes at their maximum extent

5 miles

NIGHT ROUTES

Introduced to replace night tram routes, night trolleybus services followed wholly or partly their counterpart daytime services. For many years they were referred to as 'night cars'. Initially the routes were unnumbered (a blank display was shown in the route blind box), but commencing on Wednesday 19th June 1946 route numbers were displayed, although an LT internal reference had been made to them from April to October 1943. These services were mainly for press workers, railway staff and cleaning staff, but they were also useful for employees of London Transport who needed to travel in the early hours; no premium fares were charged. Most routes ran at an hourly headway although the 665 alternated between 30 minutes and 60 minutes; the 543/643 enjoyed the luxury of a 30-minute headway throughout the night. Over the years there was little change to the timings, due to the consistent work pattern of users.

Two services were introduced on Monday 13th September 1937 (for the sake of clarity, the route numbers introduced in June 1946 are used here): route 612 from Mitcham, Fair Green to Battersea 'Princes Head' with Wandsworth depot operating it; route 628 ran from Hammersmith Grove to Clapham Junction with Hammersmith depot working it. For a short time, the turn in Hammersmith Grove was partly by battery, as initially there was no wiring facility, and as such was unique on

the night trolleybuses; a link wire was provided in due course and was the only instance of wiring being erected specially for night trolleybuses. On Monday 11th July 1938, a service from Holloway depot commenced on routes 513/613 from Hampstead Heath to Holborn Circus; an unusual aspect being that the 613 operated *from* Hampstead Heath (as opposed to Parliament Hill Fields). On Monday 6th February 1939, route 643 from Stamford Hill depot commenced to run from Stamford Hill to Holborn Circus. Journeys were introduced on the 543 routeing and there was a Monday morning 543 trip to Liverpool Street; it is unclear whether these commenced at inception but they were operating by July 1942. Route 665, from Poplar depot, commenced on Monday 10th June 1940 working from Poplar to Bloomsbury. No routes ran on Saturday night/Sunday morning. Due to Hammersmith Grove becoming only available to trolleybuses from the west, the 628 terminus at Hammersmith was altered about October 1946. Vehicles were extended along King Street to turn by way of Studland Street, which required a trolley swing and was the only such instance on the night services. There was a connection on night route 630 for 2.29am at Tooting Broadway with the 630 staff trolleybus to West Croydon; it was the only maintained connection between night and staff trolleybuses.

Routes 612 and 628 last operated on Saturday 30th September 1950. On Monday 2nd October 1950, night route 630 from Hammersmith depot was introduced, between Tooting Broadway and Hammersmith Broadway; it did not operate on Saturday nights and, like the 628, the terminus at Hammersmith was in Studland Street. The final change to the night services was that the 630 terminus in Hammersmith was revised from Monday 14th July 1958 to turn at Butterwick due to a new road layout at Hammersmith.

On Coronation Day 1953, night services operated to about 15 minute headways with increased allocations; 543/643 with seven vehicles had the highest number of vehicles ever allocated to night services on one night. An oddity was that the last 630 journey went to Clapham Junction before returning to Hammersmith depot. At Hampstead, the 513 was shown as operating, although traversing both ways round the Holborn loop. No doubt 613 was displayed for journeys via Farringdon Road. On New Year's Eve 1960, extra journeys were run on 629 from Wood Green to Enfield, 649 Liverpool Street to Edmonton, 659 Manor House to Ponders End and 662 Paddington to Sudbury, with the last of these being a 659 from Manor House to Ponders End at 1.10am. These were the only known additions to night work. Services operated through Christmas night apart from the occasions when Christmas Day fell on a Sunday; from the routes' mid-life, services finished by about 3.30am by which time day services were starting.

The first night route to be withdrawn in the trolleybus conversion programme was route 665 which last operated on 10th November 1959. Route 630 last worked on 19th July 1960. Next to go were routes 513/613 on 31st January 1961 with the last night trolleybus journeys operating on routes 543/643 on 18th July 1961.

STAFF TROLLEYBUSES

A very interesting but little known aspect of trolleybus operation was the network of staff trolleybuses. Their purpose was to take staff near to their homes after they had finished work and to pick them up for early shifts. They were crewed by staff who either worked a complete duty as a staff trolleybus or who worked the duty as partly staff work and partly passenger work. Similarly, the trolleybus itself might be used totally on staff work or partly on staff work and partly on passenger work; most staff trolleybuses returned to the depot during the night for crew relief. In a number of cases, as with night trolleybuses, a regular but elderly crew permanently worked these duties as there was an element of easement with this work. As a conductor had to be carried to operate overhead frogs, it was deemed that he might as well take what revenue was in the offing, so these journeys were available to the public; it is also thought that the police insisted on a conductor being carried. Some journeys became well known, particularly the late night ones; in the case of Edmonton depot, a Saturday night journey which was advertised as finishing at Tramway Avenue but continuing to Waltham Cross, became so well known to members of the public that an extra staff trolleybus had to be laid on specially for the staff!

It was for the reason of not inconveniencing the staff that staff trolleybuses were not advertised in the public timetable (though there was a pre-war example at Fulwell). This has also been the case with the tram and bus staff transport. With the operation of staff trolleybuses, the system was open 24 hours a day. To save a lot of route-blind changing, EXTRA or a specific route number was displayed throughout the night and gave rise to 521/621 appearing at Cricklewood. There were a few direct journeys made by staff trolleybuses which were not made by daytime services: Twickenham to Kingston Loop via Hampton Court, Chingford Mount to Woodford, Lea Bridge Depot to West India Docks, 'Nags Head' Holloway to Willesden Green and a Sunday 521 operated from Holborn Circus to Barnet.

Staff trams had operated (there tended to be complaints from residents about the noise they made during the middle of the night) and this facility was perpetuated with the trolleybuses, the number of staff trolleybuses being gradually built up over the years. During the war these journeys acted in a dual capacity, for they catered for night munition workers; at Waltham Abbey, workers were able to take the staff trolleybus from Waltham Cross.

Most depots had just one vehicle allocated to staff work, although some had more, but on a Saturday night Edmonton had no fewer than four trolleybuses scuttling around. Not every depot had a staff trolleybus – Lea Bridge and Wood Green did not. In the former case the staff work was carried out by Clapton and in the latter case by Finchley and staff motorbuses in the area. Stamford Hill only operated on a Sunday morning (Edmonton covered much of their territory). Staff journeys often ran one hour later on a Sunday morning due to the general later start of services. The timings and routeings changed very little over the years; the main changes arising from requests by the staff to meet different requirements. Many workings made connections with other staff trolleybuses, originally known as staff cars, a terminology handed down from the trams.

A number of unusual occurrences happened with this type of operation. The night was the time when overhead line renewal took place and the power would have to be switched off. To accommodate the few nocturnal trolleybuses that were operating in such vicinities, a breakdown tender would tow trolleybuses through any section that was being worked upon. One night this was happening northbound at Enfield Highway. After the last advertised journey had passed through the power was switched off, although it was known that staff trolleybuses would need to be towed through the section and consequently a pole carrier was stationed here for this. One of these was the same journey mentioned in the first paragraph of this chapter and in this instance just one staff trolleybus was being used. As there were more people than could be carried on the trolleybus who wished to make the journey, they were carried in a tower wagon specially laid on for the purpose of carrying the excess passengers, to the point beyond the rewiring. At Enfield Highway the pole carrier was hitched to the front of the trolleybus to tow it to a live section of wire; so great was the weight of the trolleybus that in its initial attempt to move the vehicle, the front wheels of the pole carrier were lifted off the ground! On another occasion the Colindale staff trolleybus was hurtling back from Barnet when the driver failed to observe some roadworks at Whetstone. The bumpy road surface caused the trolleys to shoot off the wires and unfortunately for the driver, a bamboo pole was not being carried beneath the vehicle; this led to the driver, conductor and the solitary passenger clambering onto the roof of the vehicle to rewire the trolley arms! It was the

only time that the driver did not claim an overtime docket for a late arrival at the depot! Staff journeys tended to be taken at breakneck speed and one night the Isleworth vehicle dewired at Isleworth fire station when returning to the depot from Brentford, waking up a number of nearby residents including one of the drivers on a very early shift next morning. Staff trolleybuses were also used by the staff for their own domestic purposes and many an odd item of furniture has been carried around during the night to get it to a member of staff's home. Literally in the middle of the night, three trolleybuses used the quiet Warlters Road while turning at the 'Nags Head' Holloway. At quieter locations such as Twickenham, Fulwell Junction and Kingston, where the staff trolleybus was the only vehicle in the vicinity, once the overhead frog had been negotiated, the semi-automatic frog would be pulled for the next journey, to save stepping out again.

A rather odd aspect of these journeys was that the same running time was given for them as given for the daytime peak hour services. Some turns could be rather unpleasant for the crews in the blackout and in winter, for trolley swings, battery movements or battery/gravity manoeuvres were required. Between February and April 1960, the West Ham staff trolleybus working to the now closed Lea Bridge depot had to perform most of this manoeuvre on battery power, as much of the overhead had been dismantled. The facility of allowing members of the public to ride was not continued upon the withdrawal of the trolleybuses, although in the instance of the Ilford runnings, some very late night journeys were added to the new bus timetable and at West Ham the staff journeys were made into a new night bus route. There were some instances in the conversion programme of the last vehicle into a depot being the staff trolleybus. Staff trolleybuses continued until the last day of operation in London.

REVERSERS

Only three reversers existed on the system, each being of a different configuration. The first to be introduced was at Anerley, Versailles Road which had come into operation by 1940. The second to be brought into use was at Plumstead Station which was installed in the spring of 1941. That at Crayford, Princes Road was the last to be commissioned, in 1942; Crayford and Plumstead had previously been battery reverse points. That at Anerley was useful not only for turning late running vehicles but for curtailing the service when snow and ice prevented the ascent of Anerley Hill; it was also used during the war when damage occurred to the overhead. There was only one scheduled turn here during its entire life, being the first 654 on Coronation Day 1953 which turned at 2.52am. Drivers did not always use the total amount of wire available to them here as the turning arrangements were quite awkward. A trolley swing was required before reversing and some drivers just lowered the poles, reversed by a combination of gravity and battery power and replaced the poles in the wiring stub; assistance was given to drivers in the form of 'fairy lights' on part of the reversing wire. Crayford reverser was constructed due to an increase of work at Vickers factory during the war. Consequently their employees had to be transported; trolleybuses had to reverse across the main road here. At Plumstead, vehicles moved to the left while still paralleling the main line wires before reversing into Griffin Road. Many scheduled journeys were made at Crayford and Plumstead.

London Transport stated initially that the 'triangular turns', as they described them, were successful. However, no more were constructed and problems were encountered at Plumstead, where two booms were pulled out of trolley bases in 1947. Incidents such as this may have prevented other battery turns from having reversers installed. Places such as Holly Park would have benefited from one. A suggestion was made in March 1947 that lights should be installed at all reversers but this was not proceeded with. Similarly a proposal for a reverser costing £396 at March Road, Twickenham was not pursued. Strangely enough, all three reversers came out of use after the traffic day of Tuesday 3rd March 1959 when the three routes involved, 654, 696 and 698, were withdrawn at stage one of the trolleybus conversion programme. The last use of a reverser was in the early hours of Wednesday 4th March 1959, when vehicle 405B used the one at Plumstead. It was a 696 staff trolleybus but returned via route 698 to Bexleyheath Market Place and the depot.

766B, displaying the erroneous 'PRINCESS ROAD' blind display, has just completed the reversing manoeuvre at Crayford: 390B, working as a 698 to Abbey Wood, is about to embark on the same manoeuvre. An inspector supervised reversing movements and departure times for the six evening peak hour journeys that reversed here for the benefit of Vickers works employees. Denis Battams

Far Left **The reversing stub at Anerley is clearly visible in this view in Versailles Road; 68 passes on its way to Crystal Palace. Undoubtedly the most unusual use of this or any reverser was that of a Q1 from Fulwell depot that turned here on training duties. The instructor was conversant enough with the trolleybus system not to allow it to ascend Anerley Hill.** J.H. Price

Left **431 has just reversed into Griffin Road, Plumstead. Would that be a young Steve Davis casting a sideways glance at the small amount of wiring in the reverser stub?** Denis Battams

BATTERY MOVEMENTS

All vehicles from 62-1891, apart from the SA classes, were fitted with traction batteries to give manoeuvrability in depots and flexibility around obstructions which could occur in service. It was claimed that a trolleybus could travel for half a mile on its traction batteries, albeit slowly, if they were fully charged; these batteries were also used for lighting and bell signals. Drivers changed from trolley to battery operation by placing a reverser key in a trolley/battery changeover switch. An interlock ensured that battery and trolley operation worked independently. Drivers had to place the circuit breakers, control switch and motor generator switch in the OFF position before operating the battery changeover switch. Movement occurred by the driver placing his left foot on a special pedal; forward and reverse was available. Rule 79 of the rulebook stated that an entry was to be made

on the vehicle's defect sheet each time the battery was used. There were many places where bus stops were situated at section breakers and no matter how experienced a driver was, there were occasions when he would get stuck on one of these 'dead' sections; he would then use the battery to move the vehicle up a few inches.

In the early years of the system, approval was given for many short working points to be used for battery operation but a number were soon given up; some, however, were later wired up. In the main, battery short workings were infrequently used but were retained for emergencies. The battery facility was a good feature, enabling vehicles to turn in side streets. This was particularly useful during the war and at times of power failure and overhead damage; it also enabled vehicles to be turned short of a terminus to cover a gap

in service in the opposite direction. Many battery workings were not included on the destination blinds and in such situations the nearest available display or a blank display was used with the conductor informing passengers of the destination. Most battery turns had disappeared from the blinds by the early post-war period and only three were included later, due to their frequent use. These were at 'Goldhawk Road YOUNGS CORNER', 'WALTHAMSTOW Sinnott Road' and 'HOLLY PARK' but not all blinds became fitted with these displays.

Above **398 turns at Clyde Road (Victoria Docks). Despite heavy peak hour use it was not fully wired until 1953 and until then this manoeuvre, although supervised, was rather dangerous. Unfortunately 398 was destroyed at Bexleyheath depot in June 1944.** Charles Klapper

Top **An obscure side road was the means of turning at Walthamstow Sinnott Road. It was a battery turn and 625 travels down Blackhorse Lane to join line of route at Billet Road.** David Packer

Above **Due to a power failure in Hendon on 23rd December 1961, trolleybus 1569 has been curtailed at Holly Park. Conductor Sharville is (a) in action with his bamboo pole and (b) in typical trolleybus stance of bamboo slung over shoulder and cigarette in mouth, watching Driver Armitage reverse 1569 safely into Fitzalan Road.** Peter Moore

Some battery turns embraced a reverse manoeuvre while others would circle a traffic island or roundabout. A battery turn agreed locally with the staff was at Cricklewood, Gillingham Road; there was no short working facility at Cricklewood for vehicles travelling from Harlesden, so this turn was brought into use. Some crews, however, turned at St Gabriels Church rather than cross Cricklewood Broadway and this was also done on battery power. It is believed that the battery manoeuvre of vehicle 1595 on route 666 at Gillingham Road on the night of 2nd January 1962 was the last battery turn on the system as the remaining routes' short working facilities were by wire. Some locations used part battery/part wire manoeuvring, such as Fortess Walk and Kew Bridge from the west. The battery facility also enabled wired turns to be used from the wrong direction, e.g. Golders Green and Turnpike Lane Stations, and Claughton Road, West Ham ('Boleyn'). Holly Park was used very regularly on Friday evenings, for 660s tended to get held up in traffic on that day of the week; one after another, 660s turned here, and some Stonebridge drivers became so skilled with their vehicles that they manoeuvred them on the wires until they were at right angles with them. It was only then that the poles were pulled down briefly by their conductors and a quick tap on the battery pedal brought them back to the wires on the other side of the road. HOLLY PARK appeared on destination blinds issued from April 1960 and had appeared on five line side displays; its use on blinds is intriguing (it appeared on tram destination blinds) for Holly Park is a side road and not an area, although the GPO used it internally.

At the Victory in Europe celebrations, 8th June 1946, all London Transport road services were turned short of a specific area while these took place and trolleybuses had to undertake a number of battery manoeuvres that were applicable on this day only; special arrangements were made with the appropriate authorities. They were:

513, 613, 615, 639 southbound at Pancras Road, Platt Street.

513, 517, 521, 613, 617, 621, 659 northbound at Swinton Street. – this was a very short journey and from the wrong direction.

517, 521, 617, 621, 659 southbound at Canal Bridge, Caledonian Road.

543, 643, 647, 649 southbound at Downham Road – wrong direction.

555, 557, 653 southbound at Westgate Street – wrong direction.

611, 641, 683 southbound at Chart Street.

627, 629, 653 southbound at Cobden Statue.

661, 663 westbound at Tredegar Square.

565, 567, 569, 665 were turned short at Arbour Square and 581, 609, 677 and 679 were turned short at Islington Green, but these were performed in the normal manner; the curtailment of northbound vehicles at Swinton Street enabled a shuttle service to be worked inside the closed area. The restriction at Cobden Statue was from sunrise whilst all the others came into operation at approximately 7.30am except those at Arbour Square, Tredegar Square and Westgate Street which occurred at approximately 8.30am. As soon as the celebrations were over, normal services were resumed. There were similar temporary curtailments when the Coronation was being celebrated in 1953.

NON-SERVICE MOVEMENTS

Apart from trials at Hendon works, Haydons Road in Wimbledon and West Ham, the first movement of a trolleybus under power was on 1st October 1930 when a demonstrator was tested over the newly strung overhead in the Twickenham area.

When each trolleybus route was due to be opened it had to be approved by the Ministry of Transport and Civil Aviation; each route was tested with a six-wheel vehicle beforehand. When each new trolleybus was delivered to Fulwell works, it was road tested in the locality. Prior to tram to trolleybus conversions batches of vehicles were forwarded to depots, sometimes in convoy.

No.1768 was tested on Highgate Hill in the early 1950s carrying some experimental equipment, while 1856, after accident repair at Charlton works, was tested on the isolated Bexleyheath network; this gives rise to thoughts of what other vehicles might have been used there. When the 'Diddlers' were withdrawn from training duties in 1951 they made their way under power to Finchley depot.

A little known operation that took place was the running of what were known by the staff as 'frost buses' which operated when a heavy frost took place. The depot night foreman would approach the traffic department and make a request for a number of volunteer drivers to operate trolleybuses all night so as to keep the wires clean and prevent them icing up; the number of vehicles used depended on the severity of the frost. "Ice cutting wheels will only be used in extremely severe conditions owing to the harmful effect these have on the surface of the wires" was an instruction given to supervisory staff. Each driver was allocated a section of route operated by the depot and would ply that particular section until it was time for the service trolleybuses to operate. Some depots used 'driver only' operation and each time a semi-automatic frog was encountered, the driver would step out and operate it himself. In the case of manual frogs he would coast past the apparatus and then swing the trolleys to the correct wires – the bamboo pole was slid inside the lower saloon to avoid constant bending down! Other depots used a two man crew. Different arrangements were in force at some depots where a trolleybus with 'iron' skids would run a few minutes in front of the first service vehicle on each route. Other precautions taken on frosty nights were for night trolleybuses to carry a supply of sand and for first trolleybuses to carry a supply of salt and sand.

Transferring vehicles between depots and from Fulwell and West Ham works after overhaul was carried out by a two-man

18th July 1961; trolleybuses 1344 and 1343 from Edmonton depot pass through Cricklewood Broadway on their way to the storage lines in Colindale depot. It was all rather sad: in the afternoon working on the 649 — in the evening just waiting for a visit to the scrapyard. Sid Hagarty

engineering staff, with the drivers holding a Group 8 (trolley vehicle) driving licence. Vehicles overhauled at Charlton works were towed the whole way. This was also the case at Bexleyheath whenever replacements were required. The transfer of withdrawn trolleybuses, particularly on conversion nights was also carried out by the engineering staff.

Vehicles had to be road tested after repair or adjustment at their depot and a short trip to the nearest terminus or turning loop would be made: Lea Bridge depot would go to Woodford, Clapton depot to Dalston Lane, Queensbridge Road, Highgate depot to Parliament Hill Fields and Isleworth and Hanwell depots to Brentford, Half Acre. A piece of overhead used solely by the engineering staff for testing purposes was at 'The Nelson', Fulwell, which enabled vehicles to be taken from the Stanley Road entrance of Ful-

well depot to the Wellington Road entrance. Sometimes many more than the required two-man crew went on these excursions, which tended to take place at lunchtime, with these 'outings' taking far longer than was necessary! There was also the need for vehicles to be changed over on the road when a minor defect occurred, but if this was not on the vehicle's route then the engineering staff would take a replacement to the nearest point. Sometimes a trolleybus would be taken as the means of travel to reach a stranded vehicle and Highgate would take a 'Diddler' which was kept in the depot.

The last miscellaneous movement of all took place on the final night of operation when 1521 was driven by a member of the engineering staff from Fulwell depot to Hampton Court where it was to take up service as London's last trolleybus.

It was decided in June 1961 that all unsold Q1s should be transferred to Poplar garage for storage before the Kingsland Road wires were de-energised (vehicles were towed to Poplar from Shoreditch); only the 'Zarragoza' batch did not use trade plates, running on their current tax discs. 1839 heads for Zarragoza, eastern Spain at Harlesden, Jubilee Clock on 27th April 1961 while 1378, one of four L2s allocated to Stonebridge depot for much of 1961, heads for Paddington. 1839 survived to be preserved by Zarragoza Tramways; 1378 received a one-way ticket to Colindale. Tony Belton

DELAYS AND DEWIREMENTS

Above Left **The proverbial 'stuck up the creek without a paddle' applies to the driver of 1230 whose poles have jumped the points at Manor House. He obviously had not checked to see if there was a bamboo pole beneath 1230 when he took it over. He now embarrassingly waits for another trolleybus to arrive so that he can borrow a pole.** Peter Moore

Above Right **1231 has dewired on leaving Waltham Cross terminus. The driver would have been unable to leave the lay by at any speed, so there is no apparent reason why this should have occurred. It's a nice day, so replacing the trolley arms will just be a matter of course; however, in driving rain, this was not a popular task.** Ron Lunn

Trolleybuses, like the trams before them, were reliant on an external source, that of electricity, and at times became victims of their very nature. Services could be held up by a power failure or overhead wire break while damage to overhead collector gear could immobilise the vehicle itself. However, the number of failures due to these causes was small compared to the mileage operated. The London United Tramways used trolley wheels but with the formation of the London Passenger Transport Board, the use of trolley heads commenced and continued to be used successfully.

Notices were regularly issued to staff, in order to minimise dewirements and damage to overhead:

'It is important that controllers should be shut off when passing under special work.

Much damage can be avoided by strictly observing this instruction.'

'Dewirement at frogs is caused by: (1) not continuing to press the push button at automatic frogs until the mechanism has operated; (2) pulling the handle at a manual frog before the preceding bus has cleared the junction in the overhead wires. Every effort must be made to prevent dewirements.'

London Transport has always placed a priority on mileage operated and went to great lengths to identify and remedy failures and problems that affected the trams and trolleybuses. Three different reports regularly appeared: (1) Trolley Collection and Equipment: Defects Committee, (2) Delays and Special Occurrences and (3) Delays Investigation Committee.

The Trolley Collection and Equipment

Defects Committee met monthly; damaged equipment would be inspected (mainly trolley heads) and suggestions were made to reduce or eliminate failures. Concern was regularly expressed at the number of trolley heads which had received heavy blows, particularly at overhead special work (junctions and frogs) implying that excessive speed was occurring at these points (the speed regulation was 5 mph over all frogs and crossings). Reference was made to the force required to damage trolley collector material.

Each dewirement was supposed to be reported on a 'REPORT OF DEWIREMENT' form but if there was no apparent damage to the overhead equipment or trolley booms, generally no report was made, particularly if the incident had not been witnessed by an official.

1642 already curtailed at Paddenswick Road, suffers a further delay in Horn Lane, Acton; its poles are bent and the negative traction wire has come away from a hanger.... 1660, with badly turned route and destination blinds, cautiously negotiates the obstruction under the watchful eye of an inspector. Peter Moore

In most cases there was no damage, but sometimes damage to trolley heads went unobserved and only showed up later, to the chagrin of another driver. Similarly, overhead damage could go unobserved and it would be another driver who would be the unsuspecting victim; 'Previous overhead damage' was a regular term that was used when assessing the cause. If a driver could "get away with it" he would do, as happened at Friern Barnet on the last but one trolleybus one night. The conductor of the vehicle was wanting a lift home on a specific trolleybus and urged the driver to get to Finchley depot early. A dewirement occurred resulting in the running wires becoming detached from the supporting hangers. There was only minimal damage to the booms (stripped insulating tape) and the conductor urged the driver on and succeeded in making his connection. At Finchley depot the driver waited in the shadows for the last trolleybus to arrive and asked the driver if he had experienced a problem at Friern Barnet. He said that he too had dewired, so they both went to the traffic office to say that they had both been victims of a previously unreported dewirement!

London Transport continually issued notices for all dewirements to be reported but these continued to be ignored by drivers. However, there were times when a dewirement would not be due to the fault of a driver, as the tension on a trolley boom could slacken off and consequently would continually dewire. In such circumstances a vehicle would be run into the depot for adjustment as otherwise damage would eventually occur. An example of non-adjustment occurred with vehicle 1057 at Isleworth depot, whose staff normally were very good with their maintenance. Following a dewirement on 7th May 1962, the booms had been straightened, but no check had been made on the tension. Consequently on the last evening of operation, 8th May 1962, the vehicle bent both booms under Isleworth Station Bridge and as such was the last occasion for a breakdown wagon to be called out to deal with a London trolleybus. When boom straightening had been necessary in quick succession then the tension was checked, but of course this did not happen on 9th May! When attention was needed following a dewirement, a driver would phone Control: Hackney in the north and Oval (Camberwell before the outbreak of war) in the south by means of one of the phones installed in the top of feeder boxes, to which access was available by a special key.

'Trolley collisions' were in two categories: deliberate and unintentional. In the former case, a driver would overtake a vehicle so as to get into a required position; a 649 driver doing this on the last day. It was a matter of conjecture whether both vehicles or a single vehicle would dewire in these situations. In the latter case an example is given of a driver having his stand time at Edgware and who noted the last 142 bus of the day head down the Edgware Road. He set off on his journey and noticed what he thought was the 142 waiting at the stop two away from Colindale depot. However, the '142' turned out to be a trolleybus which was sitting out a couple of minutes before entering the depot for the night. Night speeds tend to be faster than day speeds, particularly when the crew were near to finishing time and the resultant dewirements of both vehicles needed attention to heads and booms in the depot that night.

Dewirements were also caused due to vagaries of the weather. In excessive heat the wires could expand and sag, causing trolley booms to leave the overhead. Similarly, in extreme cold, frost would cause frogs to ice up and freeze and not operate properly; crews would be unaware of this and dewirements could occur. Irregularly used points, although attended to by the overhead department, could become sluggish, with the same result. Dewirements occurred at feeders where a wooden insulator broke the running wires into the required half-mile electrical sections; by taking these too fast a dewirement could occur as the smoothness of the wire was temporarily broken. If a driver positioned himself incorrectly under the wires, overtook rapidly rather than gradually or if booms became outstretched trying to pass obstructions (roadworks and parked cars) the inevitable dewirement occurred; there were also times when a hand frog did not return to its proper position and a driver would be unaware of this. Obstructions were sometimes passed by use of the battery or by placing the booms on the wires in the opposite direction. At places where booms were regularly going through upstairs windows, principally junctions, mesh guard wires were strung between traction standards to prevent such damage. This did not completely arrest the problem as booms still tended to find their way through this mesh, with top floor windows at Seven Sisters Road, 'Nags Head' being regular victims. At known dewirement spots, spare bamboo poles were placed for ease of reach. Some of these were placed there by the crews while others were hung on a rail at the top of a traction standard and retained in a clasp near its base. At times bamboo poles would be discarded and left in the gutter and often these were run over and flattened by other road traffic. This may have been due to the fact that the pole could not be replaced in its position beneath the vehicle due to other road traffic immediately behind. Discarded bamboos, either hanging from traction standards of those laying in the road, would be retrieved by crews who became aware that their vehicle was not carrying one. An incident in the blackout is recounted of a driver removing a bamboo pole the wrong way round – the way everybody did it with their back to the road. A police inspector running to the scene of an air raid tripped over the pole and fell flat on his face; he remained forever mystified as to the cause, for the driver had run off with the bamboo in the darkness.

Dewirements also occurred on entering or leaving bridges, for in many instances the wiring was brought downwards to pass underneath the bridge. It was more likely to happen on leaving the bridge, as drivers would accelerate too quickly as the booms rose; caution was required under bridges. Some drivers, when running early, would deliberately dewire so as to lose a bit of time. They got to know the locations where booms would dewire and not cause any damage. One Colindale driver would regularly do this northbound at Jubilee Clock, Harlesden. He normally worked with a conductress, so rewiring was left to him. On one of these occasions though, he was paired with a conductor, who had the trolleybus rewired very quickly. Further time-wasting practices were then required further along route 666.

It was not uncommon to see the lights of light standards, even those erected to replace trolleybus traction poles, broken by booms and even lights on light standards at pedestrian crossings became victims of trolley booms. Booms became bent by hitting span wires, heavy overhead work or traction standards. A danger when a dewirement occurred was that a flaying boom could go through a passing trolleybus top window; this was extremely rare. Another effect could be that vibration would knock off another vehicle's booms.

Trolley pole collisions normally occurred at junctions and staff had to be particularly aware that when parked on loop wires, both trolleys were not fouling the main line. When fouling did occur the result could be quite dramatic. When dewirements took place both trolleys normally left the wire; however, when a single trolley dewirement occurred the other trolley was often knocked off due to vibration or being hit by the dewired trolley. There were times when dewirements could not be avoided, such as in the case of having to brake sharply to avoid a child running into the road, which could cause the booms to leave the wires. In fact one driver from Isleworth who had been driving trolleybuses for many years, had a Q1 dewire on him for this reason and although there was no damage, it was the only occasion in his entire trolleybus driving life that he had dewired.

When a dewirement did occur, upstairs passengers were very aware of this as there was a hefty noise from above; this was then followed by a rumbling sound from underneath as the bamboo pole was withdrawn from its holder. There was no electrical danger when a dewirement occurred, although upon a dewirement in Surbiton the author observed two young children running from the top of the vehicle shouting "Get off, it's live" which of course was not the case. Conductors of smaller stature sometimes had difficulty in rewiring vehicles, for having retrieved an errant trolley boom, they would find themselves supported by the bamboo pole, at a 45° angle to the ground.

The overhead department regularly inspected all the overhead, but things could be missed, as occurred at a section breaker in Brentford. Many vehicles were suffering bad dewirements because a wooden runner had worn out. This was due to drivers taking it with power on when they should have momentarily paused and the runner became burnt out. Consequently a new wooden runner bar had to be inserted on 7th May 1962 and had just two days use! Minor overhead defects which went unobserved caused dewirements and in such circumstances no blame was incurred by the driver. It should be stressed, however, that most dewirements occurred at special work although another regular cause was attributable to new drivers being unfamiliar with overhead layouts. Any driver responsible for overhead damage or who was the first to observe any damage, would remain at the scene to warn and help other vehicles.

London Transport considered that trolley wires falling to the ground was a serious matter and justifiably so, as it could be dangerous. When this occurred, and it was only rarely, the following instructions had to be followed: 'If the body of the trolleybus concerned is in contact with the fallen wire, the vehicle must be driven by means of the battery, close to the kerb and away from the wire before the passengers alight. If the fallen wire is in contact with any person and rubber gloves are not immediately available, a dry stock, dry rope or any article of dry clothing may be used to drag the person away from the wire or the wire away from the person.' When wires did fall they could drape over the vehicle or would curl up on the ground. Rubber gloves were held in a wooden emergency box in the driver's cab with other articles of equipment. Two anecdotes of falling wires can be recounted. A Highgate driver was at a stop in Seven Sisters Road when another trolleybus overtook his vehicle; he just had to stay in the cab until the fallen wires had been cleared away. (The same driver, when he had only been driving trolleybuses for two weeks, pulled almost the entire junction down at Manor House and it took the tower wagon staff the whole day to put it up again.) He was surpassed by a Stonebridge driver who on his first day by himself as a trolleybus driver, 'pulled the lot down' outside the depot on his first journey.

Regularly discussed was the fact of an increase or decrease in 'pulled heads' – whereby a trolley head had become detached from a trolley boom and had caught in a span wire, fallen to the ground or was hanging by its retaining rope to the boom. What were termed as 'heads to ground' were always a matter of concern and the improvement or deterioration of the situation was regularly expressed and monitored. An infrequent occurrence was when both trolley heads became detached from the trolley arms, and in the period from 1947-1951 this was only recorded as happening six times. 'Heads to ground' could have serious results of trolley heads falling on cars and even people, although such occurrences were extremely rare. These incidents however, did have a lighter side in that the crew, at times, had to go searching for trolley heads. One embedded itself so heavily into the ground in Caledonian Road that it had to be dug out with a spade, while one which went through a bedroom window at Kingston, entailed the driver having to confront a young lady in her nightdress! – he literally had to go and retrieve the trolley head from the bedroom. One trolley head lost at Childs Hill was not found despite an extensive search by the crew. It was later returned to a local depot by someone who had found it in their front garden.

Trolleybuses came out of Southbury Road into Hertford Road at Ponders End too fast and dewirements caused both poles to swing round, and to regularly knock off a pair of concrete eagles on pedestals on the pillar of a house called 'Eagle House'. The dewirement of trolleybus 1319 in early September 1959 was so violent that the nearside gantry was partly pulled off its base, pulling part of the roof out of the body. It was immediately withdrawn for scrapping.

When booms were bent, the breakdown wagon would attend and the crew would straighten the booms with a 'Jimmy Crow' boom straightener; they would replace heads if necessary and booms would be re-taped with insulating tape. A near catastrophe occurred to trolleybus 1521 on 8th May 1962. It was being driven out of the depot onto the Stanley Road forecourt prior to positioning for the afternoon ceremonial run, when the positive boom became badly bent upon dewiring. Specifically chosen to be London's last trolleybus, it HAD to be repaired as the special advertisements and blinds had already been fitted.

Damage within depots was usually minimal. Due to vehicles' generally slow speed, when dewirements occurred the booms normally lodged themselves gently in the wooden troughing or the girders of the building. At Isleworth depot, a single trolley was often dewired as it passed through the special opening for the overhead in the depot doors when vehicles were being drawn onto the parking area and the entrance to Stamford Hill depot still bears the score marks of dewired trolley booms in the brickwork as drivers hurried in.

Vehicles would sometimes enter the depot with scuffed tapes (known as 'flags flying' to the staff) and drivers would give a member of the maintenance staff a florin (10 new pence) to straighten and tape the booms. This would be a sound investment and avoided making out a report and seeing the chief depot inspector. From time to time, trolley booms could become splayed at frogs, with one boom taking the intended wire and the other not doing so, but this was quickly remedied by the use of the bamboo pole. Occasionally, a driver would over-run a frog and in these situations he would either reverse or swing the poles with the aid of the bamboo pole. There were times too, when a semi-automatic frog would be pulled in an unauthorised manner. With this type of frog, the driver with the frog in his favour would not expect it to be against him and anything out of the norm could go unobserved. If he was attentive enough, he might realise the fault before the frog or just afterwards, in which case the trolleys could be swung onto the right wires. However, trolleys on wrong lines and running into bad dewirements did occur and could be quite severe as the booms would be going into a completely different direction to the vehicle. Broken booms and trolley booms being pulled out of their bases were considered to be very serious incidents but were rare.

There were times when trolley arms, upon dewiring, would come to rest so high, that it was not possible for a crew member to retrieve them. Recourse was then made in one of two ways: a) the vehicle would be moved up on battery power so that the booms would be lowered into a rewiring position by a span wire or other piece of overhead equipment, or b) another trolleybus would be stopped for the use of its bamboo pole. One bamboo pole hook would be placed as near to the top of the arm as was feasible, and while as much force as was possible was exerted on pulling down this arm, the other bamboo pole hook was then placed near to the trolley head and the vehicle would eventually be rewired.

Dewirements were an everyday occurrence on the system and happened right up until the final evening of operation. At times the bizarre could be encountered, with a boom dewiring and then rewiring itself. An account was related to the author of a Holborn Circus bound 659 at the junction of Holloway Road and Caledonian Road. The semi-automatic frog had been set erroneously and consequently the driver was not expecting this and had not looked at the frog light signal; the inevitable dewirement occurred with both booms bouncing off the wrong lines but both returning to the correct ones!

Sometimes drivers had been misled into overtaking other trolleybuses by failing to observe a trolleybus in front of a motorbus that they were overtaking. Dewirements did, however, occur even at the regulation speed of 5mph over special work, but it could be difficult to convince an official of this, as it could also be difficult to convince them that

dewirements had occurred on straight track for no reason. On conversion nights, many vehicles suffered dewirements due to ferry staff being in unfamiliar territory and even on the journey to the scrapyard, vehicles would protest at their destination by dewiring. There were times when a dewirement would occur and a bamboo pole was not to be found in its holder beneath the vehicle. Some drivers were brave enough to clamber onto the roof to rewire errant booms.

Although regarded as a nuisance by passengers and crew but as a spectacle to the onlooker, most dewirements were quickly rectified. Power failures were the main delaying factor, but these did not occur regularly. After such delays, drivers were expected to set off singly, as otherwise a section would be overloaded and the power would be cut off again; unfortunately this practice persisted with some staff who wanted to lose further mileage. When hold-ups occurred, a build-up of vehicles soon happened, such were the frequencies of the services, but the small numbers of delays overall can be measured by the following statistics. An average of 11,878 miles per dewirement for a 28-day period was typical as was an average of 6,007,272 miles run with only 513 reported dewirements.

Topics discussed included why there was excessive carbon wear on particular stretches and why there were voltage variations. In 1947, difficulties were encountered with low voltage in the Fulwell area and high voltage in the Malden, Kingston and Crystal Palace areas. At one time only 400 volts could be obtained in the Kingston area when 600 volts was required and this led to low-speed running. Flooding under Barnehurst Bridge was a popular topic for discussion. Many bridges, where there was a dip in the road, caused problems due to the accumulation of water and while drivers were told not to drive through floodwater they would do so, particularly if they were about to finish their day's work. If the water was higher than the bottom edge of the lifeguard slat (rule 78) they were not to proceed. Drivers were also instructed that in all cases of driving through floods, the speed must not exceed walking pace and trolleybuses should be kept as near to the crown of the road as possible, which was to avoid the motors being flooded and having to be dried out.

Drivers came in for special scrutiny by the committee and one reason was for using spare fuses for packing their driving seats to make the driving position higher. Six depots (BW, FY, HT, PR, WH, WW) were identified; steps were taken for this practice to cease.

The committee had positive thoughts and put forward many constructive suggestions so that the trolleybus services would run more smoothly. One suggestion was that semi-automatic frogs, many of which were already in operation, should replace the push-button type of frog. (The buttons were located on special posts or on traction standards). They had come into criticism because the buttons

tended to spring out and although a driver had read the signal light correctly (a direction light in a box situated on a forward traction pole) it would then return to an incorrect position. However, push-button frogs did survive in a few places, including that at Twickenham which lasted until 8th May 1962. With the semi-automatic (whereby the conductor pulled a lever fixed to a traction standard and returned to his vehicle before it passed the frog) and push-button variety, the frog became set for a different track from that programmed. Having passed the points, the trolley head made contact with a re-set skate which would be on either positive or negative wire, returning the track to its normal position. A manual frog meant that the conductor had to 'pull and hold' a handle, normally situated on a traction standard, until the trolleys had safely negotiated the points.

Other possibilities examined by the committee were the use of trolley retrievers which would have pulled booms down to near roof level at dewirements, anti-swing devices which would have prevented booms from flaying too far and the possibility of lights being provided for changing carbons in trolley heads. None of these suggestions was taken up.

The Delays and Special Occurrences Committee met monthly. Main reasons for delay were sub-station faults (sometimes the fault of the London Electricity Board), overhead damage and bunching of vehicles. There was an unusual cause on 24th January 1951 at 11.20pm at Green Lanes, Palmers Green where damage to overhead equipment was caused by a lorry with a high load. Further damage was caused by the same lorry at 5.15am the following morning at Silvertown Way, North Woolwich, causing dislocation of trolleybus services.

Delays were often for just a few minutes but there were times when they might be as long as 90 minutes. Such long delays were unusual and it was not often that a trolleybus was at fault. As an example, on 25th March 1961, a motor car collided with the feeder pillar in Chesnut Road, Tottenham, causing 37 northbound trolleybuses and 24 southbound trolleybuses to line up together until power was restored from an adjacent section. Astute juggling of the crews and vehicles by inspectors got the services back to normal. When a power failure occurred vehicles would just come to rest. This would normally be just over one section and at the feeder leading to that section all further trolleybuses would bank up. One dodge practised was to delay a preceding trolleybus was to pull in at a stop, pull the handbrake hard on and then depress the power pedal to its full extent, thus depriving the preceding vehicle of full power. This would then struggle at slow speed until it reached the next feeder and full power was available again. The following trolleybus, whose crew wanted an easy time, would then get into this section and the scenario was repeated!

Examples of delays are listed below:

10th January 1949. Dewirement of trolley-bus 429 at Erith, pulled trolley wire to ground, causing 25 minute passenger delay.

14th January 1949. Fitter working in Bexley depot withdrew switch in error, causing current to be off from Brook Street to Silverdale Road and a 24 minute passenger delay ensued.

21st January 1949, 5.40pm, Wallington sub-station, Redford Avenue. Bunching of trolleybuses in section caused circuit breaker to overload. Restored by traffic staff by remote control. 14 minute passenger delay.

8th September 1949, 3.11pm, pole 212, Cricklewood Lane. Pole broke at base and fell across running wires to rest against a trolleybus: 6 minute passenger delay with a 77 minute electrical delay.

25th October 1949, 5.26am, West Barnes Lane, New Malden. Linesman working on overhead during the night omitted to restore current. Driver of first trolleybus also omitted to use remote control and tester was called out. Push button control operated by tester and normal conditions were resumed: 19 minute passenger delay.

10th March 1950, 3.10pm, Seven Stars Junction. Overhead crossing burnt out, electrical fault causing dead short. Fire Brigade called by member of the public and there was a 12 minute passenger delay.

28th June 1950, 11.07am, Brentford, Kingsley, Fulwell, Twickenham and Hampton Court sub-stations. Damage to feeder No.248 in Chiswick High Road which was caused by British Electricity Authority workmen using pick on road work, led to the sub-stations being shut down and a 34 minute passenger delay occurred.

The Delays Investigation Committee issued a 'Report of Dewirements' each four weeks; the period from December 1946 to January 1951 is used below. The locations where reported dewirements most frequently happened in order of regularity, occurred at:

1) Stratford (highest single location)
2) Seven Sisters Road (highest single length of track)
3) Barking Road
4) Shepherds Bush
5) Whipps Cross
6) Barking Broadway
7) Bexleyheath Market Place
8) Plaistow High Street (Clegg Street)
9) Old Street
10) Stamford Hill
11) Manor House
12) Green Street (Upton Park)
13) 'Nags Head', Holloway
14) Shoreditch
15) Upper Street, Islington
16) Ilford High Road
17) Wood Green High Road
18) Grays Inn Road
19) Aldgate
20) Docks (Connaught Road)

Bearing in mind the complexity of 'Nags Head' Junction, its position is most surprising. Dewirements at other major junctions such as 'Angel' Islington, Walthamstow 'Bell', 'Bakers Arms', Leyton and Gardiners Corner were very small, with those at Gardiners Corner particularly being very few in number. That these five locations had such good track records implies that more care was taken at them. A merit table was in force each month

between the depots and took the form of a football league table. Positions were defined by the number of reported dewirements per service miles but those caused by bad road surface were not counted. In 1950, CN, ID, FW, HL, WD, IH averaged the best positions while PR was bottom on eight occasions. At this time, on four 28-day periods, Wandsworth depot had no reported dewirements at all while averaging 77,417 service miles.

In one in six cases both booms were damaged in a single dewirement and in one in thirty cases booms were knocked or shaken off. Reasons for dewirements and the order in which they fell were:

1)	Unknown	28%
2)	Speed at special work	14%
3)	Speed at curves	10½%
4)	Wide driving	8%
5)	Defective overhead	5%
6)	Avoiding obstructions	4½%
7)	Frog not operated or operated in error	4%
8)	Bad road surface	4%
9)	Booms knocked or shaken off	4%
10)	Defective trolley gear	3½%
11)	Previous overhead damage	3½%
12)	Neglect of frog signal by driver	3%
13)	Overtaking	3%
14)	Previous trolley damage	2½%
15)	Unauthorised frog pull	1½%
16)	Fog	½%
17)	Wrong road taken by driver	½%

Each vehicle was checked every night for the condition of the carbon inserts in the trolley heads, so that dewirements for this reason should not occur. However, in rainy weather the carbons wore down more quickly. This factor, coupled with the fact that Bexleyheath depot maintenance staff were not bothering about changing carbons near to conversion day, caused a number of vehicles to have their trolley heads screeching against the wires on the rainy last evening of operation.

Some vehicles seemed prone to dewirements and during this period, vehicle 534 of Hammersmith depot needed attention eight times. Dewirements fell into four categories which in reverse order of severity were: a) dewire but no damage, b) twisted, damaged or partly drawn head or bent boom, c) head pulled off or boom broken or pulled out, d) head pulled off and fell, shoe broken and fell, boom pulled out or broken and fell. Some vehicles appeared frequently due to bad tensioning of booms.

DRIVER TRAINING

The first staff to receive trolleybus driving instruction were the tram drivers at Fulwell depot who were given preliminary training within the confines of the depot. No doubt though, staff involved with the early trials of trolleybuses in London had tuition of some sort. The Fulwell tram drivers were trained by London United Tramways staff who themselves had undergone instruction by AEC. These tram drivers were then taken out and given instruction on the wiring that had been installed between Teddington and Twickenham, enabling the first services to start on 16th May 1931 with fully competent staff. The first of the London United Tramways trolleybus drivers were permitted 48 hours tuition but should any man fail to pass or obtain a licence, training was continued in the man's own time up to a further total of 24

hours; any man failing to pass the police test and obtain a licence after 72 hours training would be finally failed. When the tram to trolleybus conversion programme took place a large number of drivers had to be trained and some of the Fulwell men were seconded to the north side to train tram drivers there; they would stay in an area after the conversion had taken place for observation purposes and to take over from drivers who were a bit slow and therefore holding the service up. The Fulwell staff were paid a subsistence allowance for taking up residence in these areas and although some staff did do this, others would travel together in a private car from Fulwell each day but retain the allowance! In the early days an experienced driver would sit in the seat in the lower saloon near the driver's cab and give advice to the new man

about stops and frogs. About ten days instruction was all that was necessary for tram drivers to become trolleybus drivers; recruits from the conducting staff were given up to four weeks training for, in the main, such staff had not had any previous driving experience. In the initial training of tram drivers, they were in many instances sent to trolleybus depots already in commission. 'Diddlers' were used for training purposes at Bexleyheath prior to conversion and B2s were used at Sutton depot on the southern section of route 654. Once the conversion programme was completed, each depot then assumed its own responsibility for training new staff. Four drivers from Fulwell went to Bournemouth in 1935 to train Bournemouth staff to drive trolleybuses.

Bexleyheath and Stonebridge depots had training circuits within their confines and at

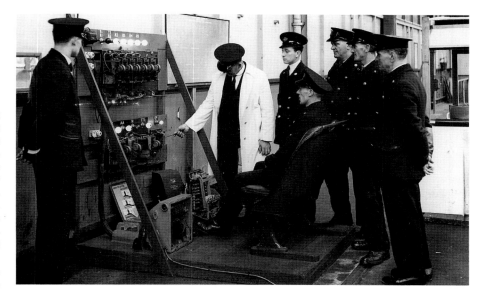

Stonebridge there was a large wooden hut which housed a driver instruction school. This contained a driving simulator and various pieces of equipment for demonstration purposes appertaining to trolleybus driving; the simulator was not used latterly. Driving over fire ramps was also practised here. It was a long trek for staff from distant depots and large numbers of learner vehicles would be seen parked in the depot forecourt with vehicles from Carshalton depot rubbing shoulders with those from Edmonton depot. Ilford depot did not bring over an SA type and a standard class vehicle would be borrowed from West Ham or Bow. Staff from Bexleyheath depot did not attend; it also appears that some novices from other depots did not attend Stonebridge School, particularly during wartime. The driver training school at Stonebridge continued during the trolleybus conversion programme although its use diminished as the number of operating trolleybus depots was reduced, but it stayed open until almost the end of 1961. Fulwell and Isleworth were the last two depots to regularly use the facility and after 1060 from Isleworth, a Leyland usurper in strong AEC territory, had ploughed its last lonely course to Stonebridge, the school closed. The last few trainees missed out on this part of the training, as the wires from Hammersmith to Stonebridge were de-energised in early January 1962.

Although trainees normally traversed wiring appertaining to the depot from which they would work, it was not unusual for drivers to be taken over wiring that was not operated by their depots. The reason for this was that it enabled them to cope with all types of traffic conditions. A Lea Bridge learner would go to North Woolwich, a Wood Green learner to Canons Park and Kingston, a Hanwell learner to Stratford and Croydon, a Finchley learner to Hampstead Heath, a Stonebridge one to Chiswick and Hanwell, a West Ham and Highgate one to Woodford and a Fulwell one to Leyton. Q1s which reached Leyton would not go into Lea Bridge depot for some reason, but strange though it may seem this class of vehicle has been driven to Dartford and Bexleyheath depot. The reason for this was that the driving instructor was involved with the sports and social side of London Transport and wanted to see a colleague at that depot. The two Fulwell Q1 learners, 1779 and 1842, worked over to Poplar depot and 1779 was left there; all trainees and the two instructors then boarded 1842 and took it over the North Woolwich free ferry using battery power on and off the vessel. Various other sorties occurred due to instructors' personal arrangements!

A mock-up contactor panel is being used to demonstrate the workings of a trolleybus in the Fulwell depot complex in October 1935. Then it is out into the depot yard to view the position of the contactors on trolleybus 143; of note are the two dots under the 'BDY' of Hammersmith on the destination blind.
London Transport Museum U18524 and U18522

Each depot was allocated one or more trolleybuses that could be adapted for driver tuition; the smaller depots would only have one whereas the larger depots might have four. These vehicles had a removable glass window behind the driver which gave the instructor easy access to the cab. There were times when these vehicles were not available; then any vehicle was used, with the glass partition behind the driver being removed and returned later. These were ordinary passenger carrying vehicles, being used in a learner capacity when required, which, generally speaking, was in the off-peak time Monday to Fridays and on Saturday mornings. In 1949, ten 'Diddlers' were allocated to various depots around the system for training purposes, thus saving vehicles that were required for service; these continued in this role until 1951. Two other vehicles, 61 and 378, which had been used for 'pay as you enter' experiments were also used as training vehicles in the early fifties; these twelve vehicles were the only ones that were ever permanently allocated to this work. The instructors were either former trolleybus drivers themselves or permanent trolleybus drivers acting as trolleybus driving instructors. They would work from any depot that required their services and were conversant with all overhead wire layouts and knowledgeable about the working of a trolleybus. Learner plates were fixed in the front cab and in the rear window, although this seldom seemed to happen in the first half of the system's life. Tests were carried out by London Transport staff who were approved by the Ministry of Transport. No more than three men per instructor were to

be seen so as to give each man adequate driving time, but it was not uncommon for just one person to be trained at a time. Conductors learning to be drivers and wanting a few more days easement would try and 'con' the instructor by deliberately dewiring, but instructors were wise to this. Drivers also received training in reversing and battery manoeuvres.

The main drawback to trolleybus tuition was that novices had to be pressed immediately into service speed, otherwise the normal service would be held up. The learner vehicles lowered poles to allow the service vehicles through, but the problem could be partly overcome by taking a different track from the following vehicle or by using a short working facility. One notable place for learner vehicles to park was in the infrequently used Hoe Street loop; here the instructor could give the novices a 'pep talk' and a break could be taken by all participants. A piece of overhead that was virtually used only by learner vehicles was a link wire from 603 wires to 604/605 wires at Norbiton Church. The novices were either direct recruits or were conductors training to be drivers. It was only in later days that staff were recruited directly to trolleybus driving from outside the industry. Very occasionally, motorbus drivers would become trolleybus drivers and had to undergo a trolleybus driving instruction course. A small number of drivers at each depot were licensed to drive motorbuses so that staff outings from trolleybus depots could use their own staff, a motorbus being borrowed from a local garage. All staff were trained in the art not only of trolleybus driving itself, but also in reading overhead layouts, frog direction signals, positions of frogs and the raising and lowering of trolleybooms.

In the days when there was plenty of staff, new drivers could be lent to local depots and would have been taken over such routes in their training; if particular routes had escaped their attention they were allowed to route-learn them. Such staff may have found themselves at a depot which operated a type with which they were unfamiliar but no special instruction was given to them: this would also apply to vehicles lent to a depot. There were exceptions and Bow staff were trained on SA types as they could be lent to Ilford depot: Stonebridge staff were trained on Q1s as they could be loaned to Hanwell. This specific training was due to these vehicles' greater width. At Ilford depot, staff were also trained on standard vehicles as these were used from time to time.

When Fulwell, Hanwell and Isleworth depots were allocated Q1s, type training was given to the drivers (for Fulwell staff they were vastly different to the 'Diddlers'). When Fulwell and Isleworth were restocked with older vehicles in 1961, the drivers were given familiarisation on them as the K1s and L3s were equipped with regenerative braking. At Ilford depot, specific training was given on the Bournemouth vehicles and 8ft wide SAs.

During the tram to trolleybus conversion programme, types and classes of trolleybuses were used for training at depots that would not normally operate such trolleybuses. No.200 was regularly allocated to these duties. It is seen being used for Hammersmith depot training purposes at Mitcham, Fair Green on 5th September 1937 (training taking place on a Sunday) passing tram 483.
John Bonell

Vehicles 484-488 were used for learner duties before being regularly allocated; 486 approaches Hampstead.
Lens of Sutton

London Transport went to considerable trouble and expense to train staff on trolleybuses during the trolleybus conversion programme, when, perforce, their time on them would be short. This was not a waste in real terms though, for once trained to drive a large passenger carrying vehicle, retraining to drive motorbuses would normally be just a formality. If London Transport had taken the course of sending new drivers to bus garages, they would have created shortfalls at trolleybus depots. If they had asked such applicants to wait until a trolleybus depot had been converted to motorbuses, such men might have taken different employment and in times of staff shortages this had to be avoided. Consequently, training was occurring at many depots almost to the time of conversion and Highgate was still training in late January 1961 despite there being enough staff who were trolleybus-trained to cover the remaining trolleybus requirements. It was considered that drivers should learn on trolleybuses when dual motorbus/trolleybus operation was occurring at various depots; senior staff had priority to work on motorbuses in these situations. Training on

trolleybuses ceased once a penultimate conversion had occurred, although this did not apply to Wood Green depot which continued training for a time after the April 1961 conversion. This policy brought about an unusual occurrence, with a Stonebridge man passing his trolleybus driving test on 1st January 1962, therefore driving trolleybuses by himself for just one day. With trainee conductors in the conversion programme, the problem of re-training did not apply, but situations did arise when trainees would commence their training on a trolleybus and conclude it on a motorbus; no specific training was given to trolleybus conductors who were to become motorbus conductors during the conversion programme.

When trolleybus drivers had passed their test, they received a Group H licence; all licences were valid for a period of three years at a fee of 3/- and a Metropolitan Stage Carriage badge was issued. These detailed the badge number and had a blue edging; the fee was the same for conductors and their badges had orange edging. Of interest was the fact that tram drivers who became trolleybus drivers continued to be issued with a tram

driver's licence, but a note on the reverse of the licence gave approval for trolleybus driving. This led to the situation of a Hendon depot trolleybus driver being issued with a tram driver's licence in July 1949 which in theory allowed him to drive trams on the last day of London's trams! All new trolleybus staff were issued with a tram and trolleybus rule book and even in 1962 such issues were still giving details of how to operate trams on Dog Kennel Hill! New trolleybus conductors were trained in the art of frog pulling and trolleyboom raising and lowering; the latter art was normally only taught to the men, it being unusual to see conductresses manipulating trolley arms – but do it they did on occasions.

The last trolleybus driving schools took place in 1962. One commenced at Fulwell in January and once these staff had passed their test, the final school was held at Isleworth depot using vehicle 1060; this commenced in February with three Isleworth conductors. All were successful, the last test being carried out on 23rd March 1962 when trolleybus conductor Terry Shaw became a trolleybus driver and the last new badge, T14876, was issued.

His licence did not expire until 22nd March 1965 but no doubt other licences, both for drivers and conductors, were renewed after this.

One of the finer points of trolleybus driving was the ability to give a smooth start. This was done by applying the first notch of power while the handbrake was still on. This ensured smooth acceleration and then the power notches would be built up gradually. This instruction was given as part of 'handling vehicles on the road' in the tram and trolleybus drivers' rule book. Drivers had to remember where to coast over a piece of overhead equipment and where they could take power at such places. Generally speaking, a driver could take power on the main line of trolleybus overhead but there were many exceptions to this and rather oddly 609s/679s entering the Islington Green turning loop from the Holloway direction had power to take the frog — this peculiarity was accentuated by the fact that this manoeuvre was performed on a downward slope. At main junctions, where there was equal use of diverging tracks, there was no hard and fast rule as to 'power priority'; the same applied to

converging tracks in the situations mentioned above. The need for good memory was paramount at places like Ilford Broadway where so much equipment was strung above in a very small area. In traffic congestion, drivers would attempt to stop before a piece of 'dead' overhead; this enabled them to obtain 'juice' before this piece of equipment was reached. This was not always possible and there was a risk of getting stuck on a dead section or causing an arc of electricity to light up by going over with power on. When a dewirement occurred, a driver was instructed to pull up as soon as possible to prevent damage to the overhead — by braking too sharply, though, the poles could whip round to the front of the vehicle and cause even more damage. All these matters were part of tuition duties.

Above **Allocated for a short period as a learner, 61 passes through North Finchley. The County School of Motoring is also giving tuition in the vehicle following it.** Don Thompson

It was important that we left the depot on time as otherwise we would be out of order at Hounslow. Early morning 657s coming up from 'The Bush' would pause before passing the depot frogwork to ensure that their preceding vehicle had left the depot in front of them. Consecutive vehicles 1778 and 1779 enact this. Tony Belton

AT THE WHEEL
A Driver's Eye View from Terry Shaw

In 1960, I decided to seek fame and fortune with London Transport, little knowing that the former would come true. I applied for a job as a bus conductor and having passed the medical and arithmetic tests was told that I would be on trolleybuses at Isleworth depot. After a few days classroom teaching at Chiswick training centre I was instructed to report to Isleworth trolleybus depot on a particular day and over the next few days a conductor-instructor showed me how I was to perform my tasks. These meant collecting fares, looking after the platform and dealing with the appropriate frog pulls. Then it was back to Chiswick for two more days and I was issued with a trolleybus conductor's licence and badge. One Saturday I reported to the depot

for work, now being a fully qualified trolley-bus conductor; I was on my own now and had to teach myself to manipulate trolley arms. As a trolleybus conductor I had to make sure that I didn't pull a frog too early and dewire the preceding vehicle or let go of a frog too soon and dewire my own. When I started, we had the 8ft wide vehicles which made life easy for conductors as there was plenty of room in the gangways. They were of the 1952 batch, but from January 1961 were replaced by those of the 1948 batch. However, they were sold to Spain in 1961, the last of ours being withdrawn on 25th April that year. Thereafter, we had K1 class vehicles drafted in from Wood Green depot; these were less popular than the luxurious Q1s. I was soon allocated

a regular rota line and had a regular driver: Isleworth operated just the one route, the 657 from Hounslow to Shepherds Bush for which we were given 40 minutes running time each way. The route was an important service as it was the only link between Hounslow and Brentford/Chiswick and the depot was always fully staffed. Having been an amateur boxer at one time I had very little trouble with the passengers and by having just one route to work you got to know your regulars. Every day was different, though, and on trolley-buses there was always plenty of activity. One instance that springs to mind during my conducting days is of the time I nearly fell in the canal. My driver had dewired eastbound at Brentford Canal Bridge and the poles had

swung out to the nearside and were in such a position that I could not rewire the vehicle from the pavement. When rewiring trolley booms it is necessary to have the bamboo pole grappling hook around the topmost part of the trolley arm; now this was only going to be possible by my standing on the bridge parapet! Disaster nearly struck! I eventually re-wired the vehicle, but as will be seen later, this location became ominous for me.

At the end of 1961, I applied to be trained as a trolleybus driver and in February 1962 two of my colleagues, 'Ginger' Waldron, Adrian O'Callaghan, and myself had to report to the depot one Monday morning where we were to enter the trolleybus driving school; this turned out to be the last such school. We were given about four weeks tuition, which saw us driving most of the time on the main wires but we did have to traverse the loops at Brentford, Half Acre and Stamford Brook Station. At this latter location, I found it very difficult to make the turn and the instructor made me do it over and over again until I got it right. We got a change of scenery from time to time when we went to Fulwell depot for our meal reliefs, because our instructor, Charlie Durrant, preferred to use the canteen there than ours at Isleworth. Working an eleven-day fortnight at the time, we had to come in on Saturday mornings; Charlie said that we were so bad that he kept us right to our full time on Saturdays. We always had trolleybus 1060 for training as the window behind the driver could be removed and enabled the instructor to communicate with us. Adrian passed his test first time, so he left us to enter the regular drivers rota at the depot; 'Ginger' passed his test at the second attempt and I too, a few days later, on 23rd March 1962. The trolleybus driving school then closed and my fame with London Transport was attained in that I had become the last man to qualify as a London Transport trolleybus driver. My driver's badge number was T14876 and I had to pay 2/6 for it and 3/- for the licence, which entitled me to drive trolleybuses in London until 22nd March 1965!

My first duty by myself was a late turn on the following day and on my first trip back from Shepherds Bush, it was just like 'wagon train' for I had a whole convoy of trolleybuses behind me. I was obviously a bit slow to start with. Inspector Jim Taylor instructed me to pull into the depot and the vehicle was turned on the turntable-traverser and I was sent back to Shepherds Bush to the relief of the other drivers who could then pick up their own timings. However, after a few more days I gained confidence and was able to keep up to schedule. I discovered that there was an initiation test for new London trolleybus drivers which I was hitherto unaware of, despite having been at the depot for some time. The drivers had worked out when I would be at Brentford Canal Bridge where there was a curve in the wires; Tony Shanny was coming in the opposite direction to me on my trip to Hounslow. He waited for me and wiggled his steering as he came round the corner; the wires swayed and my poles came off. He kept going but anchored up a bit further down the road to see me go to the rear of the vehicle and pull out the bamboo pole which was kept underneath the vehicle. I gave the bamboo pole an almighty yank and fell over on my back; all that was left in the holder was a four-foot length of bamboo, for the drivers had sawn it off! It was just like an umbrella handle, not even reaching to the destination blind box, let alone the trolleys! I had to get a pole from another trolleybus and by now there was a tail-back of traffic with me standing in the road with a four-foot length of bamboo! Having failed the test miserably I was now accepted as a fully-fledged trolleybus driver by one and all, so it is now appropriate for me to take you on a journey on 'the 657 road'.

Ten minutes are given for signing on and getting the trolleybus ready. On trolleybuses we only have one time card between conductor and driver, so I take hold of it and go out into the depot to look for the trolleybus allocated to the running number; the time card is always kept in the driver's cab, but because the partition between the cab and saloon is normally open, the conductor has easy access to it. Most of the trolleybuses are parked on the east side of the depot with a few on the west side. There are four roads on the east side, each taking five trolleybuses and as we have 24 for service on Mondays to Fridays, four of them have to be parked on the west side. From this side of the depot we have to battery out into service which is a bit awkward when going towards Hounslow. On Mondays to Fridays, 22 vehicles take up service towards 'The Wellington' (Hounslow) so at least two have to battery out of the depot in this direction. Spare trolleybuses are normally kept on the pits which are reached by the turntable-traverser. Today I am on duty 20 and want IH 24, the vehicle being 1058. I find her parked on the east side of the depot. Roads two and four are dead-end wires with road one leading out to Shepherds Bush and road three leading out to Hounslow; 1058 is parked on road four, so I get into the cab, switch in the master switch, the circuit breakers and the motor generator and wait for the air pressure flag to drop. It doesn't take long and as there is another vehicle directly behind me, I have to move 1058 up a few yards so that I have access to the trolley poles; I will need to swing them on to road three as my first trip is to Hounslow. First of all though, I put the direction lever in the forward 'trolley' position and see that the special key is in the 'trolley' position (as opposed to the 'battery' position). There is normally a bamboo pole hanging from the depot roof girders, so I take hold of this and swing the booms; it is easy swinging booms in the depot as the wiring is in wooden troughing and therefore rigid and not flaying around as it does on the road. The negative trolley is placed on the nearside wire and the positive one placed on the offside wire.

An orange neon light was set in the 'trolley indicator' housing just above eye level in the cab. The light went out if there was a power failure, a dewirement, or when the poles were pulled off the wires. The neon's greatest asset was its flickering as we went through frogs and crossings — the light momentarily went off on 'dead' sections. You would know how many flickers to expect and then you could get back onto your higher power notches.

Left **The depot's painter has put the 'IH' code in the wrong position on 1807 which is standing at the Hounslow terminus. A well groomed Tony Shanny, perusing a paper for a dog to bet on no doubt, walks towards his charge, 1778 seen behind.** Tony Belton

Due to flat batteries, 1113 has become stuck on 'the dead' on leaving the 'Half Acre' turning loop. The author had to swing the poles to the 'up track' allowing 1113 to nudge forward; conductress Phyllis Constable watches her driver replace the poles on the 'down track'. During all this commotion, traffic has built up in both directions — never mind though, it's 19th April 1962 and problems such as this will soon be a thing of the past. Hugh Taylor

Before leaving the depot, a trolleybus driver should always check that he has a bamboo pole in the holder beneath the vehicle; you never know when you might need it, either for yourself or someone else, so I go to the back of 1058 and put my fingers inside the pole holder but find that there is not one there. You now apply the rule that exists in the army: if somebody pinches your kitbag, then you pinch someone else's! I just go round to the back of another trolleybus, take out the bamboo pole from its holder and shove it under 1058.

The vehicle is due out of the depot at 7.16am; it is important to leave the depot on time when going towards Hounslow for if you got out of order you'd be lowering and raising poles at the terminus. Similarly, if you were on one of the early runnings which had come up from 'The Bush', you had to make sure that you also came up on your time at the depot, for if one came out a bit late you would find yourself out of order. So first of all it is up to Hounslow terminus; the turn is quite tight and I have to go in with a fair bit of speed and then coast and swing straight in to come to a

halt on the circle. The first round trip is reasonably busy but by the time we come up for our second trip from Hounslow, other road traffic is starting to build up. It is necessary therefore to leave on the mark as timekeeping is of the essence. At 8.54am my conductor presses a button on a traction standard which will set the traffic light signals here against all other traffic except that eastbound along the Staines Road, giving 657s fifteen seconds to make the turn before the traffic lights allow westbound traffic through. This is a unique feature on the trolleybus network and a white light appears in a special box, informing us when we can move. On the last day but one, I came in too close to the traction standard which held the special light and knocked it off; the overhead boys had to come out and strap it on again for just two days! At this time of morning it is a four-minute service through to Shepherds Bush and I make a mental note that IH 9 with Tony Shanny at the wheel is the trolleybus in front of me. It is still peak time, so my conductor has his hands on the bell cord pretty sharpish at the stops for we don't want to lag behind time. We pick up a fair number of people as we go through Hounslow; as I approach the overhead crossings at the depot, I slow up and let the vehicle coast through the first two crossings. As the momentum begins to die, I give the vehicle a couple more notches of power to see me safely through, for by driving in this way there will not be any mishap with the trolleys. A bit further down the road, there is a bend by Isleworth fire station and I drive inside of the wires here; next comes the bridge at Isleworth Station and I nurse the trolleybus through; the booms come down quite low to the top of the vehicle under the bridge and gradually rise to their normal position as we leave it. If you did come through here with a bit of speed,

1113 has been curtailed at Stamford Brook Station; the conductor, impeded by parked cars, is standing on the pavement in order to place the negative trolley arm on the dead-end wire here. For the assistance of drivers on through trolleybuses, a string of 'fairy lights' will ensure that they take the right road at this location. John Gillham

though, you were gambling that your poles would stay on the wires.

Busch Corner at Brentford is where the 657 and 667 meet. At the stop before the junction I glance to my right, across the wood-yard to see if I can view the poles of a 667 above it; however there is nothing there and I pass at a fair speed beneath the trailing frog for the 657 is on the main track. We pick up a fair crowd here, so maybe there hasn't been a 667 through for quite a time, and in a couple more stops we are almost full up. When we get down to Brentford, Half Acre there are a lot of people milling about and as boarding and alighting will take the best part of a minute, I recall an incident which I saw happen here. A 667 shed a head which flew off right through a chap's newspaper which he was reading outside the pub here; he shot off like a bullet. We had a number of runnings that turned at Brentford, Half Acre; in the afternoon eight of the ten vehicles that took up service in the afternoon peak turned here as did a few in the peak hours generally. For this turn, the conductor would have to pull and hold the frog handle down but it was quite a tight turn into Half Acre; we then turned into St Pauls Road and parked there. It could be a bit awkward coming out onto the main road and we could get stuck on a 'dead' section of wire. If that happened we would have to finish the manoeuvre on battery, but if it was flat we would swing the poles onto the east-bound wire, move up a few yards and then swing them back again.

I get three bells from my conductor now so I know we have a full standing load. By looking in my driving mirror, I notice that two 667s have come up behind me; no doubt one of them should be in front but as I have got the wires I might as well get on with it. However, after a couple more stops, I notice in my mirror that the driver of the leading vehicle is flashing his headlights at me; I know that this means he wants to overtake. He is obviously down on his time, having no doubt been delayed in traffic. I look at my watch as we approach Kew Bridge and comparing this with the time board, notice that I have a couple of minutes to spare. There was no love lost between crews of the 657 and 667; we shared the wires between Busch Corner and Youngs Corner and whichever vehicle reached each location first would carry the major part of the workload. In fact there could be a bit of rivalry and things have turned nasty from time to time between the crews, even to the extent of there being a literal punch-up between them. The most sensitive time concerned the last vehicles on each route which were timed to arrive at Busch Corner eastbound within a minute of each other; the last 667 was a minute in front of the last 657 daily. However, I am not a vindictive type so I pull up at the stop here, jump out of the cab and go to the back of 1058 and pull out the bamboo pole. At this stop the trolley poles are stretched out far to the offside of the vehicle, so when I pull the negative boom away from

the wire it swings around with a fair bit of force before I am able to pull it down beneath the retaining hook. I pull the other trolley arm away from the wire and hold it steady while the 667 overtakes and the driver gives me a wave of acknowledgement. I then hold the first arm just three or four inches beneath the wire and hit it up first time onto the wire. Removing the other boom from its retaining hook, I look behind me as I walk out into the road as there is the possibility of oncoming traffic mowing me down. When you are far out in the road, you get a different look at the shoe of the trolley head than if the vehicle were directly beneath the wires; it is at a completely different angle to the trolley arm itself. While pulling this boom down, the carbon shoe has become slightly off-centre, so I place it against the running wire and a touch of blue flame appears. The shoe is straightened and allows me to place the arm on the wire (the he-men trolleybus drivers would place the positive arm under the negative arm and then pull the negative arm away from the wires; they would then replace the negative arm followed by the positive arm). I drop the bamboo pole onto the road and as there's always a bit of play in these things, I see it bounce before I shove it back into its holder, giving it a kick to make sure it's right in. This was necessary, for now and again you would see a trolleybus with the bamboo pole sticking out a couple of feet from the vehicle. This could be dangerous, as it was quite possible for somebody to walk behind the trolleybus and trip over it. I jump into the cab again and we're away: in situations such as this, I don't bother to knock out the circuit breakers, which was advisable each time I left the cab.

The 667 is taking most of the passengers now and I am still with him when we get to Youngs Corner. My conductor alights, pulls the semi-automatic frog and reboards immediately. In front of me, mounted on a traction standard is a signal box in which are direction indicators in the form of a letter Y. It is lit in the base and right-hand side of the Y, but by my conductor pulling the frog, the light changes to the left-hand side of the Y; these lights are orange so that we can easily see them at night. The purpose of the signal box and lights is to indicate the position of the points and to show that a frog has operated correctly in our favour. As soon as I pass over the frog, there's a skate on the running wire which is actuated by the trolley head and puts the frog back to its original setting. A few yards up Goldhawk Road, we pass beneath the bridge by Stamford Brook Station where we often use the short working facility; the dead-end wire starts as soon as we pass the bridge and immediately goes off line to the main running wires. It was an awkward manoeuvre when we turned here for there were always cars parked on the nearside and we needed to swing the trolleys to the nearside set of wires. We often could not manoeuvre the trolley arms easily as we were clambering between cars, even standing on their bumpers

Terry Shaw at the depot on 7th April 1962 with 1117. Hugh Taylor

Shanny's Last Dewirement . . . from left to right: the tree, 1116, Shanny looking on proudly and Shanny's conductor putting matters to right. Despite a badly bowed boom, Shanny continued to the depot at full speed! Hugh Taylor

and were not able to get beneath the trolley booms properly. We had to get ourselves into as good a position as possible and keep on prodding away until we were successful. As often as not you would miss the wire and the trolley skid would swivel around to the wrong angle; this could all be a bit of a performance and by the time you had got both poles on the right wire, you would have aching arms. There was not a frog here, due to the proximity of the bridge; for our convenience a bamboo pole was normally available. It was hung over an arm that projected from the top of a traction pole and was kept in position near its base by a retaining clasp, also fixed to the traction pole. When curtailed here it was a very tight turn to make and there was heavy traffic going up and down the Goldhawk Road. If we were unlucky and got caught up on the 'dead', we might have to change our poles from the circle wires to the main wires. Vehicles that went straight through to Shepherds Bush enjoyed the benefit of guide lights in the overhead there, to show their drivers where the overhead was strung; these were switched on and off by a conductor at the appropriate times.

On one occasion in Goldhawk Road, a West Indian conductor with a broad accent came up to me and put his head through the partition from the saloon to the cab and told me that somebody wouldn't pay his fare. I told him to get on to the controller, saying that we required assistance. Meanwhile I whipped the poles down and this fellow went to the phone to speak to the controller. He told him that he had an uncollected fare on the trolleybus, but the controller thought he said that there was an uncontrollable fire! In a few minutes we had three fire engines and a number of police cars in attendance. Mentioning the partition between cab and saloon brings to mind the many occasions when as either driver or conductor, I played chess by trolleybus; the chessboard would be on top of the contactor box and we'd make our moves when the conductor wasn't collecting fares or the driver was at a stop or traffic lights. Another useful fitting on a trolleybus was the mirror in the driving cab which allowed the driver to see into the lower saloon. This was particularly useful for us in observing the platform, especially when the conductor had signalled us away from upstairs.

I keep my foot down now all the way to Shepherds Bush, but as I approach Goldhawk Road Station I see that trolleybus 1116 on IH9 which is supposed to be four minutes in front of me, is now approaching from the other direction. It is showing ISLEWORTH DEPOT; running numbers 1-14 stay out in the day so it is probably going in as a staff cut. By looking at my watch, I am sure that Shanny has left Shepherds Bush a couple of minutes early: I'm still quite a new boy as a driver, so I think he is trying to show me who's boss. I suggest to the inspector that I might get away a bit sharpish but he says "not you son, you hold your time". We only get two minutes stand

time at Shepherds Bush where there is a dead-end wire, occasionally used when we get out of turn; hung on to a nearby traction standard are a couple of spare bamboo poles. This trip is due away at 9.36am and I am scheduled to run into the depot. I get away on time and it is not long before I pass through Seven Stars Junction where it is just straight wires now, as we are the only trolleybus route left here; until recently routes 660/666 crossed our wires. I soon approach Youngs Corner and at the stop before the traffic lights we would often wait to see if a 667 would go over in front of us taking all the passengers as far as Brentford. I negotiate the junction here carefully as it can be very easy to dewire a trolleybus at this point. Our cue here is to come out over the manhole cover thus enabling our booms to follow the wires. We continue along Chiswick High Road and pass Chiswick works where we had to put on our best driving techniques because of all the instructors and examiners who were around. Soon I reach the Chiswick flyover and on both sides of the flyover there are manholes which we use as markers; on my journey to Hounslow I clip the inside edge of one, while on the journey to Shepherds Bush I clip the outside edge of another. This place was notorious for dewirements and we seemed to be able to take the wiring faster on the way to Shepherds Bush than in the other direction. You might notice that the orange neon light in the cab which signifies that the poles are on the wire would flicker here, indicating that they are wavering, so you ease off to come through all right. Mind you, trolley poles could even come off in a strong wind. Manhole covers played a big part in a trolleybus driver's life as did many other markings on the road; when council workmen came along mending, levelling and digging up roads, they'd take away our markers and we'd have to find other ones.

Kew Bridge is reached again and it is only very recently that the short working wires have been taken out. Beyond here I am able to get a good turn of speed past the gasworks before I reach Brentford again. Soon we reach the canal bridge at Brentford and immediately after this we have to go slowly under the railway bridge. Just beyond here there is a section breaker and on the day before the end of trolleybuses, this had to be renewed as so many of us had been going through it with power on, thereby gradually burning the wood, and there were numerous bad dewirements because of this. I can recall a couple of dewirements for which I was responsible. At Youngs Corner I thought I'd given my conductor enough time to pull the frog when it was busy; it turned out that he hadn't pulled it and I hadn't watched the Y light, so my poles went to Hammersmith as I went to Shepherds Bush. On another occasion at Kew Bridge, on a journey to 'The Bush', I saw a gap in the traffic and thought to myself "go for it"; I got past a lorry and a motorbus but failed to see that in front of it were two 667s. I hit all their

poles and they all came off except mine! When I looked in my mirror, I could see all these poles flaying around with various members of the Fulwell staff shaking their fists at me!

I will soon be reaching Busch Corner where I recall that one day there was an electrical problem and a lot of trolleybuses kept on blowing the breakers in the junction box; the electrical department ran out of spare fuses and had to go up to Stonebridge (which was then closed to trolleybuses) to get some. At Busch Corner we could take the crossover fairly quickly, but sometimes our haste was such that we'd go over with our power on and there would be a flash from the overhead. I recall one morning outside Isleworth depot when all the wires were sparking, lighting up the darkness as if daytime – there must have been an electrical fault. Now and again we might get an electric flash in the cab, for if we started off too quickly the circuit breakers would open. There would be a loud bang, making the driver and nearby passengers jump in their seats; we would just knock the circuit breakers in and continue. We were supposed to go over all frogs and crossings at 5mph but we knew which of these we could take faster than that. Shortly before the trolleybuses finished, we had a dispute which led to a work-to-rule. We carried out this rule to the letter which threw the service into chaos. Isleworth depot was so small, but we were a force to be reckoned with!

As I approach Busch Corner, I see that a trolleybus incident has occurred. Shanny had suffered a heavy dewirement at speed; he had lost both poles and he and his conductor are out with their bamboo pole, trying to sort out which are tree branches and which are trolley booms. In the depot later, he recounted: "IH9 was going into a staff cut so, as I did not have to worry about a relieving crew, I thought I'd pick up a bit of time and get my breakfast earlier. I came out of Youngs Corner away from the manhole cover and although the poles shuddered they stayed on. I went round the Chiswick flyover like a bullet out of a gun barrel and although the poles bucked and swayed, they stuck to the wire like glue. I hit all the feeders and junctions with power on, but good fortune finally left me as I went through the 667 turnout at Busch Corner at speed, sending the poles into a tree". They eventually untangled the booms but not before I overtook Shanny, who still came up behind me fairly quickly after this. Rogue that he was, he was not the type of man to lose mileage – hence his continuing to the depot with a badly bent positive boom. As a full vehicle requirement was not needed that day, 1116 was laid to rest.

On the way to the depot I remember to take my foot off the power pedal as I cross the section breakers which are situated at half mile intervals; the traction standards which hold them are distinguished by a white band around them. My conductor pulls the frog handle for the depot, I park 1058 just inside and the maintenance staff take it from here.

Terry Shaw drove a passenger carrying vehicle away from Shepherds Bush many times in his driving career with London Transport — this was the very last time he did it by trolleybus. Already the new plate for replacement route 117 is in position on the bus stop. Peter Moore

Coming into the depot from the other direction was carried out with some skill. The conductor would be off the platform and abreast of the driver as he came to the frog; he would pull the handle and we would be over the frog without having to stop. It is a very tight turn into the depot and is done at slow speed for it could be easily misjudged; it was rather deceptive, a sort of optical illusion,

for just as you thought you were in a good position to turn into the depot, you could find that you'd overshot or undershot your entrance and you'd have to re-manoeuvre accordingly.

On my second part of duty I have two round journeys to do on IH3 and have arranged to have trolleybus 1117, my favourite vehicle. I'm finished on return from Hounslow and

when I reach Isleworth depot, I get out and close the cab door behind me. I give 1117 one last look and walk into the depot. Today's date: Tuesday 8th May 1962. For obvious reasons I never drove another trolleybus.

TERRY SHAW

DEPOTS

A total of 23 establishments housed trolley-buses during the lifespan of the system although two of them were only of a temporary nature. Bexleyheath depot was the only completely new premises with all the rest being on the same sites as the tram depots they had replaced. Depots were responsible for the day to day maintenance and cleaning of the vehicles and the allocation for service. Daytime work included examining each vehicle on a rotation basis and at specific intervals each vehicle would receive a 'Dock' or 'Major Dock'. Maintenance included checking electrical items, boom tensioning, chassis greasing and attention to seats and bodywork. Each depot had a painter, and a tyre fitter was employed by the company contracted to deal with each depot's tyres. Cleaning was carried out day and night; by day, vehicles would receive a thorough external wash at regular intervals while at night they were cleared of used tickets and other matter and at some depots were hosed down. External washing was by hand, with some depots turning vehicles out better than others; Wood Green, Clapton, Lea Bridge and Isleworth always despatched smart vehicles, but those from Highgate and West Ham were generally grubby, with grease stains from trolley heads being particularly noticeable on the back emergency window. The reason for changing from red roofs to brown roofs was because of grease falling from the trolley heads.

Each night, trolley head carbons were checked and changed if necessary, only taking a few seconds by the 'skid man'; on frosty mornings, 'iron' (actually made of gun-metal) skids were inserted in the trolley heads of the first vehicle on each route to cut ice off the wires. As these wore down the wires, the carbons were replaced at an early opportunity; a vehicle would be changed at the depot or at a convenient place if the route did not pass the depot. Each night, vehicles underwent a leakage test to ensure that they were in a safe condition; this checked current leaks and insulation. In the latter days of the system, leakage tests were only carried out if there was a complaint from the staff. If a vehicle became 'live' en route, an instruction stated that the trolleys should be removed from the wires and passengers taken off the vehicle which was then to be run to the depot. A Stonebridge trolleybus became 'live' on its last day of life as the author found out when he held a handrail. The crew just let everybody have a last-day 'tingle' and did not run the vehicle into the depot. Faults reported by drivers would be rectified and the appropriate running plates allocated to each vehicle, which was positioned in such a way it would then run out in order. Vehicles needed for attention were allocated to running numbers that spent the off-peaks in the depot. Conductors were responsible for displaying the correct fare tables and route and side blinds.

At many depots a traverser moved a vehicle along its width and turned it round on a turntable; although against regulations, the moving and turning of vehicles was often done simultaneously. The tram-type controllers were marked 'traverse' and 'slew' at depots where these were installed. Although interlocked to prevent simultaneous movements, staff were able to override this feature. Turntable-traversers existed at Bow, Edmonton (2), Finchley, Hackney, Hammersmith, Hanwell, Hounslow, Poplar, Sutton, Walthamstow, Wandsworth and Wood Green; traversers without a turntable existed at Stamford Hill (2) and Holloway (3). Reversed polarity wires were installed in all depots in the early 1950s, enabling vehicle circuits to be checked. Official depot capacity was the number of vehicles which could be parked under wires but excluded unwired sections and pit areas. Pit areas were beyond traversers in depots so fitted: in some depots, these were adjacent to the running shed. Most depots had a separate feeder cable direct from the substation to supply current to their overhead wires, although Lea Bridge, Walthamstow and Ilford tapped off adjacent wires for this. Dead-end wires existed in all depots. It was not considered desirable to park trolleybuses in the open air in view of the possibility of creepage of damp over the insulators, causing considerable leakage of current.

Poplar was the last trolleybus depot to be commissioned. Located in dingy surroundings it was a long way off line of route. 1470 enters whilst 1510 takes up late for some reason and is curtailed at Arbour Square.
Fred Ivey

Generally speaking, units were changed at agreed periods rather than waiting for actual failure although in latter days they were only changed when necessary. Overhauled parts would be received from Charlton works with each vehicle having its own 'Dock' card which detailed work carried out. According to the layout of each depot, vehicles would be cleaned before being parked for the night.

Most depots had a Leyland Cub breakdown vehicle which attended to breakdowns, dewirements and punctures, although the smaller depots had to call upon larger ones to deal with these matters. Vehicles requiring to be towed back to the depot were towed by 'out of depot' sources. Now and again a defective vehicle would be substituted by one from another depot; vehicle 1280 from Wood Green depot ran from Wood Green to North Finchley on route 521 on 20th June 1960 displaying EXTRA but showing NORTH FINCHLEY which was on Wood Green depot blinds. Any vehicle suffering a defect was substituted at the depot if possible. If this was not possible a replacement was sent out and in some situations maintenance staff would attend on the spot. For example, an observant policeman noticed that the tail light was not working on an Isleworth vehicle at Kew Bridge and gave instructions for it not to move until a replacement was inserted. This led to a member of the maintenance staff travelling by service trolleybus with a replacement bulb!

Depot	Code	Date opened	Date closed	Capacity
Acton		5.4.36	9.3.37	
Bexleyheath	BX	10.11.35	3.3.59	75
Bow	BW	5.11.39	18.8.59	102
Carshalton	CN	8.12.35	3.3.59	51
Clapton	CT	11.6.39	14.4.59	90
Colindale	CE	5.7.36	2.1.62	48
Edmonton	EM	16.10.38	18.7.61	122
Finchley	FY	2.8.36	2.1.62	108
Fulwell	FW	16.5.31	8.5.62	120
Hammersmith	HB	12.9.37	19.7.60	65
Hanwell	HL	15.11.36	8.11.60	108
Highgate	HT	6.3.38	25.4.61	230
Ilford	ID	6.2.38	18.8.59	34
Isleworth	IH	27.10.35	8.5.62	37
Lea Bridge	LB	11.6.39	14.4.59	33
Poplar	PR	9.6.40	10.11.59	149
Stamford Hill	SF	5.2.39	18.7.61	97
Stonebridge	SE	5.7.36	2.1.62	86
Walthamstow	WW	18.10.36	26.4.60	107
Wandsworth		12.9.37	30.9.50	24
West Ham	WH	6.6.37	26.4.60	170
Wood Green	WN	8.5.38	7.11.61	108

Some depots had a higher allocation than their official capacity; e.g. Ilford had 43 SAs allocated with a capacity of 34. The capacities quoted relate to under-cover accommodation. Acton was operational only until work on Hanwell and Stonebridge depots was completed.

Prior to 12th July 1950, Carshalton depot was named Sutton, Clapton was Hackney, Colindale was Hendon, Highgate was Holloway, Isleworth was Hounslow and Lea Bridge was Leyton.

MISCELLANEOUS MATTERS

ROUTE NUMBERING POLICY

In 1934 it had been proposed that the design of trolleybuses should include a permanent letter 'T' to precede the route numbers and that trolleybus services be numbered from T1 upwards in the 1-99 series. Green Line coaches were to be prefixed 'G' with Central buses being designated by number only, thereby enabling the public to readily identify the three types of service. A decision was made in 1935 for trolleybuses to use the 600 series of route numbers. No precise date has been found for the renumbering of routes 1-5 but a fare chart for route 604 appeared in August 1935. In January 1938, anticipating that the number of trolleybus routes would exceed 100, authority was sought for the use of route numbers 700 to 799. This was declined, so the use of 500 to 599 was decided upon. Mr T E Thomas was instructed to consider the practicability at some future date of renumbering the trolleybuses, so that 500 to 599 series be used for routes south of the river and the 600 to 699 series be used for routes north of it.

For the tram to trolleybus conversion programme, it was thought desirable that, wherever possible, there should be a similarity between the replaced tram route number and the replacing trolleybus route number. Under the original plan for renumbering all trolleybus routes in the 600 series, tram services 55 and 57 could not receive 655 and 657 as these were already in use, so they were originally allocated the unrelated numbers 671 and 673. However, after the 500 series was introduced it was decided to widen its use beyond its original Holborn loop remit, enabling the 55 and 57 to become 555 and 557. At the same time the related 81 tram, which was to have become 681, was renumbered 581 instead.

Two other route numbers, 537 and 637, were also originally anticipated for use in north London, and details concerning them are to be found in the Hampstead chapter.

OVERHEAD FROGS

It was general practice for conductors to operate frogs where the vehicle was using nearside wires (e.g. 687/697 at Connaught Road, 697/699 at Plaistow, Clegg Street) thus obviating the need to re-board in the main road, but this was not a hard and fast rule. Consideration was given so that not too many frog pulls would apply to each route and attempts were made to equal things out. 662 pulled at Craven Park while 660/666 pulled at Jubilee Clock with 607 pulling at Acton Market and 660/666 pulling at 'Askew Arms'. In both 660/666 instances the semi-auto frogs unusually required an offside pull. With the quicker semi-automatic frogs, conductors pulled a lever which remained set for a certain position while they re-boarded the vehicle. The frog was re-set when the trolley head passed over a skate on the wire. Few heavily-used main line frogs had 'pull and hold' frogs where the vehicle was taking the offside wires. One example was the 555 for Downsell Road at 'Bakers Arms'. An onerous task on routes 609, 639, 679, 685, 697 and 699 was the necessity for seven frog pulls on a round journey – that being there and back. It did not follow that routes with the more frequent headways would have 'frog priority'; 628 had priority at Wandsworth and College Park despite being less frequent than 630. Likewise, 691 pulled at Ilford Broadway rather than 693 and 601/603 pulled at Surbiton rather than the infrequent 602. There were many anomalies in that some infrequent services had a semi-auto (e.g. 602 at Norbiton Church), while regularly-used frogs (e.g. 521/621 at Jolly Butchers Hill, 611 at Baring Street, 623 at Tottenham Hale, 641 at Winchmore Hill, 645 at Edgware, 653 at Mile End Gate) were 'pull and hold'. Unusual were semi-auto frogs for offside manoeuvres for Edmonton and Highgate depots. Rather unfairly, at Islington, 609 pulled a semi-auto frog at 'Angel' and then used a 'pull and hold' frog just round the corner at Goswell Road. Similarly, southbound 699s had to pull in quick succession at Stratford Broadway, Plaistow Station and Plaistow Broadway. Uniformity at Cricklewood saw all three semi-auto frogs requiring nearside pulls, one each for 645, 660 and 664/666. Very unusual, and surviving until March 1959, was a push-button frog at the exit of Carshalton depot. At a number of regularly used frogs, pointsmen in canvas huts were positioned to act as 'frog men' and thus speed the services; some were employed in peak hours only.

The semi-auto frog had been set incorrectly at Eden Street, Kingston but fortunately the driver has observed this; the re-set skate apparatus is clearly visible. The frog handle has now been set to its correct position and this is ratified in the 'Y' light in the signal box ahead of 1494. The driver changes the poles by hand but surely the conductor of RT2499 cannot be giving him advice about trolley manipulation. Hugh Taylor

Far Right With one hand on her hip and her tunic sleeves rolled up, a touch of femininity is given to trolleybus work as this Edmonton depot conductress gives her full attention to the 'pull and hold' frog at Ponders End for a 659 trolleybus to enter the loop that will lead to Enfield bus garage. J.H. Price

MSC PLATES

All cabs, buses and trams operating in London were required by the Metropolitan Public Carriage Act 1869 to hold a licence which manifested itself as a Metropolitan Stage Carriage Licence plate; with the introduction of trolleybuses in 1931 they, too, had to comply with this requirement. All plates issued prior to 1st July 1933 were of rectangular dimensions (6" x 9") but were known as 'square' plates; trolleybuses 1-61 gained these but they were re-issued plates. They were enamelled and a number was displayed on them, above which was a crown of the Sovereign. Initially this was a Victorian crown which gave way to an Edwardian crown displaying a lion and a unicorn; the last type was a Georgian crown (the highest numbered square plate was 12915). The plates were interchangeable between buses and trams and between trams and trolleybuses and were issued for a year. Originally trolley vehicles were exempt from a charge but from 1st July 1933 an annual fee of 10/- was payable. The plates were under the jurisdiction of the Public Carriage Office of the Metropolitan Police until 1933, when upon the formation of the LPTB they were administered at Chiswick works on behalf of the PCO. From 1st July 1933, oval plates with a letter 'N' below a number, started to replace the square plates, but this process was soon discarded and both types were used simultaneously thereafter. Their use on motorbuses gradually declined (although one was fitted to RT 1).

Trolleybuses 1-60 carried their plates below the rear window; 61 had one positioned beneath the rear registration; 62 onwards used oval plates which were placed over the used-ticket box flap on the platform; some 'Diddlers' gained oval plates which were positioned in the same place. The licence number was also carried above the fare chart holder in the lower saloon, but this practice was discontinued on standard vehicles. A particular plate may well have stayed with a vehicle throughout its life; however, if delicensed for any reason, such as overhaul at the time of its annual renewal, the plate would be returned and re-issued, with another plate being issued to the vehicle on its relicensing. A spare copy of each plate was held in stock by the authorities. Five vehicles (106, 406, 804, 861, 1001) carried three different plates during their lives. Plates would be changed if one was defaced or lost and this continued almost until the end of the system.

It was unusual to see vehicles operating without MSC plates. However, about ten C class Stonebridge trolleybuses were operating without them for a few days prior to their withdrawal in August 1959. This was unlawful. The reason for vehicle 699 running without one for a few days before withdrawal in November 1960 was probably due to it being illegally removed. A possibly unique situation occurred to trolleybus 1148, which was a very late allocation to Stamford Hill's fleet towards the end of June 1961. It had

The fine lines of trolleybus 61 are shown in this view of it waiting to enter Hounslow terminus; the MSC plate was carried in an unusual position.
F.G. Reynolds

378 gained 61's MSC plate after its withdrawal from passenger service. In so doing it became the only standard trolleybus to gain a 'square' plate.
Brian Chaplin

Below The MSC plate from trolleybus 383, of the standard oval variety.

been restored to service from the Rolling Stock Engineer's spares float and while its plate was being located, it ran with a paper tracing in the prescribed position.

The dates on which plates were changed were generally recorded at a later date by the office dealing with them; vehicle 383 was withdrawn on 6th January 1959 but the plate was not recorded as being returned until 24th February 1959. The lowest one issued to a trolleybus was 47N for vehicle 1670 in 1946. Q1s were issued with a combination of high and low numbers; 524N was allotted to 1884 with 11218N being given to 1825. Plate 9610N was fixed to trolleybus 1815, having previously been on a vehicle it replaced, trolleybus 11; the plate fixed to trolleybus 1856 (10946N) had previously been on Bournemouth 77 and tram 1850. The highest plate in circulation was 11248N, which was fitted to tramcar 2050 on 19th November 1945. The highest one allocated to a trolleybus was 11247N, issued to 392B on 12th November 1945 after its return to London subsequent to rebodying.

Trolleybus 378, which was used for a 'pay as you board' experiment in 1946, had its plate re-located to the rear when being rebuilt for this role. Trolleybus 61 at Isleworth depot carried square plate 4081N which is recorded as being removed on 18th November 1950. No.378 was allocated to Isleworth in the summer of 1951 and required a plate; 4081N was put on 378 but this time fitted to the usual

position on the platform. It became the only standard trolleybus to carry a square plate, which is recorded as being on 378 from 30th May 1951 until 26th June 1952. It is assumed that the reason for it not gaining an oval plate was that 4081N had been retained at Isleworth and when 378 was relicensed, having been a training vehicle for some time, Chiswick gave them authority to use it. The 'Diddlers', 61 and 378 when used solely for driver training did not carry a plate as this was not a requirement.

All licence plates were removed and returned to the PCO for destruction when they were no longer required. When vehicles were withdrawn during the conversion programme, the plates were meticulously removed. Those on vehicles 1, 260 and 796 stayed on the vehicles, as did 1538's which reached the scrapyard with it on despite being in store for a considerable time. The last MSC plates were in use on 8th May 1962 on trolleybuses operating out of Isleworth depot. The staff at Fulwell, on instructions, had acted illegally and removed all of that depot's plates on the night of 7th May in order that their workload would be diminished on 8th May. The last vehicle to use a Metropolitan Stage Carriage Licence plate on the public highway therefore, was trolleybus 1274 in the early hours of 9th May 1962. Very few plates survived destruction, that belonging to trolleybus 383, illustrated, being one such survivor.

THE SOUTH LONDON PROPOSALS

Had it not been for the outbreak of World War Two, the remainder of the London tramway system would have been converted to trolleybus operation as part of the New Works Programme. On Sunday June 9th 1940, just over 1,100 tramcars remained operating on 102 route miles, a third of the of the total taken over by London Transport in 1933. Most of the trams ran solely in south London, with three routes operating through the Kingsway tram subway into north London.

The London Passenger Transport Board had carried out much groundwork to convert the remainder of the tramway system to trolleybuses. Much correspondence had taken place between the LPTB and local councils, the necessary Parliamentary powers had been obtained, mainly in 1937, (they were in force for five years) and a list of replacement routes had been drawn up and frequencies determined. No vehicles had been ordered although it was anticipated that 939 vehicles would be required, making a fleet total of 2,660 trolleybuses. However, it was approved in principle by the General Manager in June 1938 that five or six low-earning tramway routes could be replaced by motorbuses. A requirement of law meant that all trolleybus vehicle route applications in the country had to be made known to the public and at strategic points along these routes, notices were placed detailing these applications. Those objecting could voice their opinions and in some instances, notably inner London, objectors were successful.

London Transport's planning for this scheme was so far advanced that extra overhead equipment had been put in place at Islington Green, Shoreditch Junction, Columbia Road (Shoreditch Church) and in two places at Mildmay Park; at Newington Green a siding wire was constructed. These related to the Kingsway Subway routes. Trolleybus 1379 was fitted with an offside entrance to permit passengers to board in the subway stations and it underwent clearance tests on Sunday 13th August 1939 when two round trips were made, running to Islington Green to recharge its batteries. Clearances were found to be tight, so alterations to the tramway subway would have been necessary. It was planned for a turntable to be constructed at the southern end of the subway to cater for emergencies and powers were obtained for trolleybuses to work through. Trolleybus possibilities were eventually aborted and the tramway subway would only ever resound to the elfin clang of the tramcar.

During the north London trolleybus conversion programme it was stated that the continuation of the subway services could not be contemplated and it was suggested that they be curtailed at 'Angel' Islington, Newington Green, Bloomsbury or Shoreditch. These possibilities were examined with the result that tram route 31 was withdrawn from Hackney and diverted to Islington. Its retention would have meant the use of Old Street and Great Eastern Street (towards Hackney) by trolleybuses, while withdrawal meant only Old Street would be used. The reason for this investigation was that London Transport wished to eliminate dual operation of trams and trolleybuses as far as possible in the northern area. It was anticipated that the subway services would be converted in June 1939 and would operate to 'some central point in the southern area such as Camberwell Green'. A 'spanner in the works', though, was an undertaking given to Westminster City Council that trams would not run on the Victoria Embankment for a longer period than three years after the commencement of trolleybuses. This could not be guaranteed.

These conversions would have brought trolleybuses to the heart of the capital, for overhead wires would have been strung along the Victoria Embankment, at Cannon Street Station and at Victoria where approval was given for two alternative routeings. The Act of 1937 specifically stated that trolley vehicles were not allowed to turn on the Victoria Embankment (which would have hindered operation). This restriction led to proposed routes 534, 540, 556, 562 and 574 being extended around the Embankment rather than turn thereon. Nor where they approved to turn at Tooley Street, north west of Bermondsey Street or at Duke Street, Bermondsey. This would have linked the Tooley Street and Southwark Street routes. Other turning points not approved were: Bloomsbury Square, London Bridge, Southwark Bridge, Bermondsey Street and St Thomas Street. Powers were obtained for operating over Westminster Bridge despite strenuous opposition from Westminster City Council; Westminster Corporation and the City of London Corporation viewed trolleybuses with disfavour.

Despite not being used in its intended role, 1379 was used at Highgate depot. Being a notable vehicle, it was requested for a tour and it is seen here at the Bloomsbury terminus, just round the corner from the northern entrance to the Kingsway Subway. Michael Dryhurst

536
VIA OLD KENT RD & NEW CROSS
ABBEY WOOD

The plan drawn up for the replacement trolleybus routes in 1939 is shown alongside. Compared to the tram network, a number of alterations would have occurred:

533 curtailed at Newington Green instead of terminating at Manor House.
534 curtailed at Battersea, so Chelsea would not be served by trolleybuses.
540 extended to Welling daily.
542 extended to South Croydon.
554 extended to Marvels Lane.
562 would have operated from Forest Hill at all times and would also have operated daily.
572 would have run to Victoria instead of Embankment.
628 would work daily to Wembley.
631 would have run to Hackney and Wandsworth, thus restoring the former tram 31 routeing that had been lost in earlier years. It was to be the only route to be extended at both ends.
612 night service would become Blackfriars Road to Mitcham.

Notes:

Tram routes 44, 66 and 84 would have been covered by other trolleybus services rather than being directly replaced. Trolleybuses 540 and 698 would have been the only new links compared with the tram routes.

Cannon Street Station would have replaced Southwark Bridge as an inner terminus. Apart from the Marvels Lane extension, another significant extension would have been that of the West Norwood routes to 'Rosendale' which presumably would have replaced the spur working on bus route 2. The proposed extension was due to the lack of a suitable turning point and standing arrangements for trolleybuses in the vicinity of West Norwood tram terminus at 'Thurlow Arms'. Consideration was given to cutting the Norwood routes back to Tulse Hill (using Thurlow Park Road, Avenue Park Road and Norwood Road) or Norwood depot.

As with all conversion schemes, a number of ideas were floated. There were plans for the 506 to work from Clapham, 'Plough' to Cannon Street, the 510 to operate from Summerstown to Cannon Street, the '542' (tram 42) to be run by motorbuses, the 552 to operate from Downham and that the 626 be diverted at Hammersmith and work to Kew Bridge.

In an internal London Transport document dated 19th November 1939, the replacement trolleybus routes were quoted as:

502	Wimbledon - Embankment via Westminster	Daily
504	Wimbledon - Embankment via Blackfriars	Daily
502A	Streatham Library - Clapham - Westminster - Clapham - Tooting, becoming 522	Mon-Sat peaks
522	Tooting - Streatham - Westminster - Streatham, becoming 502A	Mon-Sat peaks
504A	Streatham Library - Clapham - Blackfriars - Clapham - Tooting, becoming 524	Mon-Sat peaks
524	Tooting - Streatham - Blackfriars - Streatham, becoming 504A	Mon-Sat peaks
506	Wimbledon (Sats pm) Tooting - Clapham - Cannon Street Stn	Mon-Sat peaks
508	Victoria - Clapham - Streatham - Victoria (via Tooting)	Daily
520	Victoria - Streatham - Clapham - Victoria (via Tooting)	Daily
510	Tooting - Streatham - Cannon Street Station	Daily
516	Purley - Embankment via Westminster	Daily
518	Purley - Embankment via Blackfriars	Daily
533	Newington Green - West Norwood	Daily
534	Battersea - Embankment via Blackfriars am peak / via Westminster pm peak / Battersea - Camberwell Green off-peaks	Daily
535	Archway - Forest Hill	Daily
536	Abbey Wood - Embankment via Blackfriars	Daily
538	Abbey Wood - Embankment via Westminster	Daily
540	Welling Corner - Embankment via Westminster	Daily
542	Thornton Heath - South Croydon	Daily
546	Woolwich - Cannon Street Station	Daily
548	West Norwood - Cannon Street Station	Daily
552	Grove Park - Cannon Street Station	Mon-Sat peaks
554	Marvels Lane - Victoria	Daily
556	Peckham Rye - Embankment via Westminster	Daily
558	Blackwall Tunnel - Victoria	Daily
560	Goose Green - Cannon Street Station	Mon-Sat peaks
562	Forest Hill - Embankment via Blackfriars	Daily
568	Greenwich - Waterloo	Daily
570	Greenwich - London Bridge	Daily
572	Woolwich - Victoria	Daily
574	Grove Park (Sats pm) Downham - Embankment via Blackfriars	Daily
578	West Norwood - Victoria	Mon-Sat
631	Wandsworth - Hackney Station	Daily

Revised trolleybus routes:

612	Mitcham - London Bridge (via Lambeth Road)	Daily
626	Hammersmith - London Bridge	Daily
628	Wembley - Victoria	Daily
655	Hammersmith - Hanwell (Acton Market Place in peaks)	Daily
698	Eltham, Well Hall Station - Bexleyheath	Daily

Night trolleybus routes (unnumbered):

(504A)	Tooting - Clapham - Blackfriars - Clapham - Tooting, becoming 522 *	Mon-Sat
(522)	Tooting - Streatham - Westminster - Streatham - Tooting, becoming 504A *	Mon-Sat
(534)	New Cross - Embankment via Camberwell and Blackfriars	Mon-Sat
(535)	Archway - Bloomsbury	Mon-Sat
(574)	Downham - Embankment via Old Kent Road and Blackfriars	Mon-Sat
(612)	Mitcham - Blackfriars Road (via Embankment)	Mon-Sat
(626)	Hammersmith - London Bridge *	Mon-Sat

*These are thought to be the most likely configurations. Route 626 would have been the only service to regularly operate both ways along the Embankment. Route 630 would have been worked by Thornton Heath and Hammersmith depots.

The London County Council had planned to operate a new tramway between Eltham and Grove Park. London Transport indicated that this route would be trolleybus equipped, but powers were not sought.

Between 1938 and 1946 the LT allocation books detailed trolleybus capacity for each tram depot as:

Abbey Wood	58
Brixton Hill	32
Camberwell	112
Clapham	108
New Cross	250
Norwood	40
Streatham	90
Thornton Heath	60
Wandsworth	86

There were no plans, however, for Brixton Hill and Norwood tram depots to become trolleybus depots, but land was purchased for what is now Stockwell bus garage, as it was intended for this to be a trolleybus depot. By discontinuing the use of Norwood, it was proposed to build a new depot in the vicinity of Kennington Gate for 120 vehicles and a site at Lansdowne Road (now Stockwell garage) was investigated. A new trolleybus depot was required in the neighbourhood of Clapham Common and it was reported that the High School adjoining the sub-station on South Side, Clapham Common, which was to be auctioned in 1938, would make a suitable site. The trolleybus depot at Rye Lane was planned to have two exits and certain houses in Ophir Street were considered for purchasing for demolition (it was intended to close Abbey Wood, the implication being that Rye Lane would be the substitute). It is thought that Charlton tram works, which would have become Charlton trolleybus works, may have been used partly as a running depot to alleviate accommodation problems. Trolleybuses take up more room than trams and there was a general increase in vehicles upon conversion or shortly after, so spare depot capacity was immediately swallowed up and more room required. Drawings had been prepared for Clapham, Rye Lane, Stockwell and Wandsworth depots.

The trolleybus depots would have received, it is presumed, the following codes:

AW	Abbey Wood
BN	Streatham
CA	Clapham
NX	New Cross
RL	Rye Lane
SW	Stockwell
TH	Thornton Heath
WL	Camberwell

The Conversion of Tramways to Trolleybus Routes, Southern Scheme, as the plan was known, would have been a ten-stage programme and scheme A of 8th January 1945, and compiled by the Office of the Permanent Way Engineer (Trams) Chief Engineer's Department, read:

Stage One: Wandsworth to London.

Stage Two: Wimbledon & Tooting to London.

Stage Three: Completion of Clapham & Tooting.

Stage Four: Purley & Streatham.

Stage Five: Subway to Norwood.

Stage Six: Dog Kennel Hill Routes.

Stage Seven: Grove Park, Downham & Forest Hill.

Stage Eight: Jamaica Road Route.

Stage Nine: Eltham and Lee Routes.

Stage Ten: Woolwich and Embankment.

It is not known what scheme B was, or even if one was ever compiled; scheme A was very similar to the 1950-52 tram to bus conversion programme. In that scheme, the subway tram routes were originally as in the order of this scheme and the only other difference between the two was that in the 1950 plan, only two stages were required for what were the first three stages outlined above. In both cases, access to Charlton works would be maintained until abandonment. One link which might have been resurrected was the summer Sunday and Bank Holiday extension to Hampton Court for routes 502/504, giving an Embankment to Hampton Court service which had been withdrawn in 1931.

The turning circles had been applied for and in most cases approved. The necessary drawings had been prepared, although direction of use remained to be settled in a few instances and consultation with the police had taken place. Minor alterations such as corners of roads which had to be eased were noted, and at Deptford Broadway a large centre island would have replaced existing islands and traffic lights were to be erected. At Thornton Heath, it was proposed that route 542 would circle a roundabout, and there was to be a purpose-built roundabout at Marvels Lane. However, Battersea Park Road (Savona Street) and Kennington Cross were not approved and alternatives were being sought. The short working facility at Battersea Park Road was to be a battery turn and was the only one nominated as such. Residents were not pleased about the possibility of trolleybuses running along residential roads and public meetings were held to voice discontent. The residents of Sherard Road, Eltham received little sympathy from London Transport at one such meeting on 3rd June 1937 when objecting to the routeing of the Woolwich to Eltham trolleybus service.

Part of the planning involved the finding of suitable turning circles for the new trolleybus routes. Approved ones were as follows:

Balham Station, Oakmead Road: via Oakmead Road and Ravenstone Street

Battersea Park Road, Savona Street: clockwise

Beresford Square: via Plumstead Road and New Road

Blackwall Lane, Colomb Street: via Trafalgar Road, Colomb Street and Pelton Road

Blackwall Tunnel: junction of Tunnel Avenue and Ordnance Road

Brixton Church: via Effra Road, Church Road and Brixton Hill

Brockley Rise, Codrington Hill: junction of Stondon Park and Brockley Rise.

Camberwell Green: clockwise

Cannon Street: Various options were considered but no concrete proposal materialised. A common element was a stand in Queen Street.

Catford, Rushey Green: clockwise

City Terminus, Southwark Bridge: on LPTB property at junction of Cloak Lane

Clapham, Nightingale Lane: via Clapham Common South Side and The Avenue

Clapham, 'The Plough': via two sides of The Pavement and Clapham Common South Side

Deptford Broadway: clockwise

Deptford, Church Street: via Wellington Street and Church Street

Downham Way, Northover: clockwise

East Dulwich Road, Goose Green: at the junction of Grove Vale, Lordship Lane and East Dulwich Road

Eltham, Sherard Road: via Well Hall Road, Lassa Road and Sherard Road

Forest Hill, Waldram Road: via Perry Vale, Waldram Road South and Waldram Road

Greenwich Church: via Church Street, Clarence Street, King William Street and Nelson Street

Grove Park: via Chinbrook Road

Hop Exchange, Thrale Street: junction of Southwark Street and Thrale Street

Kennington Cross: via Kennington Lane, Windmill Row and Kennington Road

Kennington Gate: at junction of Kennington Park Road, Camberwell New Road and Brixton Road.

Kingsway Subway: turntable at southern entrance

Lancaster Street, Borough Road: via Lancaster Street, Southwark Bridge Road and Borough Road

Lewisham, Lewis Grove: via Lewis Grove

London Bridge: junction of Bermondsey Street and Tooley Street (permission was later granted to extend to the junction of Southwark Street and Borough High Street but with no turning facilities)

Lower Road, Rotherhithe Tunnel: via Brunel Road, Rupack Street, St Mary Church Street and Paradise Street.

Malpas Road, Shardeloes Road: via Malpas Road and Shardeloes Road

Marvels Lane Terminus: junction of Chinbrook Road and Marvels Lane

Mitcham Lane, St Leonards Church: via Babington Road and Ambleside Avenue

New Cross Gate: via Kender Street, Besson Street and New Cross Road

Norbury, Hermitage Lane: via Hermitage Lane and Green Lane

Old Kent Road, 'Bricklayers Arms': via Bartholomew Street and New Kent Road

Peckham Rye: via Hall Road, Hawkslade Road, Kelvington Road and Athenlay Road

Purley Terminus: via High Street, Purley Road and Brighton Road

South Croydon, 'Red Deer': via Sanderstead Road, Bynes Road and Rolleston Road

Southwark Bridge Road, Union Street: clockwise

Southwark, Trinity Street: via Borough High Street, Trinity Street and Great Dover Street

South Wimbledon Station, 'Grove Hotel': via Cecil Road, Balfour Road and Merton Road

Stamford Street, Burrell Street: via Burrell Street, Bear Lane and Southwark Street

Stangate: via Lambeth Palace Road, Stangate and Westminster Bridge Road

Stockwell Green, 'The Swan': via Stockwell Terrace and South Lambeth Road

Thornton Heath Terminus: at roundabout

Tower Bridge, Parish Street: via Parish Street, LPTB property and Barham Street

Victoria Terminus: (a) via Gillingham Street, Wilton Road, Victoria Street and Vauxhall Bridge Road or (b) via Warwick Street, Wilton Road and Vauxhall Bridge Road

Waterloo Terminus: via Mepham Street, York Road and Waterloo Road

Well Hall Roundabout: clockwise

Westhorne Avenue Roundabout: clockwise

West Norwood Terminus: via Robson Road, Park Road, Rosendale Road, Myton Road and Martell Road

Woolwich Academy, Prince Imperial Monument: clockwise

In the 1939 LPTB Act, two emergency points were granted on the Victoria Embankment. One was near the eastern end of Temple Place and the other was between Horseguards Avenue and Northumberland Avenue. They could only be used in traffic emergencies and were specifically not allowed to turn "for the more convenient working of the trolley vehicle system of the Board".

Sites had been inspected for substations at:
Brixton
Brockley, Malpas Road
Camberwell, Ashbourne Grove
Camberwell, Old Kent Road
Catford, Culverley Road
Charlton
Clapham
Deptford
Eltham
Greenwich
Oval, Harleyford Road
Peckham, Glengall Mews
Streatham High Road

Despite the ten-stage plan of 8th January 1945, the General Manager of London Transport had requested on 17th August 1944 that his senior staff consider and report on the benefits likely to be secured through dealing with the situation of tram replacement by means of enlargement and re-arrangement of the central bus fleet. The report was to cover the changes in services, routes and terminal points and the economies likely to be secured.

In a report by the Department of the Chief Development and Research Officer dated 26th April 1946, a number of salient points appertaining to the choice of vehicle to replace the south London trams were detailed. One was crew costs; in 1937, the wage differential was £1 per week less for tram and trolleybus crews as opposed to motorbus crews. By 1946 this had narrowed to just 4/- per week. It was foreseen that crew costs on the road services would soon be equalised and the lower crew costs of the trolleybus would be lost. London Transport's engineers maintained neutrality as to which was to be the preferred vehicle. They quoted the fact that maintenance costs of the trolleybus were lower and gave it a distinct advantage; however, they went on to say that these savings were offset by maintaining the overhead equipment and ancillary items. They did make the point though, that they thought that the possibilities of technical development lay with the motorbus. Operationally, it was considered that buses would cause more congestion in the central area particularly at major traffic points such as Elephant & Castle, Vauxhall and Blackfriars. (Buses were quoted as 56-seaters; trolleybuses as 70-seaters). The need to protect the capital investment was much less strong in 1946 because the equipment was that much older and therefore closer to life-expiry. The surplus capacity that would be thrown up in the electrical generating stations, was almost exactly the amount needed to feed the new Central Line extensions of the Underground.

A matter now rearing its head was that of civic amenities. Town planning was now emerging from its slumbers and it was considered in the post-war period that there might be public reaction against the installation of overhead wires, not merely along the Victoria Embankment and over famous river bridges, but also beside the Houses of Parliament. If trolleybuses were adopted, there would have had to be the erection of poles and overhead wires over a considerable mileage in south London generally. A report was submitted to the London Passenger Transport Board on 6th June 1946 by the department of the Chief Development and Research Officer, recommending that the south London trams be replaced by buses; that day, the Board approved the recommendation that this policy should be adopted 'in principle'. Despite more buses being required than trolleybuses it was decided that it would be the 56-seater motorbus that would become the replacement vehicle. Ease of fare collection was brought in as a factor for there was a higher incidence of uncollected fares on trolleybuses as opposed to motorbuses, but the main argument that influenced this decision was the mobility offered by the motorbus. It was later stated by the same department that the expiry of the lives of any south London trolleybuses would occur eight years after the expiry of the lives of the trolleybuses in north London and that if a decision was taken in due course to adopt bus operation to replace the north London trolleybuses, then a simultaneous conversion in south London would hardly be practicable in view of the capital losses that would be sustained. On 3rd October 1946, the Board received official notification that the Minister of Transport had approved the proposal. On 15th November 1946, an announcement was made that there would be no more tram to trolleybus conversions and that the remaining trams would be replaced by motorbuses when they became available. It was stated that buses were "eminently flexible and much cheaper".

The Parliamentary powers were extended twice. On the first occasion, during the war, they were automatically extended under Defence Regulations and on the second occasion, in late 1945, they were extended by the Minister of Transport when the Board had to re-apply for powers (the Extension of Powers proposals went through the Board on 1st November 1945). The powers finally expired on 20th July 1948.

In the late 1940s and early 1950s London Transport deliberated further whether to replace the trolleybuses by new motorbuses or new trolleybuses. Although there was little to choose by way of costs, the determining factor for the choice of motorbuses was their flexibility. On 28th April 1954 this decision was announced and the system closed in the early hours of 9th May 1962.

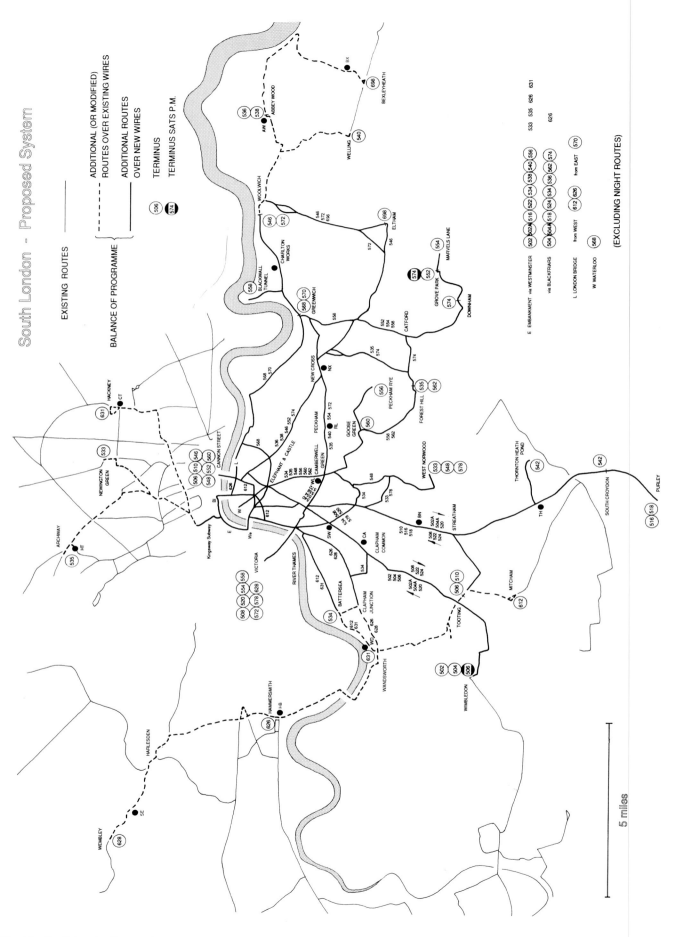

South London – Proposed System

EXISTING ROUTES ———

BALANCE OF PROGRAMME
- ADDITIONAL (OR MODIFIED) ROUTES OVER EXISTING WIRES - - - -
- ADDITIONAL ROUTES OVER NEW WIRES ———

TERMINUS ◯

TERMINUS SATS P.M. ⬤

(EXCLUDING NIGHT ROUTES)

DESTINATION BLINDS

Due to their availability in recent years there has been a surge of interest in blinds generally. Such availability did not occur during the heyday of the trolleybus and it was only during the conversion programme that depot staff allowed others to obtain them. For many years, obsolete blinds from all road services had to be returned to the blind shop. In wartime, redundant blinds were much sought after and the engineering staff were allowed to take them home on a rotational basis. Linen blinds were used for extra bedding material and in later years to lag pipes in lofts. Latterly, many ended up as rags or wrapping material for other blinds but some Clapton/Lea Bridge linen destination blinds were used by Highgate for repairing motorbus blinds. George Cohen & Son, who scrapped most of London's trolleybuses, sold what blinds came into the scrapyard and although enthusiasts were able to buy them for about 2/6 (bamboo poles were 10/-) Cohens would only sell a certain percentage of them in this way as they had orders from barbers who used them as stuffing in their chairs; how many readers have unknowingly had their hair cut sitting on a SMITHFIELD display? In the conversion programme some depots removed the blinds whilst others left them in. It was particularly hard on the Fulwell staff on the night of conversion stage nine, when they had to first de-blind most of their Q1s, then remove Highgate blinds from newly-arrived L3s and finally re-blind them with those from the Q1s. The result was that hundreds of blinds appeared that night on the depot floor and it was no wonder some vehicles went out next day with blinds upside down or none at all in some apertures!

The first trolleybus blinds made were for the LUT 'Diddlers' although their manufacturer is unknown. Prior to entry into service, 'Diddlers' 1 and 2 were fitted with wooden boards and roof-mounted route plates but these were soon removed in favour of blinds. The 'Diddlers' had two blind boxes, front and side, yet some blinds were marked FULWELL DEPOT FRONT AND REAR. The side blinds were very difficult to fit — it was as if the trolleybus had been built around the blind box! Original 'Diddler' blinds were distinctive, but the LPTB introduced a new print style for them which was the same as for standard vehicles.

Charlton works produced all trolleybus requirements from 1933, their last issue being for Edmonton depot in early 1952. Their blinds were made of linen with the blind shop printing them by a silk screen process on long tables. Some destination and side blinds were of such extreme length, that it was necessary to produce them in sections that were then sewn together. In contrast, several number blinds could be printed on a single length of linen and then cut appropriately. This method lent itself to layout variations, for each word was laid out individually. One employee might set out a display in a different manner to a colleague. One week's work could differ from another's when the layout was reassembled after washing down and cleaning. An order for blinds could take two weeks to complete and identical blinds would receive closely spaced dates. All were checked for accuracy and few errors occurred.

Until 1941/42 light bulbs in trolleybus blind boxes were blue so as to distinguish them after dark from motorbuses. This practice ceased as the bulbs became unobtainable and white ones had to be used. As part of the experimentation which preceded the changeover to 'paper' blinds, Chiswick works produced sets of blinds with blue wording on a black background, thus reviving the earlier practice; these had printed paper labels stuck onto a coarse cotton material and were fitted to the 1948 batch of Q1s at Fulwell. They were not particularly legible and were soon discontinued. However, the print type was perpetuated in white on black. There was also an experiment at Hounslow depot in 1946 with 'blue' paper blinds produced at Chiswick. Further trials, using paper blinds, were carried out in the early post-war years at Hammersmith and West Ham which led to Aldenham taking over the production of all trolleybus blinds, first issues appearing in 1951 (linen blinds were sent to Aldenham for the blind shop to copy). With the transition from linen to paper blinds, the lettering changed from thick and bold to the more restrained 'Johnston' style but both were very legible. Linen and paper blinds became intermixed on vehicles but 1207 at SF still carried a complete set of linen blinds until withdrawal on 18th July 1961. Linen destination blinds were last used on 18th/19th July 1961, linen side blinds on 2nd/3rd January 1962 and route blinds on 8th/9th May 1962; the last 602 of all, vehicle 1491, carried a linen blind in its front route box. Aldenham only printed paper blinds.

Vehicles 64-754, 756-779 and 905-919 had the front destination blinds altered by the conductor; on 755, 780-904, 920 onwards and rebodied vehicles, they were changed by the driver from the cab. With one exception it was the conductor's responsibility to alter route and side blinds, for which a special key was used. Side blinds were turned alongside the rearmost nearside upstairs seat on standard vehicles; on the 'Diddlers', SAs and Q1s they were altered by winding the details from the platform. Rear blinds were changed from the staircase. The conductor viewed the 'tell-tale' back-stamp tab through a peep hole; the back-stamp details were printed in miniature form on the reverse of the blind and the wording was identical or similar to the actual blind display. The tabs were printed on cotton cloth at Charlton, while Aldenham used gummed paper labels; from the end of 1960 details were inked on. Tabs had to be accurately positioned in order that part of the next display did not show. Five line linen side blinds and linen destination blind tabs were numbered (additions to numbered tabs were given an A/B/C suffix). Linen destination blinds had four tabs: one for the driver's use (by periscope), one for the rear box and one for each of the different peep hole positions on vehicles with conductor-operated front blinds. The latter two were viewed by the conductor through either (a) a peep hole which was situated in the blind box pull-out flap up to, it is believed, the D class, or (b) through a peep hole situated in the ledge above the blind box housing on the remainder of vehicles with conductor-operated front blinds. The reason for the change was probably due to requests from the staff as the 'flap' position was awkward to use — it required the conductor to almost get down on the floor! The tab for the 'ledge' position was in mirror image form and upside down as the conductor looked into a mirror in the blind box housing. On paper blinds the tab for the position in the pull-out flap was omitted; no doubt the blind shop thought the 'ledge' position had replaced the 'flap' position whereas in fact both types were in use. As no guide was now available on 'flap' vehicles, it became almost standard practice for the conductor to pull out the flap on vehicles where blinds required to be changed — in this way the blinds could be more accurately positioned. On the SA1/SA2 classes, the conductor opened a flap which was retained by clips and changed the rear blind from within the blind box; SA3 rear blinds were changed from the platform. The exception referred to above concerned the SA3s — the front route blind was changed by the driver, there being two handles in the cab. 'Diddler' front blinds were wound from inside the box. Route blinds on standard vehicles had a tab each side — one for the front and one for the rear.

Charlton blinds were dated and stamped LPTB (later LTE) and the depot name usually appeared in full whereas on Aldenham blinds the date and depot code were shown. Paper destination blinds sometimes had panels sewn in and were stamped 'REN' to show they had been renovated. Sewing machines existed in larger depots, such as HT, for repairs. Inserts could be sewn in and good parts from damaged blinds could be sewn together to make one good blind. Aldenham sewed paper and linen destination blinds together for WH and WW and route blinds were similarly dealt with. Special blinds were made for vehicles 61, 63 and those from Bournemouth. The shortest blinds were route blinds for CN (22½ ins) and the longest were 37 ft linen destination blinds for WW (including an insert) with HT having a 36 ft long paper destination blind.

Front and rear destination blind box apertures on standard trolleybuses measured 33½ ins by 14½ ins and route box apertures 26½ ins by 9 ins. Despite the different aperture widths, both route and destination blinds were printed on material of 36 ins width. The display depth was 14 ins on destination blinds and 9 ins on route blinds. The side box measured 28 ins wide by 25 ins deep, the display area being 29½ ins by 25 ins. A metal route plate also was originally displayed in a carrier mounted above the rearmost nearside window (on classes L, M and N below it). Similar plates were carried on the offside on most classes but all became disused in 1939/40. The nearside plates were repositioned in brackets on the ledge behind the nearside long seat and remained in use until 1949.

Some depots shared joint blinds initially (BW/PR, CE/SE, LB/CT, WD/HB and HL with Acton); this was for economy but clashed with a desire to include as many turning points as possible. After the initial FW/IH joint paper blinds, all were made singularly for each depot. Linen blinds were very stout, needing little attention, but paper blinds could tear at the most frequently used labels. When vehicles stayed on routes for long stretches, e.g. 607, 653, 654, blinds would 'yellow' from the heat of blind box bulbs and tended to 'rust' due to water ingress. Less commonly used displays remained in pristine condition.

ROUTE BLINDS

The first route blinds embraced a rounded type of numeral; the last '6' of 696 and the '8' of 698 looked similar and caused confusion to the public. An experiment occurred and it is thought that the 698 was printed as black on white. Consequently, in 1936, less rounded numerals appeared. A completely new style was brought into use upon the introduction of paper blinds and two different types of print were used with the second style being of a tall compressed nature. On these blinds most of the printed labels carried two route numbers and both styles might be used on one blind. Blinds were marked on the white ends at the top and bottom as TROLLEYBUS SERVICE NOS, SER NUMBERS or a similar abbreviation on linen blinds and as ROUTE NUMBERS on paper blinds. Initially EXTRA was the last display, but soon became the top one; EXTRA was not used on 'Diddler' blinds. The last route blinds made were for Fulwell on 27th August 1961.

SIDE BLINDS

Five via points were used before route numbers were added in 1949 although occasionally only four were used. Four via points were given with the introduction of route numbers although sometimes there were only two or three. With the new system, the via points were re-arranged and a half turn of the blind gave a short working display. This eliminated the shortest of short workings, the illustrated Acton to Hammersmith example for CE/SE being the most poignant; its inclusion was both superfluous and wasteful as CE/SE had no such scheduled journeys. Formerly there were many separate displays for short workings with route 655 having five examples. Routes 612, 653 and 692 showed both termini as via points. There were instances of via points in two lines: SILVERTOWN WAY, HIGH STREET WHITECHAPEL, WADDON AERODROME, NORTHUMBERLAND HEATH, GUNNERSBURY STATION, ISLEWORTH (SPRING GROVE), TEMPLE FORTUNE. Linen blinds were marked as SIDE BLIND or TROLLEYBUS SIDE BLIND***DEPOT and paper blinds as SIDE BOX. On paper blinds, route strips were used and the 603 example is illustrated. FW had no route or side blinds issued between 1952 and 1961. WW, the main operating depot for the 625 had just one display, yet WN with just a few journeys on the route had two. An odd 699 via point retained on PR/WW paper blinds was STADIUM despite WW being the distant 699 depot. A PRIVATE display was used on some late issue linen and early issue paper blinds. Rather oddly, Charlton produced two displays for route 612 at HB in March 1951. With the arrival of L3s at FW, former Q1 blinds returned to Aldenham for inserts were returned with back-stamps.

Of interest is the fact that where a route was operated by more than one depot, the side and destination details differed on a number of displays which were common to both depots. When some former Hanwell Q1s were allocated to Isleworth in 1961, they retained HL blinds. By being transferred from one vehicle to another, HL side and route blinds remained in use until 8th May 1962. The last side blinds made were for Fulwell on 19th October 1961. One final side blind issue was for vehicles 1 and 1521 for their ceremonial run on 8th May 1962; these were made so that they could be fixed to the blinds in the vehicles but were actually applied to the outside of the blind boxes.

SA CLASS BLINDS

Special blinds were made for the SA classes. SA1s/SA2s used a very large box, front and rear and the blinds measured 45 ins by 16 ins; the side box was of a different (unknown) dimension to that of standard vehicles. The linen destination blind was a one-piece arrangement although only two displays, totalling 33 ins in length were made and then sewn together. The paper one was a two-piece affair which consisted of route details being taped to adjacent destination details. SA3s had a route number box at the front, the nearside and the rear — an offside one was not used. These blinds measured 13½ ins wide by 11½ ins deep, while the destination blind was 33½ ins by 12 ins. No route 695 displays existed for SA3s. SA3s showed destinations at the front only. Charlton issues for SA1s/SA2s were titled EX DURBAN while SA3s showed EX JOHANNESBURG T/BUS; Aldenham's issue for SA3s quoted AEC. None were back-stamped although main destinations had primitive pencil abbreviations to give drivers an indication of display locations.

DESTINATION BLINDS

Early Charlton blinds included SPECIAL but was soon superseded by a PRIVATE display which varied over the years. PRIVATE was usually the first display but there were instances of additions above it. Inserted sections led to blinds being profusely marked, such as LPTB JULY 6 1939 HACKNEY AND LEYTON DEPOTS TROLLEYBUS FRONT AND REAR WITH DEL'S & ADD'S MAY 7 1940. A WORKMAN display was used on trams and trolleybuses, being shown in the rear destination box to inform passengers that workman fares were in force. (All blinds were fitted with this display, so it could also be seen at the front when winding through). Conductors knew to which fare stage these fares were available and meticulously at 8am altered the blind to show the destination. Despite this facility being withdrawn from 1st October 1950, blinds continued to be printed with WORKMAN until early 1951. Although removed from some blinds, it could still be observed as late as 1961. An enthusiast who obtained a CT/LB blind after conversion was unaware of its meaning and traversed the CT/LB routes asking where the 'WORKMAN' pub was situated.

As with side blinds, early Aldenham blinds used a thicker style of 'Johnston' lettering until 1955 when a thinner version was introduced; SF never received any blinds with the thicker print due to the longevity of their linen blinds. Generally, Charlton blinds were marked FRONT & REAR while Aldenham's were titled FRONT BOX & REAR BOX or FRONT & REAR. A few displays were not included on early issues as some turning circles were not constructed initially. Two separate sets of blinds were originally supplied for BW, HT, WH and WW depots. At HT these were stamped for either 60 or 70-seat vehicles while those at WW stated if they were for AEC or Leyland vehicles. UNIVERSAL was quoted when this practice ceased. At Highgate, due to excessive destination blind length causing frequent tearing, the display depth on later paper versions became shallower, thus shortening the blind length. This resulted in the boxes on the vehicles having to be masked in black at top and bottom, although some complete blinds and boxes remained of full depth. With the arrival of newer stock in 1959/60 the masking was overlooked, which gave an untidy appearance to many displays where the 'shortened' blinds had been installed. Conversely, with the transfer out of HT of 'masked-box' vehicles, destination displays at the new depots were partly obscured.

The last destination blinds made were for Finchley on 17th May 1961. The last labels made were those pasted onto the destination boxes of 1521, London's last trolleybus. If they had been correctly applied onto the tops of the blinds, the apertures would have been illuminated.

Left **Fulwell and Isleworth depots had the only instances of 'L.T. DEPOT' being used. In Fulwell's case, there was also a FULWELL L.T. DEPOT VIA TEDDINGTON display.** Right **EXTRA was incorrectly printed over the whole width of some Wood Green depot route blinds.** LT Museum U6635/Hugh Taylor

Stamford Hill depot used 'DALSTON Shacklewell Lane' for vehicles turning at Dalston Junction. 1201 passes through Stoke Newington on its way there. Sold to Cohen's the scrap merchants, it was immediately re-sold to a motor dealer at Shepherds Bush where it was used as a store-cum-office. In 1968 it was sold again, this time to the London Trolleybus Preservation Society. Most Edmonton vehicles showed DALSTON STOKE in the absence of an accurate display — how this was made up is shown on page 174. The display is seen on 1341 at the 'Dalston Stoke' terminus, alias Dove Road. Tony Belton/Hugh Taylor

Left **The final linen BX destination blinds made economic use of an intermediate display in the make-up of BEXLEYHEATH DEPOT.** Right **Conductor Fuller stands on the staircase of 1554 at Waltham Cross and turns the blind for the last ever run of a trolleybus to Highgate depot, 25th April 1961. His blind key is shiny which was no doubt due to being kept in his pocket with his coinage; retiring that night, he wears his red trolleybus cap badge to the end.** Hugh Taylor

Col 1 (blind):

PRIVATE

CLERKENWELL
GREEN

SMITHFIELD

ROSEBERY AVE
GREEN TERRACE

ISLINGTON
GREEN

SHOREDITCH
CHURCH

HACKNEY
KING EDWARD RD

BALLS POND RD
MILDMAY PARK

DALSTON LANE
QUEENS ROAD

LEYTON
DOWNSELL ROAD
VIA CAMBRIDGE HTH
& LEA BRIDGE RD

BLOOMSBURY
VIA CAMBRIDGE HTH

WOODFORD
NAPIER ARMS
VIA ESSEX RD
& LEA BRIDGE RD

BLOOMSBURY

HACKNEY
STATION

WORKMAN

LEYTON
BAKERS ARMS

WEST INDIA DOCKS
VIA GOSWELL ROAD
& DALSTON

SMITHFIELD
CHINGFORD MT
VIA CAMBRIDGE HTH
& LEA BRIDGE RD

LIVERPOOL ST STN

KENNINGHALL
ROAD

LEA BRIDGE RD

MARKHOUSE RD

LEYTON
GREEN

WHIPPS
CROSS

WALTHAMSTOW

CROOKED BILLET

SOUTH HACKNEY
LAURISTON ROAD

BURDETT ROAD
STATION

Col 2 (blind):

PRIVATE
TO HIRE A BUS
APPLY 55 BROADWAY SW1
ABBEY 1234

SMITHFIELD

SHOREDITCH
CHURCH

CLERKENWELL
GREEN

KENNINGHALL
ROAD

LEYTON
DOWNSELL ROAD

BLOOMSBURY
VIA LEA BRIDGE RD
CAMBRIDGE HTH

WOODFORD
NAPIER ARMS
VIA ESSEX RD
& LEA BRIDGE RD

BLOOMSBURY

BAKERS ARMS

LEYTON
GREEN

WORKMAN

KING EDWARD RD
HACKNEY
STATION

ROSEBERY AVE
GREEN TERRACE

WHIPPS
CROSS
ISLINGTON
GREEN

DALSTON LANE
QUEENS ROAD

BALLS POND RD
MILDMAY PARK

WEST INDIA DOCKS
VIA GOSWELL ROAD
& DALSTON

SMITHFIELD
BURDETT
ROAD

CHINGFORD MOUNT
VIA CAMBRIDGE HTH
& LEA BRIDGE RD
LIVERPOOL ST STN

WALTHAMSTOW
CROOKED BILLET
LEA BRIDGE RD
MARKHOUSE RD

Col 3 (blind):

PRIVATE
TO HIRE A BUS OR COACH
APPLY: 55 BROADWAY S.W.1
ABBEY 1234

SMITHFIELD

SHOREDITCH
CHURCH

CLERKENWELL
GREEN

KENNINGHALL
ROAD

LEYTON
DOWNSELL ROAD

BLOOMSBURY
LEA BRIDGE RD
CAMBRIDGE HTH

WOODFORD
NAPIER ARMS
ESSEX ROAD
LEA BRIDGE RD

BLOOMSBURY

BAKERS ARMS

LEYTON
GREEN
KING EDWARD RD

HACKNEY
STATION

ROSEBERY AVE
GREEN TERRACE

WHIPPS
CROSS
ISLINGTON
GREEN

DALSTON LANE
QUEENSBRIDGE ROAD

BALLS POND RD
MILDMAY PARK

WEST INDIA DOCKS
GOSWELL ROAD
DALSTON

SMITHFIELD
BURDETT
ROAD

CHINGFORD MOUNT
CAMBRIDGE HTH
LEA BRIDGE RD

LIVERPOOL ST STN

WALTHAMSTOW
CROOKED BILLET

LEA BRIDGE RD
MARKHOUSE RD

FINDON ROAD
GREEN ST

CRAYFORD
PRINCESS ROAD

Col 4 (blind):

PRIVATE
TO HIRE A BUS OR COACH
APPLY: 55 BROADWAY S.W.1
ABBEY 5600

WALTHAMSTOW CROOKED BILLET
AND
LEYTON DOWNSELL ROAD

GREEN ST
WEST HAM
DEPOT
WALTHAMSTOW

CROOKED BILLET
MARKHOUSE ROAD
FOREST GATE & GRN ST

CANNING TOWN
WALTHAMSTOW
SINNOTT ROAD

CROOKED BILLET
AND
LEA BRIDGE RD

VICTORIA DOCKS
VIA CANNING TOWN

SILVERTOWN STN

WANSTEAD
FLATS
MANOR HOUSE
SEVEN SISTERS RD
FOREST ROAD

EPPING FOREST
NTH CIRCULAR RD
VIA TOTTENHAM HALE

WINCHMORE HILL
WOODFORD
NAPIER ARMS
VIA FOREST ROAD
LORDSHIP LANE

WOOD GREEN
TOTTENHAM
HALE
VIA CUSTOM HOUSE

PLAISTOW STN
VIA PRINCE REGENT LANE

STRATFORD
BROADWAY
WALTHAMSTOW

DEPOT
DOCKS
FOREST GATE
CUSTOM HOUSE

CHINGFORD MOUNT
CUSTOM HOUSE
STRATFORD

DOCKS
STRATFORD
PRINCE REGENT LANE

CHINGFORD MOUNT
CAMBRIDGE HEATH
LEA BRIDGE RD

LIVERPOOL ST STN
DOWNSELL ROAD

LEYTON
BAKERS ARMS

LEYTON
GREEN

SHOREDITCH
CHURCH
KING EDWARD RD

HACKNEY
STATION
KENNINGHALL
ROAD

Col 5 (blind):

CHURCH END
HOLLY PARK
COLDERS GREEN
CRICKLEWOOD
HENDON

BURNT OAK
HENDON
WELSH HARP
DOLLIS HILL
CRICKLEWOOD

CHURCH END
HOLLY PARK
TEMPLE
FORTUNE
COLDERS GREEN

COLDERS GREEN
CRICKLEWOOD
WILLESDEN Gn
HARLESDEN
ACTON

HENDON
CRICKLEWOOD
WILLESDEN Gn
HARLESDEN
ACTON

HENDON
CRICKLEWOOD
WILLESDEN Gn
HARLESDEN
KENSAL GREEN

WEMBLEY
STONEBRIDGE Pk
HARLESDEN
WILLESDEN Jn
KENSAL GREEN

CRAVEN PARK
HARLESDEN
KENSAL GREEN
WESTBOURNE Pk
PADDINGTON

HARLESDEN
WILLESDEN Ln
HORN LANE
ACTON
STARCH GREEN

HARLESDEN
Nth ACTON STN
WILLESDEN Ln
ACTON STATION
HORN LANE

ACTON VALE
ASKEW ROAD
STARCH GREEN
PADDENSWICK Rd
GLENTHORNE Rd

CHISWICK
KEW
BRENTFORD
ISLEWORTH
(SPRING GROVE)

Cols 1-3

Comparative Leyton blinds for 1939/1950/1955 — of interest is the type of lettering used for BLOOMSBURY in the 1939 and 1955 issues; the Aldenham blind shop appears to have copied the 1939 style rather than the 1950 issue. 'King Edward Rd HACKNEY' was mis-spelt — King Edwards Rd is correct; it was a 555 turn but also used by 677s at 'SOUTH HACKNEY Lauriston Road', located at the other end of King Edwards Road. Of note is the amendment at the renaming of Queens Road to Queensbridge Road. Of further note are the different layouts and orders of displays on the 1939 and 1950 issues. BURDETT ROAD STATION became BURDETT ROAD after the station's closure.

Col 3

(Box) Two examples of spelling mistakes are shown. Correct spellings are Finden Road and Princes Road.

Col 4

WW destination blind 1.1.59. It was unusual to have qualifying points on two lines (as in the first display) on trolleybus blinds; there are just five known displays with this style. Displays for 'Crooked Billet' and Canning Town were unique in having three via points; this display is in a thicker style of print than most of the rest of the blind. The layout for Winchmore Hill does not permit a proper display; there was no Palmers Green display. GREEN ST WEST HAM served a dual purpose — providing for turns at Finden Road and 'Boleyn'. DEPOT WALTHAMSTOW was the only example of an inverted 'depot' display. Many displays commenced in one line format, but ended up in two lines, TOTTENHAM HALE being one such example. The top few items give overlapping displays.

Col 5

Early side displays at CE/SE and FW without route numbers; (SPRING GROVE) may be the only instance of brackets on side blinds.

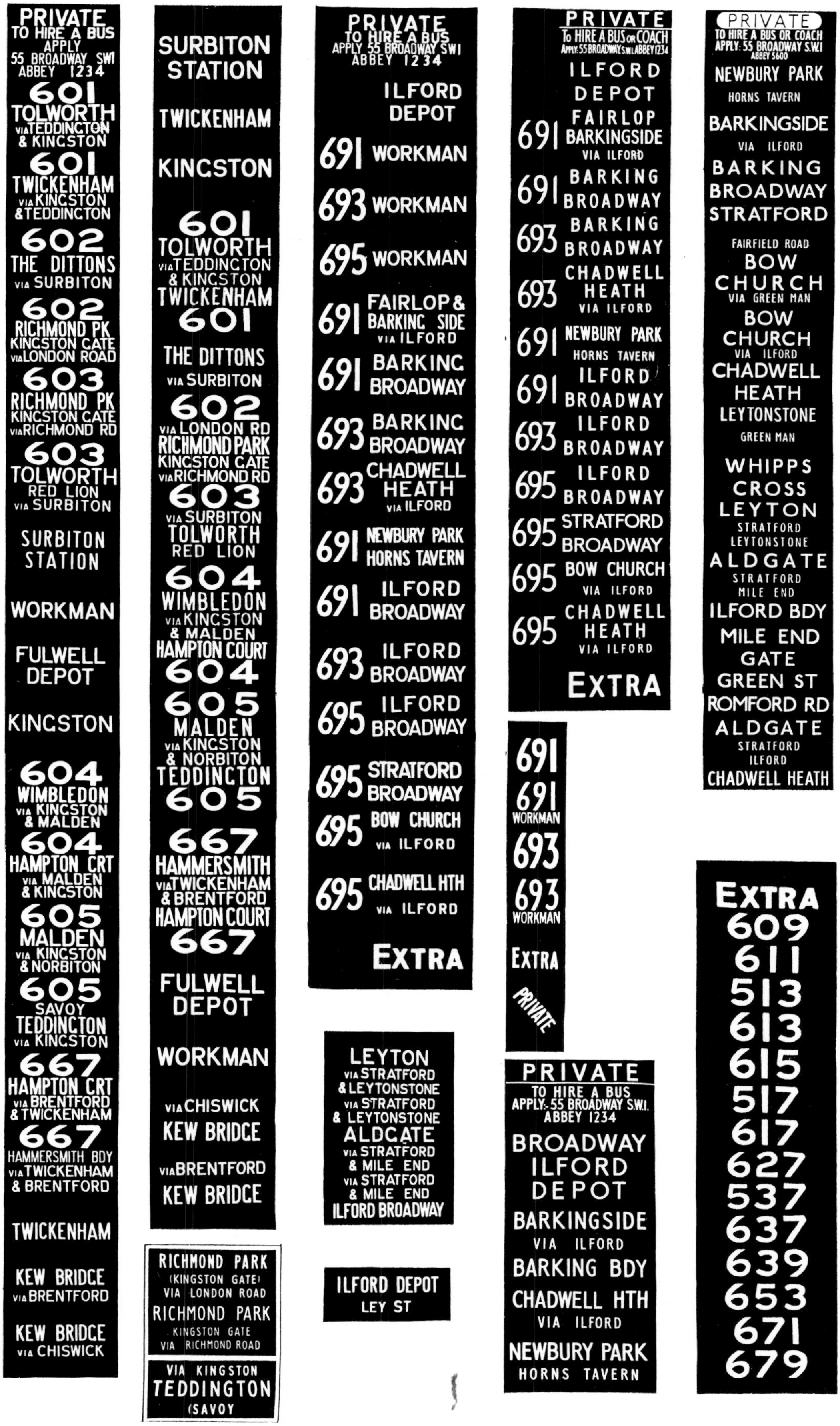
PRIVATE
TO HIRE A BUS
APPLY
55 BROADWAY SW1
ABBEY 1234
601
TOLWORTH
VIA TEDDINGTON
& KINGSTON
601
TWICKENHAM
VIA KINGSTON
& TEDDINGTON
602
THE DITTONS
VIA SURBITON
602
RICHMOND PK
KINGSTON GATE
VIA LONDON ROAD
603
RICHMOND PK
KINGSTON GATE
VIA RICHMOND RD
603
TOLWORTH
RED LION
VIA SURBITON
SURBITON STATION
WORKMAN
FULWELL DEPOT
KINGSTON
604
WIMBLEDON
VIA KINGSTON & MALDEN
604
HAMPTON CRT
VIA MALDEN & KINGSTON
605
MALDEN
VIA KINGSTON & NORBITON
605
SAVOY
TEDDINGTON
VIA KINGSTON
667
HAMPTON CRT
VIA BRENTFORD & TWICKENHAM
667
HAMMERSMITH BDY
VIA TWICKENHAM & BRENTFORD
TWICKENHAM
KEW BRIDGE
VIA BRENTFORD
KEW BRIDGE
VIA CHISWICK
SURBITON STATION
TWICKENHAM
KINGSTON
601
TOLWORTH
VIA TEDDINGTON & KINGSTON
TWICKENHAM
601
THE DITTONS
VIA SURBITON
602
VIA LONDON RD
RICHMOND PARK
KINGSTON GATE
VIA RICHMOND RD
603
VIA SURBITON
TOLWORTH
RED LION
604
WIMBLEDON
VIA KINGSTON & MALDEN
HAMPTON COURT
604
605
MALDEN
VIA KINGSTON & NORBITON
TEDDINGTON
605
667
HAMMERSMITH
VIA TWICKENHAM & BRENTFORD
HAMPTON COURT
667
FULWELL DEPOT
WORKMAN
VIA CHISWICK
KEW BRIDGE
VIA BRENTFORD
KEW BRIDGE
RICHMOND PARK
(KINGSTON GATE)
VIA LONDON ROAD
RICHMOND PARK
KINGSTON GATE
VIA RICHMOND ROAD
VIA KINGSTON
TEDDINGTON
(SAVOY
PRIVATE
TO HIRE A BUS
APPLY 55 BROADWAY SW1
ABBEY 1234
ILFORD DEPOT
691 WORKMAN
693 WORKMAN
695 WORKMAN
691 FAIRLOP & BARKING SIDE VIA ILFORD
691 BARKING BROADWAY
693 BARKING BROADWAY
693 CHADWELL HEATH VIA ILFORD
691 NEWBURY PARK HORNS TAVERN
691 ILFORD BROADWAY
693 ILFORD BROADWAY
695 ILFORD BROADWAY
695 STRATFORD BROADWAY
695 BOW CHURCH VIA ILFORD
695 CHADWELL HTH VIA ILFORD
EXTRA
LEYTON
VIA STRATFORD & LEYTONSTONE
VIA STRATFORD & LEYTONSTONE
ALDGATE
VIA STRATFORD & MILE END
VIA STRATFORD & MILE END
ILFORD BROADWAY
ILFORD DEPOT
LEY ST
PRIVATE
TO HIRE A BUS OR COACH
APPLY 55 BROADWAY S.W.1 ABBEY 1234
ILFORD DEPOT
691 FAIRLOP BARKINGSIDE VIA ILFORD
691 BARKING BROADWAY
693 BARKING BROADWAY
693 CHADWELL HEATH VIA ILFORD
691 NEWBURY PARK HORNS TAVERN
691 ILFORD BROADWAY
693 ILFORD BROADWAY
695 ILFORD BROADWAY
695 STRATFORD BROADWAY
695 BOW CHURCH VIA ILFORD
695 CHADWELL HEATH VIA ILFORD
EXTRA
691
691 WORKMAN
693
693 WORKMAN
EXTRA
PRIVATE
PRIVATE
TO HIRE A BUS
APPLY:- 55 BROADWAY S.W.1.
ABBEY 1234
BROADWAY
ILFORD DEPOT
BARKINGSIDE
VIA ILFORD
BARKING BDY
CHADWELL HTH
VIA ILFORD
NEWBURY PARK
HORNS TAVERN
PRIVATE
TO HIRE A BUS OR COACH
APPLY: 55 BROADWAY S.W.1
ABBEY 5600
NEWBURY PARK
HORNS TAVERN
BARKINGSIDE
VIA ILFORD
BARKING BROADWAY
STRATFORD
FAIRFIELD ROAD
BOW CHURCH
VIA GREEN MAN
BOW CHURCH
VIA ILFORD
CHADWELL HEATH
LEYTONSTONE
GREEN MAN
WHIPPS CROSS
LEYTON
STRATFORD
LEYTONSTONE
ALDGATE
STRATFORD
MILE END
ILFORD BDY
MILE END GATE
GREEN ST
ROMFORD RD
ALDGATE
STRATFORD
ILFORD
CHADWELL HEATH
EXTRA
609
611
513
613
615
517
617
627
537
637
639
653
671
679

Cols 1 & 2
'Diddler' blinds: the first one shows HAMMERSMITH BDY in the same size print as the intermediate points; the second one illustrates rationalisation of blind material. No display is given for BRENTFORD HALF ACRE which was far more likely to be used than the KEW BRIDGE displays.

Col 2 (Box)
At FW, two styles of Aldenham print incorporated consecutively on the same blind plus 'bracket loss'.

Cols 3 & 4
Charlton and Aldenham blinds for SA1/SA2 trolleybuses. The SA blinds were the only exact replicas on the change from linen to paper blinds. As can be seen BARKING SIDE is mis-spelt on the linen SA1/SA2 blind. Col 3 also shows wasteful duplication of intermediate data at BW. The foot of col 3 shows the only depot display to have a qualifying point. The lower half of col 4 shows Charlton route blind and Aldenham destination blind for SA3 class.

Col 5
Aldenham BW blind, December 1958. The bottom two displays are for the 663 extension from the following month. The HT number blind shows planned but unused route numbers 537, 637 and 671.

PRIVATE
TO HIRE A BUS OR COACH
APPLY: 55 BROADWAY S.W.1
ABBEY 5600 OR ANY LOCAL OFFICE

ACTON VALE
(BROMYARD AVE)
VIA HANWELL

ACTON
MARKET PLACE

SOUTHALL
DELAMERE RD
HAYES END RD
VIA HANWELL

SHEPHERDS BUSH
ACTON
HANWELL

UXBRIDGE
BRENTFORD
HALF ACRE
HANWELL
BROADWAY

CLAPHAM JUNCTION
BRENTFORD
HAMMERSMITH

ACTON VALE
BRENTFORD
HANWELL

HAMMERSMITH BDY
BRENTFORD
CHISWICK

HANWELL BDY
VIA HORN LANE

ACTON
MARKET PLACE
VIA BRENTFORD

KEW BRIDGE
VIA CHISWICK

STAMFORD BROOK
STATION
HAMMERSMITH
BROADWAY

FULHAM PALACE RD
EDGARLEY TERRACE

HILLINGDON CHURCH
AND
STRATFORD BDG

HAMPTON COURT
BRENTFORD
TWICKENHAM

HAMMERSMITH BDY
TWICKENHAM
BRENTFORD

SHEPHERDS BUSH
BRENTFORD
CHISWICK

HOUNSLOW

DOWNHAM RD
DALSTON
STOKE
NEWINGTON

DOWNHAM ROAD
DALSTON
STOKE
NEWINGTON

DOWNHAM RD
KINGSLAND ROAD
DALSTON
SHACKLEWELL LANE

649A
STAMFORD HILL
TOTTENHAM
BRUCE GROVE
LORDSHIP LANE

627
MANOR HOUSE
HIGH ROAD
TOTTENHAM

607
SHEPHERDS BUSH
ACTON
HANWELL
SOUTHALL
HAYES
607

655
HANWELL
BRENTFORD
HAMMERSMITH

655
HANWELL
BRENTFORD
HAMMERSMITH
WANDSWORTH

667
CHISWICK
KEW
BRENTFORD
TWICKENHAM
HAMPTON
667

657
CHISWICK
KEW
BUSCH CORNER
ISLEWORTH
HOUNSLOW
657

602
EDEN STREET
SURBITON STN

603
EDEN STREET
SURBITON STN
EWELL ROAD

602
PARK ROAD
EDEN STREET
PENRHYN ROAD
SURBITON
603

517
KINGS CROSS
CALEDONIAN RD
HOLLOWAY RD
HIGHGATE
617

660
HARROW ROAD
WILLESDEN
CRICKLEWOOD
HENDON
664

PRIVATE
TO HIRE A BUS
APPLY
55 BROADWAY SW1
ABBEY 1234

612
WANDSWORTH
EARLSFIELD
TOOTING
MITCHAM
612

628
WANDSWORTH
PUTNEY
HAMMERSMITH
HARLESDEN
ACTON

626
MITCHAM
TOOTING
WANDSWORTH
HAMMERSMITH

630
TOOTING
WANDSWORTH
PUTNEY
HAMMERSMITH

628

660
JUBILEE CLOCK
OLD OAK LANE
NTH ACTON STN
ACTON

665
WEST INDIA DOCKS
COMMERCIAL ROAD
567

665
WEST INDIA DOCKS
567

697
HIGH ROAD LEYTON
STRATFORD BDY
PLAISTOW STN
BALAAM STREET
FREEMASONS RD
CUSTOM HOUSE
697

690
PORTWAY
PLASHET ROAD
GREEN STREET
EAST HAM

689
PORTWAY
PLASHET GROVE
EAST HAM
STRATFORD BDY

685
MARKHOUSE ROAD
GRANGE PARK RD
FOREST GATE
GREEN STREET

685
SILVERTOWN WAY
CANNING TOWN
BARKING ROAD

685
BARKING ROAD
CANNING TOWN
SILVERTOWN WAY

669

FINSBURY PARK
MORNINGTON CRES
TOTTENHAM CRT RD

MANOR HOUSE
SNELLS PARK
EDMONTON DEPOT
WALTHAM CROSS
STAMFORD HILL
LIVERPOOL ST

GOLDHAWK ROAD
YOUNGS CORNER
CHISWICK
YOUNGS CORNER
STAMFORD BROOK
STATION

HILLINGDON
STRATFORD BDGE

HILLINGDON CH
& STRATFORD BDG

BLOOMSBURY
CANNING TOWN
COMMERCIAL RD
BARKING

BARKING BDY
CANNING TOWN
COMMERCIAL ROAD
BLOOMSBURY

CLERKENWELL
GREEN
VIA COMMERCIAL ST
SMITHFIELD

SMITHFIELD
VIA COMMERCIAL ST
CLERKENWELL
GREEN

VICTORIA DOCKS
SILVERTOWN WAY

VICTORIA DOCKS
SILVERTOWN WAY
VIA CANNING TOWN

CLAPHAM JUNC
VIA BRENTFORD
& HAMMERSMITH
CRAVEN PARK

STADIUM
WEMBLEY HILL RD

SUDBURY
VIA CRAVEN PARK
WEMBLEY
HILL ROAD

WEMBLEY
HILL ROAD

STADIUM
WEMBLEY
HILL ROAD

WINDSOR
TERRACE
CITY ROAD

HIGHGATE
ARCHWAY
STATION

HIGHGATE VGE
VIA NEW NORTH RD
& HIGHBURY

HIGHGATE
VILLAGE
VIA NEW NORTH RD

VIA NEW NTH RD
HIGHGATE VGE

VIA WELLING
& BEXLEYHEATH
WOOLWICH FERRY

VIA WELLING
& BEXLEYHEATH
WOOLWICH FERRY

Col 1

HL destination blind 2.8.60. The 'AND' in the lazy display was erroneous for Stratford Bridge was only two stops down the hill from Hillingdon Church; it was probably confused with 'lazy' displays. Of note is the PRIVATE display; it is a Country bus department label for single-deckers and signifies a temporary shortage of trolleybus PRIVATE labels at the time.

(Box) EM (top 2), SF (bottom) details for Dalston Junction. The EM blind shows how the DALSTON STOKE display came about. SF could have provided a more accurate display than 'DALSTON Shacklewell Lane' and used EM's initiative to show 'Kingsland Road DALSTON'. An idiosyncrasy was the prominence given to DOWNHAM ROAD.

Col 2

The SF blind for route 649A was the only example of a display incorporating a route number suffix. The EM blind illustrates 'High Road Tottenham' in two lines. The HL blind has two displays for the regularly used 607 route, two for the rarely used 667 and two for the 657 which it did not operate; the 655 HANWELL/ HAMMERSMITH display was in essence a lazy display for the Hanwell/Brentford shuttle. 1951/1961 FW display differences — route and side blinds had been in Q1s for such a long time that they had become brittle and many of them tore when being removed and placed in L3s — upon repair a joint 602/603 panel appeared.

Col 3

HT blind illustrates 'RD' in different styles. CE had only a few 660 workings and could not give a proper 660 display. 26.6.51 HB blind gives withdrawn 612 details. A unique destination display on side blinds existed at WH; it was for route 665 but could also be used for 567. An incorrectly assembled display showed both routes simultaneously.

Col 4

WH shows two styles of printing for its lower 697 panel; East Ham circulars had different displays. 685 displays for WW and WH illustrate the same details but in reverse order. (Box 1): One line displays printed for HT for football specials — possibly never used. (Box 2): One location being shown in three different ways in the same era — appearing at IH, HL and FW/HL/IH respectively.

Col 5

Items 1 & 2 show correct and incorrect displays for the Hillingdon turn; in the second it is erroneously treated as a lazy display. Items 3 & 6 are PR while items 4 & 5 are WH; different styles for the same displays. Items 7 & 8 show alternative 669/685 displays, one with a qualifying point and one without. Item 9 was for a proposed 655 Clapham Junction to Craven Park working that did not materialise. Items 10-13 include the Wembley Hill Road turning point shown in four different ways. Items 13-15 are the only examples of short workings that used three lines. Items 16-18 illustrate the three different displays printed by Charlton works for Highgate Village. Items 19 & 20 are alternative displays for Woolwich Ferry.

Destination Blinds

MOORGATE via KINGS CROSS & HIGH ST CAMDEN TOWN

MOORGATE viaKINGS CROSS & CAMDEN HIGH ST

via CAMDEN TOWN & KINGS CROSS **MOORGATE**

MOORGATE viaKINGS CROSS

MOORGATE VIA KINGS CROSS

MOORGATE viaKENTISH TOWN & KINGS CROSS

WANDSWORTH HIGH STREET

WANDSWORTH STATION

WANDSWORTH STN

HARROW ROAD SCRUBS LANE

NR WILLESDEN JUNCTION via PUTNEY

SCRUBS LANE

SCRUBS LANE

HARLESDEN COLLEGE PARK

HARLESDEN (COLLEGE PARK) via PUTNEY

BARING ST NEW NORTH RD

BARING STREET NEW NORTH ROAD

HAMPSTEAD HEATH viaCAMDEN TOWN

HAMPSTEAD HEATH via ROYAL COLLEGE ST

NEW SOUTHGATE STN

NEW SOUTHGATE

LEYTON DEPOT via STRATFORD & LEYTONSTONE

UPPER EDMONTON SNELLS PARK

SNELLS PARK TOTTENHAM HALE

SNELLS PARK TOTTENHAM

SNELLS PARK **TOTTENHAM HALE**

TOTTENHAM SNELLS PARK

TOTTENHAM SPURS GROUND

JUNCTION ROAD MONNERY ROAD **HOLLOWAY ROAD** PEMBERTON GARDENS

JUNCTION RD MONNERY ROAD **HOLLOWAY RD** PEMBERTON GDNS

CHINGFORD MOUNT CUSTOM HOUSE STRATFORD **DOCKS** STRATFORD PRINCE REGENT LANE **CHINGFORD MOUNT**

via STRATFORD **LEYTON GREEN** via FOREST GATE

via STRATFORD **LEYTON GREEN** via FOREST GATE

EDGWARE STATION RD viaCRICKLEWOOD & HENDON **CANONS PARK**

CANONS PARK STANMORE CIRCUS HENDON CRICKLEWOOD **BARNET** CRICKLEWOOD NORTH FINCHLEY

COLDERS GREEN STN viaNORTH FINCHLEY & WHETSTONE **BARNET**

CRICKLEWOOD ST GABRIELS RD **CANONS PARK** via HENDON & CRICKLEWOOD

WILLESDEN GREEN STN

---

via UPPER ROAD & SILVERTOWN WAY **STRATFORD BDY**

via UPPER RD & SILVERTOWN WAY **STRATFORD BDY**

WOOD GREEN STN via SHOREDITCH & STAMFORD HILL **HOLBORN** via SHOREDITCH & GRAYS INN ROAD **HOLBORN CIRCUS**

via HIGHGATE & FARRINGDON ST **HOLBORN CIRCUS** via HIGHGATE & CRAYS INN RD

via FINSBURY PK & CRAYS INN RD **HOLBORN CIRCUS** via FINSBURY PK & FARRINGDON ST

via KINGS CROSS & CRAYS INN ROAD **HOLBORN CIRCUS** via KINGS CROSS & FARRINGDON ST

via FARRINGDON RD **HOLBORN CIRCUS** via CRAYS INN RD

via FOREST ROAD & LORDSHIP LANE **WOOD GREEN** viaLORDSHIP LANE & CHESNUT RD **TOTTENHAM HALE** via BROAD LANE & SEVEN SISTERS ROAD **MANOR HOUSE** via FOREST RD & FERRY LANE **TOTTENHAM HALE**

CRAVEN PARK via HARLESDEN & HAMMERSMITH **NTH ACTON STN**

HARLESDEN JUBILEE CLOCK

HANWELL HOSPITAL GATES

COSWELL ROAD SEBASTIAN STREET

viaFINSBURY PK **EDMONTON STATION**

WEST CROYDON viaSOUTH NORWOOD & SELHURST

SUTTON DEPOT

LORDSHIP LANE PERTH RD

KENTISH TN FORTESS WALK

CHALK FARM MOTHER SHIPTON

CITY ROAD CANAL BRIDGE CALEDONIAN RD

SEVEN SISTERS CORNER

LYONSDOWN ROAD

LYONSDOWN ROAD **NEW BARNET** STATION ROAD

TALLY HO CORNER

NTH FINCHLEY TALLY HO CORNER

NORTH FINCHLEY

viaMILDMAY PARK & WOOD GREEN **PALMERS GREEN**

PALMERS GREEN

PALMERS GREEN

WOODFORD (NAPIER ARMS) via FOREST RD

ISLEWORTH (SPRING GROVE) via BRENTFORD

FULHAM PALACE RD (EDGARLEY TERRACE)

HAYES END RD via HANWELL

ACTON DEPOT

BOW DEPOT

STONEBRIDGE DEPOT

BEXLEYHEATH DEPOT

Col 1

Items 1-5 are 639 displays with items 4-6 belonging to the 615; those with two via points were earlier printing styles. Items 7-9: HL/HB/SE blinds illustrate Wandsworth in three different ways and are splendid examples of the lack of conformity on trolleybus blinds. Items 10-15: The turn at Scrubs Lane was named differently over the years and is illustrated in the progressive way in which it changed. Items 16&17: HT (above) and WN (below) used different layouts for the turn at Baring Street. Items 18&19: In early days Hampstead Heath was given a via point — its removal in later years made it a less informative display. Items 20&21: The New Southgate displays for FY illustrate that one blind compiler wanted to give pinpoint accuracy by adding STN to his work. Item 22: The only 'depot' display to incorporate two via points was the BW display for Leyton Depot.

Col 2

Items 1-6 refer to the Snells Park turning loop; items 1-4 are from EM, item 5 from SF and item 6 from HT. Items 7&8: In the latter days of operation these variants could be seen at HT. Item 9: Legibility trials at WH; the narrower style of intermediate printing was adopted. Items 10&11: A particular vehicle could show these different layouts simultaneously for they were issued in the same era and may have been fitted in the front and back of a trolleybus. Items 12&14: An early FY blind gives different details for 645 termini — the Barnet display actually belongs to route 651. Item 13: CE used different via points each the 645 terminus. Item 15: CE blind for 1951. 'Cricklewood St Gabriels Rd' had previously been known as 'Willesden Green' but was later renamed 'Cricklewood St Gabriels Church'. Item 16: The same turning point was at first described as 'Willesden Green Stn' — which was about 400 yards away.

Col 3

Items 1&2: These two displays were on the original WH blind and illustrate that two blind compilers working on the same batch of blinds would print RD in different styles. Item 3: An unusual compilation was HOLBORN and HOLBORN CIRCUS on the same blind at SF. Items 4-6: Farringdon St was continually quoted in error instead of Farringdon Rd. Item 5 shows the back-stamp position which was used for a short time at FY and HT. It enabled the driver to see the back-stamp against the daylight, but as it gave an untidy appearance, the blinds were soon meticulously painted to eradicate it. Item 7: At HT, Farringdon Rd is spelt correctly but the removal of 'via Kings Cross' gives a rather hollow effect to the blind. Item 8: At WW there is inconsistency in the compilation of 'Forest Rd' — accentuated in that 'Seven Sisters Road' is spelt in full. Item 9: Short working points with two via points were unusual — NTH ACTON STN was one example. Item 10: No wire or battery turn was possible at Jubilee Clock so its inclusion on blinds is a mystery. Item 11: Despite route 655 only being temporarily extended to Hanwell Hospital Gates, a display was given. Item 12: An anomaly was that 'Goswell Road, Sebastian Street' never appeared at CT for route 677 but did appear at PR for its intended allocation to the route; however PR never worked route 677 and these details were eventually removed. Item 13: 'Edmonton Town Hall' was previously known as 'Edmonton Station'. Item 14: The wiring layout at West Croydon precluded this display from being used. Item 15: Despite Sutton depot being renamed Carshalton depot in 1950, SUTTON DEPOT was printed circa 1952.

Col 4

Items 1-7 are early battery movement displays that were soon removed from blinds. Items 8-10: 'NORTH FINCHLEY' was quoted in many different ways over the years with these three being early examples. Items 11-13: An informative short working display for Palmers Green gave way to a plain display — later on it appeared as 'PALMERS GREEN, Hedge Lane'. Item 14: A unique feature was the make-up of (NAPIER ARMS) in that the amplification was printed in the same size as WOODFORD. Items 14-16: The use of brackets on linen blinds was rare and these are three examples of such use. Item 17: The via point has appeared in larger lettering than the destination. Items 18-21: Four depot displays. The SE display has been squeezed into one line but would have looked tidier if it had appeared as in the style of the BX display.

There were many instances of alternative displays for the same location on blinds from different depots and the knowledgeable could tell at a glance from which depot a particular vehicle came. However, there were also instances of using labels from other depots. While many of the changes may have gone unnoticed by the general public, one aspect that would have been apparent was the renaming of some trolleybus depots which resulted in new displays at CE, CN and IH. Displays for the old and new names appeared concurrently for a time. Displays for the old and new names appeared concurrently for a time. There was some display inadequacy e.g. CT/LB did not have a 'GOSWELL ROAD Sebastian Street' display; in situations such as this, a blank display or the previous short working was used and the conductor verbally indicated the destination. Some displays were not given initially; upon the commencement of route 567, a traffic circular instructed that CLERKENWELL GREEN should be displayed for Smithfield journeys.

1891, the last London Trolleybus built, was always allocated to Isleworth depot. To reduce the number of movements on the night of conversion stage 9, it was sent to work at Fulwell depot for its final few days service in London. It is seen here in Kingston with an FW plate over its IH painted code. Fred Ivey

12th May 1962. The last trolleybus has gone, but the light at Hounslow terminus which indicated to the conductor that the traffic lights were now in the trolleybus's favour was still operational. The indicator was activated by the conductor pressing the button which can be seen below it. On this occasion, however, it was pressed by the author. Hugh Taylor